Limitation of Actions

Preston and Newsom on

Limitation of Actions

Fourth edition

John Weeks, MA, QC
of the Inner Temple

© Longman Group UK Ltd 1989

Published by
Longman Group UK Ltd
21/27 Lambs Conduit Street
London WC1N 3NJ

Associated offices
Australia, Hong Kong, Malaysia, Singapore and USA

First published 1953
Fourth edition 1989

A CIP catalogue record for this book is available from the British
Library.

ISBN 0 85121 5769

Typeset by Kerrypress Ltd, Luton
Printed in Great Britain by
Mackays of Chatham Ltd., Chatham, Kent

Contents

Preface

Over thirty-five years have passed since the third edition of this work. In that time there have been five major decisions by the House of Lords, seven reports to Parliament, four Acts amending the Limitation Act 1939, a consolidation Act (the Limitation Act 1980) and three Acts amending the Limitation Act 1980. The result is that the third edition, though a work of great scholarship, is not of much assistance to those who want or need to discover the current law. The title Limitation of Actions in Halsbury's Laws of England (4th Edition) is similarly out of date, having been published before the Limitation Act 1980, the Latent Damage Act 1986 and the Consumer Protection Act 1987 were passed. No general textbook on the English law of limitation has been published since 1959. The writer hopes that this edition will provide at least a source where the statutes currently in force can be found and at best some assistance in understanding them. The law is stated as at 1 January 1989.

JHW   *Lincoln's Inn*

'A man's gotta know his limitations'

Eastwood C.

Table of Cases

Table of Statutes

Table of Statutory Instruments

Chapter 1

The legislation

1.1 History

1.1.1 The basic principle of the English law of limitation is that a plaintiff must start his action within a particular period running from the date of the accrual of his cause of action. The period is known as the limitation period. The statutes which prescribe periods of limitation for existing causes of action are called statutes of limitation: *Gregory* v *Torquay Corporation* [1911] 2 KB 556 per Pickford J at p 559.

1.1.2 In recent years the subject of limitation has attracted, and may sometimes have benefited from, increasing legislative and judicial attention. The general tendency has been to strive for justice in individual cases at the expense of certainty for all. 'Parliament has now decided that uncertain justice is preferable to certain injustice': per Ormrod LJ in *Firman* v *Ellis* [1978] QB 886 at p 911. Until 1940 the principal statutes of limitation in force were the Limitation Act 1623, the Civil Procedure Act 1833, the Real Property Limitation Acts 1833 and 1874 and the Public Authorities Protection Act 1893. These were replaced on 1 July 1940 by the Limitation Act 1939, which the editors of the first edition of this work predicted would far outlast the span of the youngest living practitioner in 1939. In fact it lasted until 1 May 1981 when the Limitation Act 1980 came into force.

1.1.3 In 1953 the editors of the third edition reached the conclusion that the 1939 Act worked simply and was a success. Less enthusiasm was found in the House of Lords in *Cartledge* v *E Jopling & Sons Ltd* [1963] AC 758, where their Lordships were forced to a conclusion which they all regarded as wholly unreasonable and unjustifiable. It was found necessary to modify the 1939 Act by the Limitation (Enemies and War Prisoners) Act 1945, the Law Reform (Limitation of Actions, etc) Act 1954, the Limitation Act 1963, the Law Reform (Miscellaneous Provisions) Act 1971, the Limitation Act 1975 and finally the Limitation Amendment Act 1980. The whole system was then repealed by the Limitation Act 1980 which came into effect on 1 May 1981.

1.1.4 The Limitation Act 1980 has also fallen short of perfect. In *Pirelli General Cable Works Ltd* v *Oscar Faber & Partners* [1983] 2 AC 1 at p 19, Lord Scarman agreed that the law was as set out in Lord Fraser's speech and continued, 'But it is no matter for pride. It must be . . . unjustifiable in principle that a cause of action should be held to accrue before it is possible to discover any injury (or damage). A law which produces such a result . . . is harsh and absurd'. This particular absurdity was dealt with by the Latent Damage Act 1986, an Act which the then Lord Chancellor regarded in bill-form as his 'ewe-lamb', a description which did not disarm all the critics.

1.2 Existing legislation

1.2.1 The basic legislation is therefore the Limitation Act 1980 which received the Royal Assent on 13 November 1980 and came into effect on 1 May 1981. The Act has been amended, principally by the Administration of Justice Act 1985 (to implement the recommendations of the Faulks Committee on Defamation), the Latent Damage Act 1986 (to implement the recommendations of the Law Reform Committee on latent damage) and the Consumer Protection Act 1987 (to implement the European Community's Directive on Product Liability). The Act is reprinted as amended in Appendix 1. Special topics are dealt with by the Limitation (Enemies and War Prisoners) Act 1945 and the Foreign Limitation Periods Act 1984 which are reprinted in Appendices 2 and 3 respectively. Finally, those parts of the Latent Damage Act 1986 which did more than amend the Limitation Act 1980 are reprinted in Appendix 4.

1.3 Policy

1.3.1 Various intentions in passing the statutes of limitation have been ascribed to the legislature. In *A'Court* v *Cross* (1825) 3 Bing 329, Best CJ gave two: first, that they were meant to protect persons who had paid their debts but had destroyed proof of payment and second, that 'long dormant claims have often more of cruelty than of justice in them'. In *Board of Trade* v *Cayzer Irvine & Co Ltd* [1927] AC 610 at p 628, Lord Atkinson gave a third, that 'the whole purpose of this Limitation Act is to apply to persons who have good causes of action which they could, if so disposed, enforce, and to deprive them of the power of enforcing them after they have lain by for the number of years respectively and omitted to enforce them'. Apart from the protection of defendants and the punishment of dilatory claimants, there is also an element of public interest in allowing sleeping legal dogs to lie and not requiring the courts to determine disputed facts on stale and unreliable evidence: *R B Policies at Lloyd's* v *Butler* [1950] 1 KB 76, *Edwards* v *Edwards*

[1968] 1 WLR 149 and *Biss* v *Lambeth Health Authority* [1978] 1 WLR 382.

1.3.2 Opinions on the morality of pleading the Statutes have differed widely. In *Green* v *Rivett* (1702) 2 Salk 421, the Court of Queen's Bench observed that 'the Statute of Limitations, on which the security of all men depends, is to be favoured'. In *Reeves* v *Butcher* [1891] 2 QB 509, Fry LJ took a neutral position saying at p 511, 'We have not to determine whether the defence here set up is handsome or conscientious but whether it is good in law'. In *Midland Bank* v *Hett, Stubbs & Kemp* [1979] Ch 384 at p 394, Oliver J referred to a plea of limitation as 'an unattractive plea at the best of times'. Other judges can see nothing unfair or reprehensible in raising a defence of limitation: *The Gaz Foundation* [1987] 2 Lloyd's Rep 151.

1.4 Scope of the Act

1.4.1 The Limitation Act 1980 applies to 'actions of the various classes mentioned': s 1(1). 'Action' is defined as including 'any proceeding in a court of law, including an ecclesiastical court': s 38(1). Counterclaims and set-offs are within the definition, as is an application for a distress warrant for arrears of rates: *China* v *Harrow UDC* [1954] 1 QB 178. The Act does not extend to proceedings which could not be called an action, eg a criminal prosecution or an inquest, nor does it include the execution of a judgment as distinct from suing on a judgment, which is within the definition: *W T Lamb & Sons* v *Rider* [1948] 2 KB 331. The Act does apply to arbitrations: s 34.

1.4.2 The Act applies only to actions of the various classes mentioned in Part I of the Act and does not apply to actions for which a period of limitation is prescribed by any other enactment: s 39. Among the former omissions are petitions for divorce, probate actions (*Re Flynn deceased* [1982] 1 WLR 310) and some applications for relief from forfeiture (*Thatcher* v *C H Pearce & Sons* [1968] 1 WLR 748). Among the latter exemptions are the following:
  (*a*) applications to the court under the Town and Country Planning Act 1971;
  (*b*) proceedings under the Post Office Act 1969;
  (*c*) election petitions under the Representation of the People Act 1983;
  (*d*) summary civil proceedings under the Magistrates' Courts Act 1980;
  (*e*) claims for financial provision under the Inheritance (Provision for Family and Dependants) Act 1975;
  (*f*) claims under the Defective Premises Act 1972;
  (*g*) claims under the Nuclear Installations Act 1965;
  (*h*) claims under the Merchant Shipping (Oil Pollution) Act 1971;
  (*i*) claims for overpaid rent under the Rent Act 1977;

(*j*) claims under the Mines and Quarries (Tips) Act 1969;

(*k*) certain applications under the Companies Act 1985;

(*l*) applications for a new business tenancy under the Landlord and Tenant Act 1954;

(*m*) applications for relief for forfeiture under the Common Law Procedure Act 1852 or the County Courts Act 1984;

(*n*) proceedings in respect of discrimination under the Sex Discrimination Act 1975 or the Race Relations Act 1976;

(*o*) proceedings under the Forfeiture Act 1982;

(*p*) certain applications under the Insolvency Act 1986;

(*q*) petitions for nullity under the Matrimonial Causes Act 1973;

(*r*) proceedings in respect of penalties under the Taxes Acts;

(*s*) shipping claims under the Maritime Conventions Act 1911, the Merchant Shipping Act 1974 or the Merchant Shipping (Liner Conferences) Act 1982;

(*t*) claims arising out of international transport of passengers or goods by air, rail, road or sea under the Carriage by Air Act 1961, the Carriage of Goods by Road Act 1965, the Carriage of Goods by Sea Act 1971, the Carriage of Passengers by Road Act 1974, the Carriage by Air and Road Act 1979, the Merchant Shipping Act 1979 and the International Transport Conventions Act 1983.

(*u*) Applications to tribunals under, for example, the Employment Protection (Consolidation) Act 1978 have their own individual time limits. Where no time limit is specified and the claim is contractual, the period is six years: *Greenwich Health Authority* v *Skinner* (1989) *The Times,* 19 January EAT.

1.4.3 The Limitation Act 1939 did not apply to admiralty actions in rem (s 2(6)) but this exception was not repeated in the Limitation Act 1980 which excludes only 'proceedings in respect of the forfeiture of a ship': s 37(2)(*c*). It is not clear whether this exclusion applies only where the proceedings are by or against the Crown.

1.4.4 The courts of equity were not bound to act in obedience to the statutes of limitation and evolved their own practice of refusing relief on the ground of laches or acquiescence. The Limitation Act 1980 provides that the time limits prescribed under certain sections shall not apply to any claim for specific performance or an injunction or other equitable relief except insofar as equity might have applied a corresponding time limit by analogy before 1 July 1940: s 36(1). Section 36(2) provides that nothing in the Act shall affect any equitable jurisdiction to refuse relief on the ground of acquiescence or otherwise. A claim to enforce a statutory charge is 'other equitable relief' (*Poole Corporation* v *Moody* [1945] KB 350) and the appropriate period is therefore twelve years under s 20 and not six years under s 9.

1.5 The Crown and public authorities

1.5.1 The Limitation Act 1980 binds the Crown except in a few instances: s 37(1). The Crown for this purpose includes the Queen as Duke of Lancaster, the Duke of Cornwall, Government Departments and officers of the Crown: s 37(3).

1.5.2 The exceptions include questions relating to gold and silver mines (s 37(6)) and proceedings for the recovery of duties or taxes or forfeiture proceedings under the Customs and Excise Acts: s 37(2). Special periods of limitation are prescribed for actions by the Crown to recover land: Part II of Schedule 1. The recovery of penalties for non-payment of taxes is outside the Act: *IRC* v *Stoke Commissioners* [1974] TR 207.

1.5.3 The Limitation Act 1939 contained a special one-year period of limitation for the benefit of public authorities: s 21, re-enacting the Public Authorities Protection Act 1893 which continued to apply in Scotland (*Burmah Oil Ltd* v *Lord Advocate* [1965] AC 75). This controversial provision was abolished by the Law Reform (Limitation of Actions, etc) Act 1954 and since 4 June 1954 the periods of limitation for actions against public authorities have been the same as those applicable to actions against private persons. Causes of action which were barred on 4 June 1954 remain barred: *Arnold* v *Central Electricity Generating Board* [1988] AC 228 where the plaintiff sued in 1984 on a cause of action which accrued in 1943 at the latest.

1.6 Private International Law

1.6.1 The English common law rule was that issues of limitation were classified as procedural and therefore formed part of the lex fori to be applied whatever the lex causae might be: *Harris* v *Quine* (1869) LR 4 QB 653, approved by the House of Lords in *Black-Clawson International Ltd* v *Papierwerke AG* [1975] AC 591. Hence the rules of English domestic law could bar an action brought in England even though the action might have been permissible under the law governing the substantive issues. Conversely, actions could be brought in England although barred under the law governing the substantive issues, provided they were not barred by English domestic law. The law was thus an invitation to forum-shopping and subjected to severe criticism. The only exception to this rule was where the foreign law extinguished not only the remedy but also the right: *Huber* v *Steiner* (1835) 2 Bing NC 202.

1.6.2 The Foreign Limitation Periods Act 1984 changed the position fundamentally by going to the opposite extreme. As from 1 October 1985 where under the rules of private international law a foreign law is applied to the substantive issues in the case, the rules of that foreign law relating to matters of limitation are to be applied to the exclusion of the English law of limitation: s 1(1). Section 1(2) qualifies the general principle where there is a rule of double reference, one reference being to English law. The most important example of a double reference occurs when a tort is committed abroad; the English court is then required to take into account the actionability of the conduct both under the law of the country where it was committed and under the English law of tort: *Boys* v *Chaplin* [1971] AC 356.

1.6.3 Section 2(1) of the Foreign Limitation Periods Act 1984 provides that in any case where the application of the foreign law would conflict with public policy, s 1 shall not apply. The doctrine of public policy is regarded as an 'unruly horse' in English law and in the context of private international law is normally invoked only where the foreign rule is morally repugnant (for example the sale of slaves) or where the application of the rule impinges on the national or international interests of the United Kingdom. It is difficult to see how either situation could arise in the context of limitation, even if the court did regard the foreign law as creating an inordinately long or exceptionally short period. However, s 2(2) provides that the application of s 1 shall conflict with public policy to the extent that its application would cause undue hardship to any party or potential party to the action. This provision had no counterpart in the draft bill attached to the Law Commission Report 'Classification of Limitation in Private International Law' (Law Com No 114, 1982, Cmnd 8570) and seems to introduce an element of ad hoc discretion ill-suited to the commercial law and incompatible with Art 16 of the EEC Convention on the Law Applicable to Contractual Obligations (1980, Cmnd 8489). All the more so if 'undue hardship' is construed as widely as in s 27 of the Arbitration Act 1950.

1.6.4 Section 1(3) of the Foreign Limitation Periods Act 1984 requires English law to be applied to determine the finishing point of a foreign limitation period, thus absolving English courts from investigating foreign procedural rules. Sections 1(5) and 4(2) avoid the possibility of a reference back to English law under the doctrine of renvoi. Section 1(4) directs the English court to exercise any discretion conferred by a foreign law by adopting the approach that the relevant foreign court would take. Where the Act applies the English court must usually have regard to any suspensive provisions forming part of the foreign law but under s 2(3) it must disregard any extension or interruption of the period allowed because of the absence of a party to the proceedings from any particular jurisdiction or country. Presumably this refers to voluntary absence only and not to provisions corresponding to the Limitation (Enemies and War Prisoners Act) 1945. The discretion to refuse equitable relief is preserved by s 4(3) but must be exercised with due regard to the foreign law.

1.6.5 A general requisite for the recognition of any foreign judgment is that it must be a judgment which was conclusive on the merits. It has been held that a judgment based on a foreign law barring the plaintiff's remedy without extinguishing his right is not a judgment 'on the merits' for the purpose either of recognition at common law or under the Foreign Judgments (Reciprocal Enforcement) Act 1933: *Harris* v *Quine* (1869) LR 4 QB 653 and *Black-Clawson International Ltd* v *Papierwerke AG* [1975] AC 591. This enabled the plaintiff to re-litigate in England. Section 3 of the Foreign Limitation Periods Act 1984 reverses the position and requires a foreign judgment based on limitation to be treated as a judgment on the merits.

1.7 Transitional

1.7.1 The Limitation Act 1980 came into force on 1 May 1981. It does not enable any action to be brought which was barred before 1 August 1980 or affect any action commenced before that date: para 9 of Schedule 2. The amendments made by the Administration of Justice Act 1985 in relation to defamation took effect as from 30 December 1985 but they do not apply if the cause of action arose before that date: para 14 of Schedule 9 to the Administration of Justice Act 1985. The amendments made by the Latent Damage Act 1986 took effect on 18 September 1986 (s 5(3)) and affect causes of action accruing before, as well as after, that date: s 4(2). They do not, however, enable any action to be brought which was barred before 18 September 1986 or affect any action commenced before that date: s 4(1). The amendments made by the Consumer Protection Act 1987 came into effect on 1 March 1988 and apply to the new rights created by that Act. For the presumption against retrospective effect see *Yew Bon Tew* v *Kenderaan Bas Mara* [1983] 1 AC 553 and *Arnold* v *Central Electricity Generating Board* [1988] AC 228.

1.7.2 The Limitation Acts can operate to bar actions immediately on coming into effect (*Pegler* v *Railway Executive* [1948] AC 332) and it may be correct to plead the Limitation Act 1980 even though time may have expired before it came into force: *Rhyl UDC* v *Rhyl Amusements Ltd* [1959] 1 WLR 465 but see *Arnold* v *Central Electricity Generating Board* [1988] AC 228.

1.7.3 The Foreign Limitations Periods Act 1984 came into operation on 1 October 1985. It does not apply to any matter in respect of which the limitation period under English law had then expired or to any action already commenced: s 7.

Chapter 2

General principles

2.1 The beginning of time

2.1.1 The general rule is that time starts to run from the accrual of the plaintiff's cause of action. The advantages of this rule are that it produces a starting point which is likely to be reasonably close to the incidents giving rise to the claim and one which is usually (but not always) unmistakable and readily ascertainable. The disadvantages are that expert evidence is sometimes needed to determine it and its occurrence is not necessarily apparent to the plaintiff; hence the problem of latent damage and the possibility of a victim finding that his action is barred before he knew of his right to sue.

2.1.2 The time limits in the Limitation Act 1980 ss 2 (tort), 4A (defamation), 5 (contract), 7 (awards), 8 (specialties), 9 (sums recoverable by statute), 10 (contribution), 11(4)(*a*) (personal injuries), 15 (recovery of land) and 21(3) (trust property and breach of trust) are all linked to the date on which the cause of action accrued. In the case of contribution and land there are specific provisions for determining when the cause of action accrued (ss 10(2), 15(6) and Schedule 1) but otherwise the matter is left to the general law.

2.1.3 'Cause of action' is 'every fact which it would be necessary for the plaintiff to prove, if traversed, in order to support his right to the judgment of the court': per Lord Esher MR in *Read* v *Brown* (1888) 22 QBD 128 at p 131 quoted with approval in *Sevcon Ltd* v *Lucas CAV Ltd* [1986] 1 WLR 462. A cause of action arises therefore at the moment when a potential plaintiff first has a right to succeed in an action against a potential defendant. There must be a plaintiff who can succeed and a defendant against whom he can succeed: see *Thomson* v *Lord Clanmorris* [1900] 1 Ch 718, especially per Vaughan Williams LJ at pp 728–729. The fact that the potential plaintiff could not identify his opponent does not prevent a cause of action accruing: *R B Policies at Lloyd's* v *Butler* [1950] 1 KB 76. On the other hand in *Re Russo-Asiatic Bank* [1934] Ch 720, time never ran at all because at the relevant time the potential defendant had been dissolved by the Soviet Government and did not exist in law. An executor's title commences on the death of the testator but an administrator's title derives from the grant and does not relate back to the death: *Ingall v Moran* [1944] KB 160. There is therefore no person capable of suing or being sued as administrator until a valid grant (*Chan Kit Sang v Ho Fung Hang* [1902] AC 257), but for the purposes of recovery of land only an administrator's title is deemed to have commenced on the death: Limitation Act 1980, s 26. A person protected by diplomatic privilege cannot be sued: *Musurus Bey v Gadban* [1894] 2 QB 352. An alien enemy cannot sue (*SS Waalhaven* [1943] AC 203) but he can be sued: *Porter v Freudenberg* [1915] 1 KB 857.

2.1.4 A cause of action can accrue although some statutory bar remains to be satisfied: *Coburn v Colledge* [1897] 1 QB 702. In an action for false imprisonment the cause of action arises on the imprisonment, not when the conviction is quashed: *O'Connor v Isaacs* [1956] 2 QB 288. A cause of action in conversion arises when a car is stolen, not when it (or the thief) is found: *RB Policies at Lloyd's v Butler* [1950] 1 KB 76. Evidence of essential facts must be distinguished from the facts themselves: *Central Electricity Board v Halifax Corporation* [1963] AC 785. When the essential facts include an omission to act, the cause of action (probably) arises at the last moment when it was possible for the act to be done effectively: *Midland Bank v Hett Stubbs & Kemp* [1979] Ch 384.

2.2 The length of time

2.2.1 There is an arbitrary element in the selection of any limitation period and the Law Reform Committee recognized the conflict between the general convenience of having one single period covering the great majority of cases and the practical advantage to particular classes of litigant of having tailor-made periods suitable to particular causes of action. The standard period in English law is six years, but the range runs from two to sixty years. The tendency in recent years has been for different periods to proliferate and for the period to depend on the cause of action selected rather than the factual situation, so that one given set of facts can attract several different periods of limitation.

2.2.2 In computing the period the day on which the cause of action arose is excluded: *Marren v Dawson Bentley & Co Ltd* [1961] 2 QB 135 and *Kirby v Leather* [1965] 2 QB 367. If on the last day the court office is closed all day, time is extended to the first day on which the office re-opens: *Pritam Kaur v S Russell & Sons Ltd* [1973] QB 336 and *The Clifford Maersk* [1982] 1 WLR 1292 but see *Swainston v Hetton Victory Club* [1983] 1 All ER 1179.

2.3 Time runs continuously

2.3.1 Time which has once begun to run continues to do so, even though subsequent events occur which make it impossible to bring an action. 'Where an action has once accrued and the Statute has begun to run, there being a capacity of suing and being sued, the Statute continues to run': per Lord Abinger CB in *Rhodes* v *Smethurst* (1838) 4 M & W 42 at p 59 and see *Homfray* v *Scrope* (1849) 13 QB 509. The death of a potential party does not prevent time running for or against his personal representative when constituted. There was an anomalous rule that, where a person entitled to a right of action died before action brought and the person liable to be sued became his administrator, the running of time was suspended so long as the dual capacity continued: *Seagram* v *Knight* (1867) LR 2 Ch 628. The rule did not apply to an executor: *Bowring-Hanbury's Trustee* v *Bowring-Hanbury* [1943] Ch 104. It has been abolished by the Administration of Estates Act 1925, s 21A and inserted by the Limitation Amendment Act 1980, s 10 as from 1 August 1980.

2.3.2 In respect of debts provable in personal or corporate insolvency, time ceases to run against the creditor on the making of the relevant order or the passing of the relevant resolution: *Re Fleetwood and District Electric Light and Power Syndicate* [1915] 1 Ch 486. Time, however, continues to run for all purposes other than proof of debts: *Re Benzon* [1914] 2 Ch 68 and *Cotterell* v *Price* [1960] 1 WLR 1097. Time does not cease to run in favour of debtors to the insolvent: *Re Mansell* (1892) 66 LT 245.

2.3.3 There appears to be an exception for mortgages where 'the hand to pay and to receive' become the same and interest is constructively paid (*Hodgson* v *Salt* [1936] 1 All ER 95) but the existence of any general exception on this ground was denied in *Bowring-Hanbury's Trustee* v *Bowring-Hanbury* [1943] Ch 104.

2.3.4 The existence of a state of war or rebellion does not prevent time from beginning or continuing to run: *Prideaux* v *Webber* (1661) 1 Lev 31. However, statutory provision has been made for suspending the Act while a necessary party to an action is an enemy or detained in enemy territory: Limitation (Enemies and War Prisoners) Act 1945. Disabilities, such as infancy or mental incapacity, may prevent time starting to run, but they will not operate to suspend it once time has started to run: Limitation Act 1980, s 28. A statutory instrument preventing the recovery of a debt may suspend the operation of the Act while the debt is irrecoverable: *Bell* v *Gosden* [1950] 1 All ER 266.

2.4 The end of time

2.4.1 The running of the period is stopped by beginning proceedings. Subsequent delays are then immaterial for the purpose of limitation. An action is normally begun by writ and in such cases the material date is the issue of the writ, ie the date when it is sealed by the court: RSC Ord 6, r 7(3). In the County Court the issue of proceedings even in the wrong court will stop time: *Sharma* v *Knight* [1986] 1 WLR 757. The term 'action' includes any proceeding in a court of law: Limitation Act 1980, s 38(1). Where the proceedings are not started by writ, time ceases to run at the date of issue of process, as for instance an originating summons. In the County Court receipt of an application by the court may be sufficient: *Aly* v *Aly* (1984) 128 SJ 65. In arbitration the relevant date is the service of the notice requiring the appointment of the arbitrator or, if the arbitrator is specified, requiring the submission of the dispute: Limitation Act 1980, s 34(3). A writ will stop time running even if it is not properly indorsed: *Grounsell* v *Cuthell* [1952] 2 QB 673. A writ on behalf of a plaintiff already dead is a nullity and has no effect on time: *Kamouh* v *British Aircraft Corp Ltd* (1982) *The Times*, 17 July.

2.4.2 Under RSC Ord 6, r 8 a writ remains in force for twelve months beginning with its date and the court has power to renew it for a further period of up to a year at a time. In computing the twelve months the day of issue *is* counted: *Trow* v *Ind Coope (West Midlands) Ltd* [1967] 2 QB 899. Service of the writ on one defendant within the period will not make the writ valid for service on another defendant outside the period: *Jones* v *Jones* [1970] 2 QB 576. The court will not usually exercise its power so as to renew an expired writ where a new writ would be too late. The court exercises this jurisdiction with caution and will not grant an extension unless there is good reason. Acceptable reasons are an agreement with the defendant to defer service or difficulty in effecting service, especially evasion of service: *Kleinwort Benson Ltd* v *Barbrak* [1987] AC 597 and *Waddon* v *Whitecroft Scovell Ltd* [1988] 1 WLR 309.

2.4.3 The result is that not all defendants are immediately aware of the fact that time has ceased to run and in some cases the limitation period is effectively a year longer. Lord Diplock thought the rule anomalous but too well established to upset: *Thompson* v *Brown* [1981] 1 WLR 744. The Law Reform Committee rejected the alternative of the date of service on practical grounds. A defendant who comes to hear of the writ may now require that it be served on him within fourteen days: RSC Ord 12, r 8A.

2.5   The effect of time

2.5.1   With three exceptions the effect of the English law of limitation is to bar the remedy and not to extinguish the right itself. The exceptions are the provisions governing extinction of title in relation to chattels (s 3(2), Limitation Act 1980) and in relation to land (s 17, Limitation Act 1980) and the extinction of rights under the Consumer Protection Act 1987 after ten years (Limitation Act 1980, s 11A(3)). The long-stop in latent damage cases bars the remedy only: Limitation Act 1980, s 14B.

2.5.2   The running of time is therefore regarded as a procedural matter rather than one of substantive law and limitation has to be pleaded by way of defence: RSC Ord 18, r 8(1) and *Rodriguez* v *Parker* [1967] 1 QB 116. The practical results are seen in those cases where the defendant, by oversight or otherwise, omits to plead limitation (eg *Ketteman* v *Hansel Properties Ltd* [1987] AC 189) in relation to the payment of debts, particularly secured debts. A right of action once barred by the Act is no longer revived by any subsequent acknowledgment or payment: Limitation Act 1980, s 29(7). It is also important in contribution claims to know whether time has extinguished the right or the remedy: Civil Liability (Contribution) Act 1978, s 1(3).

2.5.3   Statute-barred debts are due even though payment of them cannot be enforced by action or set-off. Money paid to a creditor without appropriation may be appropriated by him to the statute-barred debt: *Mills* v *Fowkes* (1839) 5 Bing NC 455. An executor of a solvent estate does not commit a devastavit by paying a statute-barred debt, unless it has been so declared by a competent court: *Re Midgley* [1893] 3 Ch 282. A trustee may pay his own statute-barred costs even if the beneficiaries object: *Budgett* v *Budgett* [1895] 1 Ch 202. A personal representative may set off a statute-barred debt against a pecuniary legacy or share of residue (*Re Akerman* [1891] 3 Ch 212) but not a specific legacy: *Re Taylor* [1894] 1 Ch 671 and *Re Savage* [1918] 2 Ch 146. A personal representative is bound to plead the Act only if required to do so by a beneficiary or creditor: *Coombs* v *Coombs* (1866) LR 1 P & D 288, *Re Wenham* [1892] 3 Ch 59 and *Re Thomson's Mortgage Trusts* [1920] 1 Ch 508. Statute-barred debts cannot be admitted in personal or corporate insolvency or, without the contributories' consent, in the winding up of a solvent company: *Re Art Reproduction Co Ltd* [1952] Ch 89.

2.5.4   A security may be enforceable even if given for a statute-barred debt and if the creditor has any lien or charge for his debt he can enforce the lien or charge after the debt is barred: *Spears* v *Hartley* (1800) 3 Esp 81. Thus, if a solicitor has client's documents upon which he has a lien an order for taxation of his costs should include any statute-barred items: *Re Brockman* [1909] 2 Ch 170.

2.6   Negotiations and agreements

2.6.1   The fact that negotiations have taken place does not prevent a defendant from pleading the Act, even though the negotiations may have led to delay. It is negligent for a solicitor to allow the period to expire while negotiations are in progress: *Fletcher & Son* v *Jubb* [1920] 1 KB 275. The defendant may however disqualify himself from relying on the Act either by contract (*Lubovsky* v *Snelling* [1944] KB 44 and *Abouchalache* v *Hilton International Hotels (UK) Ltd* (1982) 126 SJ 857), by waiver (*Kammins Ballrooms Co* v *Zenith Investments Ltd* [1971] AC 850 and in the Court of Appeal at [1970] 1 QB 673, especially per Sachs LJ) or by estoppel (*Paterson* v *Glasgow Corporation* (1908) 46 SLR 10, *Turburville* v *West Ham Corporation* [1950] 2 KB 208, *Kaliszewska* v *J Clague & Partners* (1984) 5 Con LR 62 and *The August Leonhardt* [1985] 2 Lloyd's Rep 28).

2.6.2   It is generally open to parties to a contract to stipulate that a claim for any breach must be brought within a specified period of its occurrence, a period which may be much shorter than the statutory six years. The Misrepresentation Act 1967 and the Defective Premises Act 1972 avoid provisions restricting liability under those Acts, and a shorter period could fall foul of those sections. An agreement restricting liability to passengers in vehicles may be void under s 148(3) of the Road Traffic Act 1972 and a term limiting liability for personal injuries or to consumers or other customers may be invalidated under ss 2, 3 or 6 of the Unfair Contract Terms Act 1977.

Chapter 3

Contract and tort

3.1 General rule

3.1.1 Since 1623 the general rule has been that common law actions must be brought within six years of their accrual. The Law Reform Committee considered reducing the period to five years to conform with Scots law but preferred to retain the familiar period.

3.2 Contract

3.2.1 Section 5 of the Limitation Act 1980 provides that an action founded on simple contract shall not be brought after the expiration of six years from the date on which the cause of action accrued. The phrase 'simple contract' is not defined, but the word 'simple' is probably used to distinguish contracts under seal which are 'specialties' and subject to the twelve-year period in s 8. In *Re Diplock* [1948] Ch 465 at p 514, the Court of Appeal was prepared to assume that actions founded on simple contract included actions for money had and received, and Edmund Davies J applied that assumption in *Chesworth* v *Farrar* [1967] 1 QB 407: see also *Re Mason* [1929] 1 Ch 1. The expression includes actions on foreign judgments (*Berliner Industriebank AG* v *Jost* [1971] 2 QB 463) but not English judgments which are governed by s 24 of the Limitation Act 1980. The expression does include actions by shareholders to recover amounts due by way of dividends declared or capital repayable under a scheme of arrangement: see *Re Compania de Electricidad de la Provincia de Buenos Aires Ltd* [1980] Ch 146.

3.2.2 It is well settled that in contract the cause of action arises on the breach: *Battley* v *Faulkner* (1820) 3 B & Ald 288, *Gibbs* v *Guild* (1881) 8 QBD 296 and *Lynn* v *Bamber* [1930] 2 KB 72. There is in theory no need to plead or prove damage and if none is proved the plaintiff is still entitled to nominal damages. The rule that the cause of action is complete on the breach has led to difficulties where the breach consists of a failure to act. In *Midland Bank* v *Hett Stubbs &*

14

Kemp [1979] Ch 384, where the breach consisted of not registering an option Oliver J held that the breach occurred when the contract 'ceased to be effectively capable of performance', ie when it was too late to register the option. An analogy could perhaps be drawn with a continuing tort.

3.2.3 If a date or condition is specified for repayment in an action for money lent, time runs from the date specified or from the fulfilment of the condition. However, if no date was specified or the loan was expressed simply to be repayable 'on demand' at common law, time ran in favour of the borrower from the date of his loan: *Garden* v *Bruce* (1868) LR 3 CP 300, *Reeves* v *Butcher* [1891] 2 QB 509 and *Re Brown's Estate* [1893] 2 Ch 300. The justification for the rule was that the cause of action accrued from the first moment the lender could have taken steps to reclaim his money and the writ operated as the demand. On the recommendation of the Law Reform Committee the rule was changed by s 6 of the Limitation Act which postpones the running of time until a written demand is made, where money is lent and no date is specified for its repayment and no security is given.

3.2.4 Bankers are not trustees for their customers and money advanced by a customer to a bank (and vice versa) is a loan and constitutes a debt: *Foley* v *Hill* (1844) 2 HL Cas 28. In the case of all accounts at a bank or building society time does not run against the customer until demand: for deposit accounts see *Atkinson* v *Bradford Third Equitable Benefit Building Society* (1890) 25 QBD 377 and for current accounts see *Joachimson* v *Swiss Bank Corporation* [1921] 3 KB 110. On the other hand, time does run against the bank from the latest dealing on an overdrawn account and a bank cannot recover a dormant overdraft more than six years after the last advance: *Parr's Banking Co Ltd* v *Yates* [1898] 2 QB 460. In practice banks do not leave overdrafts outstanding for six years without taking steps, by obtaining an acknowledgment or otherwise, to prevent time running.

3.2.5 Promissory notes, cheques and bills of exchange are unaffected by s 6 of the Limitation Act 1980. The right of action on them normally accrues when payment is due. If the bill or note is payable on demand, no demand is necessary to enforce payment and time runs from the date of the bill or note, or its delivery if later: *Savage* v *Aldren* (1817) 2 Stark 232 and *Norton* v *Ellam* (1837) 2 M & W 461. A bill payable at sight need not be presented unless the place of payment is specified. If it is, the period of limitation runs from its presentment. In the case of a bill payable at a fixed time after date or a specified period after sight or demand, time runs from the expiration of the relevant period.

3.2.6 Where there is a contingent promise, the contract becomes enforceable on the happening of the contingency and not before: *Waters v Earl of Thanet* (1842) 2 QB 757. In a contract of guarantee the words 'on demand' are to be given their ordinary meaning and time does not run in cases of indirect liability until demand is made and the liability under the guarantee arises: *Bradford Old Bank Ltd* v *Sutcliffe* [1918] 2 KB 833. Therefore, as between the surety and the creditor, time runs when the surety becomes liable to make a payment to the creditor.

3.2.7 The right of action on a general contract of indemnity does not accrue until the liability has been determined and ascertained: *County & District Properties* v *Jenner* [1976] 2 Lloyd's Rep 728, *R & H Green & Silley Weir Ltd* v *British Railways Board* [1985] 1 WLR 570 and *Telfair Shipping Corporation* v *Inersea SA* [1985] 1 WLR 553. The decision in *NHBC* v *Fraser* [1983] 1 All ER 1090 is probably irreconcilable. As between co-sureties the right of contribution arises when the liability is ascertained by the first surety being compelled to pay the creditor: *Wolmershausen* v *Gullick* [1893] 2 Ch 514. Special provision is made for the right of contribution which arises under the Civil Liability (Contribution) Act 1978: Limitation Act 1980, s 10. A surety who pays a statute-barred debt cannot recover from the principal debtor: *Re Morris* [1922] 1 IR 136.

3.2.8 In the absence of any agreement for credit a cause of action for goods sold arises on delivery. If credit is granted, the cause of action arises when the period of credit expires: *Helps* v *Winterbottom* (1831) 2 B & Ad 431. Similarly, in the absence of any agreement that payment should become due at any other date, time runs for payment for work done from the date when the work is completed: *Emery* v *Day* (1834) 1 CM & R 245. Rights of action for breach of express or implied terms by the seller also arise on delivery.

3.2.9 An assignment of an existing debt cannot affect the running of time, nor can events giving rise to subrogation (*Central Insurance Co* v *Seacalf Shipping Corp* [1985] 2 Lloyd's Rep 25) but a novation of a contract may give rise to a new cause of action: *Chatsworth Investment Ltd* v *Cussins (Contractors) Ltd* [1969] 1 WLR 1. So may an account stated: *Ashby* v *James* (1843) 11 M & W 542. When the period has expired the action is barred and the creditor is deprived of any remedy by action or set-off. His right to recover interest is also barred even though the interest may have accrued due during the period: *Cheang Thye Phin* v *Lam Kin Lang* [1929] AC 670 and *Elder* v *Northcott* [1930] 2 Ch 422.

3.3 Tort

3.3.1 The basic period is six years from the date on which the cause of action accrued: Limitation Act 1980, s 2. Some torts are actionable per se, ie without proof of special damage. In those cases time runs from the tortious act. In other cases damage is an essential part of the cause of action and in such cases time runs from the occurrence of the damage. At common law the date when the damage is discovered is immaterial: *Archer* v *Catton & Co Ltd* [1954] 1 WLR 775 and *Cartledge* v *E Jopling & Sons Ltd* [1963] AC 758.

3.3.2 Trespass is actionable per se and time therefrom runs from the day when the trespass was committed. However, trespass may be continuing and in that case a new cause of action accrues every day.

3.3.3 In libel a fresh cause of action accrues upon every publication: *Duke of Brunswick* v *Harmer* (1849) 14 QB 185. In those types of slander where it is necessary to prove special damage (see ss 2 and 3 of the Defamation Act 1952) time also runs from publication. In every case of defamation the period is three not six years from the date when the cause of action accrued: Limitation Act 1980, s 4A, added belatedly on the recommendation of the Faulks Committee on Defamation (1975 Cmnd 5909). Under s 32A of the Limitation Act 1980, with the leave of the High Court, an action can be brought outside the three-year period and beyond any extension allowed on the ground of disability if
  (*a*) all or any of the facts relevant to the cause of action did not become known to the plaintiff until after the expiration of the period, and
  (*b*) the action is brought before the expiration of one year from the earliest date on which he knew all the facts relevant to the cause of action.
There is no reported case in which leave has been sought under this section and the problem of latent damage is not serious in the field of defamation.

3.3.4 The action of deceit is founded upon fraud: *Derry* v *Peek* (1889) 14 App Cas 337. In other torts 'fraudulent' may be nothing more than an abusive epithet: *Beaman* v *ARTS Ltd* [1949] 1 KB 550 per Lord Greene MR at p 558. Section 32 of the Limitation Act 1980 applies whenever the action is based on fraud and postpones time until the plaintiff has discovered the fraud or could with reasonable diligence have discovered it.

3.3.5 In negligence and nuisance damage is an essential part of the cause of action and time does not run until damage occurs. It then runs whether or not the damage is known to the victim: hence the problem of latent damage which is discussed in the next two chapters. For personal injuries the rule was established by *Cartledge* v *E Jopling & Sons Ltd* [1963] AC 758, which led to the report of the Edmund Davies Committee on Limitation of Actions in Cases of Personal Injury (1962 Cmnd 1829) and eventually to what are now ss 11–14 and 33 of the Limitation Act 1980, which make time run from the date of knowledge and confer a discretion to disapply the time limit. For injuries to property the rule was established by *Pirelli General Cable Works Ltd* v *Oscar Faber & Partners* [1983] 2 AC 1, which led to the Law Reform Committee Report on Latent Damage (1984 Cmnd 9390), the Latent Damage Act 1986 and ss 14A and 14B of the Limitation Act 1980. For economic loss the rule was established by the Court of Appeal in *Forster* v *Outred & Co* [1982] 1 WLR 86 and *DW Moore & Co Ltd* v *Ferrier* [1988] 1 WLR 267. When damage 'occurs' it is not always obvious and the rule is easier to state than to apply.

3.3.6 Conversion now includes every act which would have been detinue: Torts (Interference with Goods) Act 1977, s 2 and *Howard E Perry & Co* v *British Railways Board* [1980] 1 WLR 1375. In cases of conversion time runs from the first act of conversion. Therefore, where a chattel is lost time runs in favour of the finder only when he converts the chattel — ie treats it as his own — a date which sometimes may be difficult to discover. Where a chattel is stolen time used to run under the Limitation Act 1939 from the date of the theft; after the expiration of six years from the date of the first conversion the owner's title was extinguished and no action could be brought against the first wrongdoer or against anyone else who might have received the property in the meantime.

3.3.7 The Law Reform Committee found it unacceptable that a thief or a receiver should be able to establish a valid title to stolen goods. The rules that time runs from the first conversion and that title is extinguished once time has run are preserved by ss 3(1) and 3(2) of the Limitation Act 1980, but there is a special rule introduced by s 4 for cases of theft. The section is a masterpiece of opacity but in effect it provides that a thief or any person claiming through him (other than a purchaser for value in good faith) cannot set up a limitation defence against the true owner. A purchaser for value of stolen property will acquire title six years after his purchase and will have a defence to any claim for conversion but the original owner will still be able to sue the thief or any other handler for its value without limit of time. 'Thief' for this purpose includes a person who obtains property by deception or blackmail, and theft includes conduct abroad which would be theft in England: Limitation Act 1980, s 4(5).

3.3.8 A breach of statutory duty is treated as a tort for the purpose of the relevant limitation period: *Clarkson* v *Modern Foundries Ltd* [1957] 1 WLR 1210. So is a claim by a preferential creditor against a receiver appointed by debenture holders: *Westminster Corporation* v *Haste* [1950] Ch 443. Some Acts, such as the Defective Premises Act 1972, contain special provision for determining when the cause of action accrues: s 1(5).

3.3.9 Where a tortious act creates a state of affairs which causes more than one incident of damage, the victim can recover in respect of those incidents which occur within the six years before action: *Backhouse* v *Bonomi* (1861) 9 HL Cas 503 and *Darley Main Colliery Co* v *Mitchell* (1886) 11 App Cas 127. Where continued or repeated tortious conduct creates damage, the victim can recover for so much of the damage as was caused within the limitation period: *Berry* v *Stone Manganese & Marine Ltd* [1972] 1 Lloyd's Rep 182. The onus is on the defendant to show how much damage occurred outside the relevant period: *Clarkson* v *Modern Foundries Ltd* [1957] 1 WLR 1210. The fact that suffering continues over a period does not make the tort a continuing one: *Cartledge* v *E Jopling & Sons Ltd* [1963] AC 758. If there is no tortious act within the period, the plaintiff can recover only in respect of fresh damage arising within the period: *Darley Main Colliery* v *Mitchell* (1886) 11 App Cas 127 esp per Lord Halsbury at p 133. It is a question of fact and degree whether the damage is sufficiently distinct to result in a separate cause of action (*Mount Albert BC* v *Johnson* (1979) 2 NZLR 236) but such cases are very rare.

3.4 Concurrent liability

3.4.1 There are situations, particularly in negligence, where a plaintiff can plead contract or tort or both: *Forsikring Vesta* v *Butcher* [1988] 3 WLR 565. In the nineteenth century it appears to have been the rule that in such situations the plaintiff, whether he pleaded in assumpsit or case, was entitled only to the shorter limitation period: *Howell* v *Young* (1826) 5 B&C 259, *Smith* v *Fox* (1848) 6 Hare 386 and *Bean* v *Wade* (1885) 2 TLR 157. In the twentieth century until 1976 it was thought that the cause of action lay in contract only: *Groom* v *Crocker* [1939] 1 KB 194 and *Bagot* v *Stevens Scanlan & Co Ltd* [1966] 1 QB 197. In *Midland Bank Trust Co Ltd* v *Hett Stubbs & Kemp* [1979] Ch 384, Oliver J, relying on *Esso Petroleum Co Ltd* v *Mardon* [1976] QB 801, decided that there could be concurrent liability in tort and contract and assumed that the longer period was available. The Court of Appeal reached the same decision in *Batty* v *Metropolitan Property Realisations Ltd* [1978] 1 QB 554 and proceeded on the same assumption in *Forster* v *Outred Co* [1982] 1 WLR 86 and in *DW Moore & Co Ltd* v *Ferrier* [1988] 1 WLR 267. The Privy Council in *Tai Hing Ltd* v *Liu Chong Hing Bank* [1986] AC 80 at p 107, while recognising that different consequences followed in the field of limitation according to whether the liability arose in contract or tort, was not prepared to accept that the parties' obligations in tort could be any greater than those to be found in their contract and discouraged 'searching for a liability in tort where the parties are in a contractual relationship'.

3.4.2 It has been said that 'since *Hedley Byrne & Co* v *Heller & Partners* [1964] AC 465, all breaches of contract which might with reasonable care have been avoided became torts overnight'. The Privy Council has signalled a retreat from that position but the Supreme Court of Canada has turned a blind eye to the signal: *Central Trust Co* v *Rafuse* (1986) 31 DLR (4th) 481. In two cases involving sub-contracts the Court of Appeal has found no reason to interfere with the contractual chain of liability by imposing direct tortious liability: *Simaan General Contracting Co* v *Pilkington Glass Ltd (No 2)* [1988] QB 758 and *Greater Nottingham Co-operative Society Ltd* v *Cementation Piling and Foundations Ltd* [1989] QB 71. In *National Bank of Greece* v *Pinios Shipping Co* [1989] 1 All ER 213 at p 223 Lloyd LJ said that, 'It has never been the law that a plaintiff who has the choice of suing in contract or tort can fail in contract yet nevertheless succeed in tort'. However, no question of limitation arose there. It seems odd to impose a tortious duty on a contracting party simply so as to extend the period of his liability or to increase the amount of recoverable damages, but see *Banque Keyser Ullmann SA* v *Skandia (UK) Insurance Co Ltd* [1987] 2 WLR 1300. *Pirelli General Cable Works Ltd* v *Oscar Faber & Partners* [1983] 2 AC 1 was itself a case of concurrent liability but it was argued in the House of Lords on the basis that the defendants were liable in both contract and tort.

Chapter 4

Personal injuries and death

4.1 Personal injuries

4.1.1 Section 11 of the Limitation Act 1980 provides a special three-year period which applies to

any action for damages for negligence nuisance or breach of duty (whether the duty exists by virtue of a contract or of provision made by or under a statute or independently of any contract or any such provision) where the damages claimed by the plaintiff for the negligence nuisance or breach of duty consist of or include damages in respect of personal injuries to the plaintiff or any other person.

This three-year period was first introduced by Parliament in 1954 on the recommendation of the Monckton Committee on Alternative Remedies (1946 Cmnd 6860).

4.1.2 The period applies to personal injuries caused by any tort, not only nuisance or negligence: *Letang* v *Cooper* [1965] 1 QB 232 and *Long* v *Hepworth* [1968] 1 WLR 1299. It applies whenever the damages claimed include damages in respect of personal injuries, but it does not apply where the claim is at one remove from personal injuries, eg for negligence in the conduct of a personal injuries claim: *Ackbar* v *CF Green & Co Ltd* [1975] QB 582. Nor does the period apply to a claim for purely financial loss caused by the failure to carry out a medical operation properly: *Pattison* v *Hobbs* (1985) *The Times*, 11 November CA. Similarly, the period does not apply to claims for contribution between individual tortfeasors even though the claim against them is in respect of personal injuries but it does apply where one of the defendants has himself suffered personal injuries and claims for those against his co-defendant: *Kennett* v *Brown* [1988] 1 WLR 582. A claim for damages for property alone may be made after the time for claiming has expired in respect of personal injuries caused by the same act.

4.1.3 'Personal injuries' includes any disease and any impairment of a person's physical or mental condition: Limitation Act 1980, s 38(1).

This clearly covers shock caused by other injuries and possibly distress caused by false imprisonment or other torts. Damages cannot be awarded for injured feelings arising out of an ordinary breach of contract: *Bliss* v *South East Thames RHA* [1987] 1 Lloyd's Rep 700.

4.2 The three-year period

4.2.1 Section 11(4) of the Limitation Act 1980 provides that except in cases where death ensues, the period is three years from the date on which the cause of action accrued or the date of knowledge (if later) of the person injured. The date on which a cause of action accrues has been considered in Chapters 2 and 3 above. In cases of continuing torts a fresh cause of action arises so long as the wrongful state of affairs subsists. Thus, a plaintiff may be able to recover for injuries so far as they were caused within (and not so far as they arose outside) the period: *Berry* v *Stone Manganese & Marine Ltd* [1972] 1 Lloyd's Rep 182.

4.2.2 Time cannot begin to run until the injured person's 'date of knowledge': Limitation Act 1980, s 11(4). This date may coincide with the accrual of the cause of action but it may be much later. The date of knowledge is defined in s 14 as the date on which the victim first had knowledge of four facts. Knowledge that any acts or omissions did or did not as a matter of law involve negligence, nuisance or breach of duty is expressly stated to be irrelevant. It is not essential that the plaintiff should know that he has a cause of action. This resolves one of the most contested issues on the wording of the Limitation Act 1963, an Act which Lord Reid thought had a strong claim to the distinction of being the worst drafted Act on the statute book: *Central Asbestos Co Ltd* v *Dodd* [1973] AC 518 and *Re Harper* v *National Coal Board* [1974] QB 614.

4.2.3 The four facts of which the victim must be aware are:
    (*a*) that the injury in question was significant;
    (*b*) that the injury was attributable in whole or in part to the act or omission which is alleged to constitute negligence, nuisance or breach of duty;
    (*c*) the identity of the defendant; and
    (*d*) if it is alleged that the act or omission was that of a person other than the defendant, the identity of that person and the additional facts supporting the bringing of an action against the defendant: Limitation Act 1980, s 14(1).

4.2.4 The word 'significant' is defined in s 14(2):

an injury is significant if the person whose date of knowledge is in question would reasonably have considered it sufficiently serious to justify his instituting proceedings for damages against a defendant who did not dispute liability and was able to satisfy a judgment.

The reference is to proceedings generally and not to the particular action in question. It is assumed that the defendant can and will pay, and attention is directed to the nature and degree of the injury. The test is both subjective and objective in that it requires consideration of the reasonable man but one with the plaintiff's characteristics and in his circumstances. The questions are: would this plaintiff have considered the injury sufficiently serious and would he have been reasonable if he did not regard it as sufficiently serious: *McCafferty* v *Metropolitan Police District Receiver* [1977] 1 WLR 1073. The use of the conditional implies that it is not necessary for the plaintiff to have given actual consideration to the question but, if he has, it is no excuse that he is reluctant to 'sponge' or to sue the particular defendant: *Buck* v *English Electric Co* [1977] 1 WLR 806. Where the injury appears to be trivial, time will not run against the plaintiff unless and until he becomes aware of a real risk of more serious consequences: *Knipe* v *British Railways Board* [1972] 1 QB 361. Per contra if the initial injury is sufficiently serious to warrant suing, subsequent deterioration will not prevent time from running: *Goodchild* v *Greatness Timber Co Ltd* [1968] 2 QB 372 and *Miller* v *London Electrical Co Ltd* [1976] 2 Lloyd's Rep 284. Where there is more than one injury, it is the first that is material for this purpose: *Bristow* v *Grout* (1986) *The Times*, 3 November.

4.2.5   The second fact of which the plaintiff must be aware is that the injury was attributable in whole or in part to the act or omission complained of: Limitation Act 1980, s 14(1)(*b*). 'Attributable' means capable of being attributed to the relevant act, not 'caused by'. Knowledge of the law is immaterial and the plaintiff need know only that the act or omission is one of the possible causes of his injury: *Wilkinson* v *Ancliff (BLT) Ltd* [1986] 1 WLR 1352. If the plaintiff is unaware that the injuries are caused by any act or omission of the defendant, he clearly does not have the requisite knowledge.

4.2.6   The third fact of which the plaintiff must be aware is the identity of the defendant. This covers situations such as the hit-and-run driver and the garage which fails to repair another driver's car properly: *Walford* v *Richards* [1976] 1 Lloyd's Rep 526. It also covers the situation where the defendant is one of a group of companies and the plaintiff cannot at first identify which to sue: *Clark* v *Forbes Stuart (Thames Street) Ltd* [1964] 1 WLR 836 and *Simpson* v *Norwest Holst Southern Ltd* [1980] 1 WLR 968.

4.2.7   The fourth fact of which the plaintiff must be aware is relevant only in cases of vicarious liability. The plaintiff must know the identity of the person who committed the act or omission and 'the additional facts supporting the bringing of an action against the defendant'. It is curious that the identity of the person should be considered material. If a person is knocked down by a railway train, the victim does not really need to know the name of the driver before he sues British Rail. However, it is difficult to read 'identity' in s 14(1)(d) as having a different meaning from 'identity' in s 14(1)(c). Knowledge of the law of vicarious liability is clearly not required.

4.3 Knowledge

4.3.1 Once the plaintiff knows the first three (and if relevant the fourth) matters listed in s 14(1) time begins to run against him. Knowledge for this purpose may be actual or constructive. In most cases the plaintiff's actual knowledge is a question of fact, as readily ascertainable as the state of his digestion. There are, however, border-line cases where a plaintiff, particularly one who has to rely on expert opinions, may suspect that a state of affairs exists but may not know it: *Davis* v *Ministry of Defence*, (1985) *The Times*, 7 August CA. On the other hand there are situations where a plaintiff's suspicions, even though unconfirmed by expert opinion, may amount to actual knowledge: eg *Wilkinson* v *Ancliff (BLT) Ltd* [1986] 1 WLR 1352.

4.3.2 Constructive knowledge is defined in s 14(3) of the Limitation Act 1980.

For the purposes of this section a person's knowledge includes knowledge which he might reasonably have been expected to acquire (a) from facts observable or ascertainable by him; or (b) from facts ascertainable by him with the help of medical or other appropriate expert advice which it is reasonable for him to seek; but a person shall not be fixed under this subsection with knowledge of a fact ascertainable only with the help of expert advice so long as he has taken all reasonable steps to obtain (and, where appropriate, to act on) that advice.

This roughly covers the four types of constructive knowledge identified in *Re Montagu's Settlement Trusts* [1987] Ch 264 at p 277.

4.3.3 The first limb of this subsection fixes the plaintiff with knowledge of any facts which are reasonably observable or ascertainable by him. The test is not purely objective. The plaintiff's own characteristics must be taken into account and the question is not what would a reasonable man have known but what it would have been reasonable for this man to have known. His education, state of health and 'walk of life' are therefore relevant: *Re Pickles* v *National Coal Board* [1968] 1 WLR 997,

Newton v *Cammell Laird & Co Ltd* [1969] 1 WLR 415 and *Davis* v *City and Hackney Health Authority* (1989) *The Times*, 27 January.

4.3.4 The second limb in effect imposes a duty on the plaintiff to take expert advice where it is reasonable for him to do so. Since a plaintiff's knowledge of the law is immaterial a solicitor is not an expert for this purpose (*Fowell* v *National Coal Board* (1986) *The Times*, 28 May CA but erroneous legal advice will not save the plaintiff if all the facts were available to him: *Farmer* v *National Coal Board* (1985) *The Times*, 27 April CA. On the other hand, if a person who does not know all the facts is advised by a solicitor not to take the matter further, time will not run unless the facts are ascertainable by him without legal advice: *Simpson* v *Norwest Holst Southern Ltd* [1980] 1 WLR 968 and *Leadbitter* v *Hodge* [1982] 2 All ER 167. A person who consults his union may be acting reasonably in not seeking more expert advice: *Knipe* v *British Railways Board* [1972] 1 QB 361 and *Howell* v *West Midlands Passenger Transport Executive* [1973] 1 Lloyd's Rep 199.

4.3.5 The proviso to section 14(3) protects a plaintiff who consults an expert who fails to discover all the facts that he might have discovered: eg *Marston* v *British Railways Board* [1976] ICR 124. It seems that the operative date for constructive knowledge is the date when the victim could reasonably be expected to put the facts before a solicitor: *Jones* v *Bennett* [1976] 1 Lloyd's Rep 484.

4.4 Discretion to disapply

4.4.1 The court has power to direct that the three-year period shall not apply to an action if the court thinks it equitable to allow the action to proceed. Section 33(1) of the Limitation Act 1980 provides that, if it appears to the court that it would be equitable to allow an action to proceed having regard to the degree to which first, the provisions of ss 11, 11A or 12 prejudice the plaintiff or any person whom he represents and secondly, any decision of the court under s 33(1) would prejudice the defendant or any person whom he represents, the court may direct that ss 11, 11A or 12 shall not apply to the action, or to any specified cause of action to which the action relates. The discretion does not extend to time limits imposed by statutes other than the Limitation Act 1980.

4.4.2 The power is to be exercised by weighing the prejudice caused to the plaintiff by the operation of the three-year period against the prejudice suffered by the defendant if the period is extended. Where the three-year period is extended by other provisions, such as disability, the power can be invoked after the extended period: Limitation Act 1980, s 33(8). The court can exercise its discretion differently as between different causes in the same action, but not as between separate allegations constituting one cause of action.

4.4.3 The power, although probably intended by the Law Reform Committee for the 'occasional hard case', is not confined to exceptional cases, and the discretion is unfettered: *Thompson* v *Brown* [1981] 1 WLR 744. The time limit can be extended only if the plaintiff has *not* commenced proceedings within the three-year period. If he has begun an action in time and for whatever reason does not proceed with it, s 33 does not enable leave to be given for a second action: *Walkley* v *Precision Forgings Ltd* [1979] 1 WLR 606 (effectively overruling the decision in *Firman* v *Ellis* [1978] QB 886) and *Chappell* v *Cooper* [1980] 1 WLR 958. The reason is that it is the plaintiff's own conduct in the first action and not the limitation period which has led to the failure of his cause of action: *Deerness* v *John R Keeble & Son (Brantham) Ltd* [1983] 2 Lloyd's Rep 260. The rule does not apply if the first action was wholly ineffective, for example, because the defendant was a company in liquidation: *Wilson* v *Banner Scaffolding* Milmo J (1982) *The Times*, 22 June and *White* v *Glass*, (1989) *The Times*, 18 February CA.

4.4.4 In the normal case there will be prejudice to the plaintiff if an order is refused and the degree of prejudice will depend largely on his prospects of success in the action: *Thompson* v *Brown* [1981] 1 WLR 744. However, if the plaintiff has already a strong case against one defendant he will not suffer any serious prejudice by the refusal of leave to sue another: *Liff* v *Peasley* [1980] 1 WLR 781. Equally, a defendant will normally suffer prejudice if an order is made, but he will only have lost a windfall unless his ability to defend has been affected by the delay: *Thompson* v *Brown* (supra). Consequently, if the delay (however long) does not seriously affect the evidence, the power will generally be exercised: eg *Brooks* v *J & P Coates Ltd* [1984] 1 All ER 702 and *Hutcheson* v *Pontinental (Holiday Services) Ltd* [1987] BTLC 81. The plaintiff is therefore more likely to obtain leave if the evidence is largely documentary or if a system of work, rather than an isolated incident, is in issue.

4.4.5 Some guidance as to the exercise of the discretion is given by s 33(3) which requires the court to have regard to all the circumstances of the case. In particular, six matters (which Lord Diplock described as a curious hotchpotch) are to be considered. These are:
  (*a*) the length of and the reasons for the plaintiff's delay;
  (*b*) the extent to which the evidence is likely to be affected by the delay;
  (*c*) the defendant's conduct including his response to requests for information or inspection;
  (*d*) the duration of any disability of the plaintiff;

(*e*) the extent to which the plaintiff acted promptly or reasonably after discovering that he might have a cause of action; and

(*f*) any steps taken to obtain expert advice and the nature of that advice.

4.4.6 In this context it is only delay after the expiry of the initial three-year period that is relevant: *Eastman* v *London Country Bus Services* (1985) *The Times,* 23 November CA. 'Disability' probably means legal disability, ie mental incapacity: s 38(2) but see *Pilmore* v *Northern Trawlers Ltd* [1986] 1 Lloyd's Rep 552. References in s 33(3) to the plaintiff and the defendant include their respective solicitors and agents where the context admits: *Firman* v *Ellis* [1978] QB 886 at p 909.

4.4.7 The existence of a remedy against the plaintiff's solicitor is an important but not overriding factor: *Thompson* v *Brown* [1981] 1 WLR 744. If the case against the solicitors is weak it will be disregarded: *Deeming* v *British Steel Corporation* (1979) 123 SJ 303. The extent to which either party is insured may be a relevant factor and the court will treat the party and his insurer as a composite unit: *Davis* v *Soltenpur* (1983) 133 New LJ 720. The ability of the defendant to satisfy judgment and of the plaintiff to pay costs are also material: *Lye* v *Marks & Spencer* (1988) *The Times,* 15 February CA.

4.4.8 The plaintiff's motive for not suing earlier and any serious deterioration in his condition (as for example in *Miller* v *London Electrical Manufacturing Co* [1976] 2 Lloyd's Rep 284) are relevant factors: *McCafferty* v *Metropolitan Police Receiver* [1977] 1 WLR 1073. Where a plaintiff is seeking leave to proceed under s 33, the court is entitled to know in general terms what legal advice the plaintiff has been given and the plaintiff may have to answer interrogatories on that point: *Jones* v *GD Searle & Co Ltd* [1979] 1 WLR 101. The court will be influenced by its view of whether or not the plaintiff has behaved reasonably: *Cornish* v *Kearley & Tonge* (1983) 133 New LJ 870. The court is likely to be particularly sympathetic to persons who do not know their legal rights, a class for whom the discretion was probably originally intended: *Firman* v *Ellis* [1978] QB 886.

4.4.9 The matter is one of discretion and the Court of Appeal will not normally interfere unless satisfied that the judge has proceeded on wrong principles: *Conry* v *Simpson* [1983] 3 All ER 369 and *Bradley* v *Hanseatic Shipping* [1986] 2 Lloyd's Rep 34.

4.5 Death

4.5.1 Death at common law was the ultimate limitation point because a personal action died with the plaintiff. Two statutes allow damages to be recovered where the victim of a tort or other breach of duty has died. The Law Reform (Miscellaneous Provisions) Act 1934 transfers the plaintiff's right to damages in respect of any tort to his estate on his death and so permits recovery by his personal representatives. The Fatal Accidents Act 1976 gives a substantive right to damages to the victim's dependants; the claim is not that of the deceased and the death is the source of liability. Damages recoverable under the two Acts are cumulative where both apply, but double recovery for loss of earnings is prevented by s 4 of the Administration of Justice Act 1982, reversing *Gamell* v *Wilson* [1982] AC 27.

4.6   Law Reform Act claims

4.6.1   The basic period is three years from the date of death or the date of the personal representative's knowledge, whichever is the later. Section 11(5) of the Limitation Act 1980 provides that, if the person injured dies while time is running under s 11(4), ie during the initial three-year period from the cause of action accruing or the victim's date of knowledge, the limitation period for the purposes of the Law Reform (Miscellaneous Provisions) Act 1934 shall be three years from the death or from the date of the personal representative's knowledge, whichever is the later. The relevant knowledge is that of the 'personal representative' which includes any person who is or has been a personal representative of the deceased, including an executor who has not proved the will (whether or not he has renounced probate) but not a special personal representative: Limitation Act 1980, s 11(6). Regard must be given to any knowledge acquired before or after the person became a personal representative: s 11(6). If there is more than one personal representative, the earliest date of knowledge is taken: s 11(7).

4.6.2   The purpose of s 11(5) is to give the personal representative a reasonable chance to start an action which was still available to the deceased at his death. The estate gets the benefit of a new period running at the earliest from the death, and the running of time depends on the personal representative's knowledge.

4.6.3   If the deceased died outside the initial three-year period, any action begun by his personal representative is barred by s 11(4) and does not apply. The court then has a discretion under s 33 to disapply s 11 if it appears equitable to allow the action to proceed. The prejudice to the defendant must be weighed against the prejudice to the persons entitled to the deceased's estate, being the persons whom the personal representative represents for the purposes of s 33(1)(a). The court has to have regard to the conduct of the deceased as well as that of the plaintiff in exercising its discretion under s 33: Limitation Act 1980, ss 33(4) and (5). The relevant factors in s 33(3) therefore relate to the deceased up to his death and to the personal representatives thereafter.

4.6.4 If the victim dies within the initial three-year period and the personal representative begins an action more than three years after the death or the date of his own knowledge, it is barred by s 11(5). Again, the discretion in s 33 can be invoked but in this case only the conduct of the personal representative will be relevant.

4.7 Fatal Accidents Act claims

4.7.1 The basic period is again a three-year period running from the death or the date of knowledge, whichever is the later, but in this case the relevant person for the purposes of knowledge is the person for whose benefit the action is brought: Limitation Act 1980, s 12(2). Possible beneficiaries include any spouse, parent, child or grandchild of the deceased. If any of them is an infant or of unsound mind at the death he has a period of three years from the date when he attains eighteen or becomes sane in which to bring his action: s 12(3). A claim under the Act can be made on behalf of a number of dependants although only one action lies in respect of the same subject-matter of complaint: Fatal Accidents Act 1976, s 2(3). If so, the knowledge of each dependant is relevant and the court may direct that any dependant shall be excluded from those for whose benefit the action is brought: Limitation Act 1980, ss 13(1) and (2). No such direction shall be given if the dependant in question is entitled to an extended period or can persuade the court to disapply s 12: Limitation Act 1980, s 13(3).

4.7.3 If the action was barred before the death of the person injured, the dependants' action is barred by s 12(1) of the Limitation Act 1980. However, the court may be persuaded to exercise its discretion to disapply s 12 under s 33 of the Limitation Act 1980. In exercising its discretion the court must have regard to all the circumstances of the case, including the length of and the reasons for the delay on the part of the deceased, and must apply s 33(3) as if references to the plaintiff included references to the deceased: s 33(5). The court cannot extend time if the deceased was barred by a time limit not in s 11 of the Limitation Act 1980: s 33(2).

4.7.4 If the person injured dies within the initial three-year period but an action under the Fatal Accidents Act is brought more than three years from the date of death or of the dependants' knowledge, the action is barred by s 12(2) of the Limitation Act 1980. Again, there is a discretion under s 33 to disapply s 12. Under s 33(5), s 33(3) of the Act has effect as if references to the plaintiff included references to the dependants. The guidelines in s 33(3) must therefore be applied concurrently in relation to the plaintiff and each dependant.

Chapter 5

Latent damage

5.1 The problem

5.1.1 The possibility of time running before a person discovered his injury was revealed by *Cartledge* v *E Jopling & Sons Ltd* [1963] AC 758 and dealt with eventually by making time run from the date of knowledge and allowing a residual discretionary period. In August 1980 the Lord Chancellor asked the Law Reform Committee to report on the law of limitation in negligence cases involving latent defects other than latent disease or injury to the person. Before the Committee reported (1984 Cmnd 9390) the House of Lords decided in *Pirelli General Cable Works Ltd* v *Oscar Faber & Partners* [1983] 2 AC 1 that in cases of latent damage to buildings the plaintiff's cause of action accrues, and time begins to run when damage occurs to the building. At common law discovery or discoverability is immaterial.

5.1.2 The test in *Pirelli* is easier to state than to apply and has given rise to four difficulties which have not been solved by the Law Reform Committee. The committee did tackle the major problem after concluding that the law in *Pirelli* was unjust to both sides. The preferred solution, enacted in the Latent Damage Act 1986, was to allow the plaintiff an alternative period of three years from the date of discovery, or discoverability, of significant damage and to give the defendant a 'long-stop' which bars the plaintiff from suing more than fifteen years after the defendant's breach of duty.

5.1.3 Section 1 of the Latent Damage Act 1986 inserts two new sections (14A and B) into the Limitation Act 1980. These sections apply to actions for damages for negligence other than those to which s 11 of the Act applies. Actions in which claims for both damages to the person and to property are made are within s 11 and the rules explained in the last chapter apply. There is however nothing to prevent a plaintiff from bringing a separate action for damages to property to which the time limits in ss 14A and B will apply.

5.2 The *Pirelli* rule

5.2.1 The Latent Damage Act preserves the rule that a cause of action in negligence accrues at the date on which damage occurs and unless the damage is not discovered or discoverable within the first three years of this date time will expire as in other tort actions at the end of the usual six-year period: Limitation Act 1980, s 14(A)(4).

5.2.2 The first problem with the *Pirelli* rule is the difficulty of ascertaining when damage occurs, particularly when it is a continuous process. The damage must be both relevant and significant (*London Borough of Bromley* v *Rush & Tompkins* (1985) 35 Build LR 94) and expert evidence is often necessary to determine the point of time when this occurs. In borderline cases the result can turn on the onus of proof and it is for the plaintiff to show that his cause of action accrued within the relevant period: *London Congregational Union Incorporated* v *Harris & Harris* [1988] 1 All ER 15. The Law Reform Committee took the view that no reform of the law could eliminate these factual uncertainties.

5.2.3 The second problem with the *Pirelli* rule is caused by Lord Fraser's reference to buildings 'doomed from the start'. In *Pirelli* Lord Fraser said, [1983] 2 AC at p 16,

There may perhaps be cases where the defect is so gross that the building is doomed from the start, and where the owner's cause of action will accrue as soon as it is built, but it seems unlikely that such a defect would not be discovered within the limitation period. Such cases, if they exist, would be exceptional.

The scope and even the existence of this exception are far from certain. In *London Congregational Union Incorporated* v *Harris & Harris* [1988] 1 All ER 15 the Court of Appeal followed *Pirelli* and, although they accepted that damage was inevitable sooner or later from the defective design, held that the 'doomed from the start' exception did not apply. Sir Denys Buckley dissented on the ground that economic loss had been suffered from the outset because the defects were sufficiently serious to require immediate attention. In *Ketteman* v *Hansel Properties Ltd* [1987] AC 189 the House of Lords discouraged reliance on the exception. Lord Keith said that Lord Fraser's comments were obiter and that any contention that a building suffering from a defect which would inevitably cause damage later was 'doomed from the start' and was inconsistent with the result in *Pirelli* itself. Lord Brandon did not know what special cases Lord Fraser had in mind. See also *Jones* v *Stroud DC* [1986] 1 WLR 1141, *Kensington and Chelsea and Westminster Area Health Authority* v *Wettern Composites Ltd* [1985] 1 All ER 346 and *Tozer Kemsley & Milburn (Holdings) Ltd* v *J Jarvis & Sons Ltd* (1985) 4 Con LR 44.

5.2.4 The third problem with *Pirelli* is its relationship with economic loss emphasised in Sir Denys Buckley's dissenting judgment in *London Congregational Union Incorporated* v *Harris & Harris* [1988] 1 All ER 15. In *Pirelli* Lord Fraser rejected the argument that economic loss did not occur until discoverability on the ground that an owner could dispose of an apparently sound building without loss. He did not, however, deal with the contrary argument that loss does occur when an owner acquires a defective article because he has a right of action to recover the cost of putting the defect right: *Junior Books Ltd* v *Veitchi Co Ltd* [1983] AC 520. In *Dove* v *Banhams Patent Locks Ltd* [1983] 1 WLR 1436 Hodgson J rejected the argument that time ran from the installation of a defective security gate because loss was inevitable sooner or later (in effect the 'doomed from the start' argument) but again did not deal with the problem of economic loss accruing on the installation. The problem was recognized by Bingham LJ in *Simaan General Contracting Co* v *Pilkington Glass Ltd (No 2)* [1988] QB 758 and the answer may be that the scope of the decision in *Junior Books Ltd* v *Veitchi Co Ltd* must be restricted to vanishing point: *D & F Estates Ltd* v *Church Commissioners* [1988] 3 WLR 368 and *Department of the Environment* v *Thomas Bates & Son* (1988) *The Times*, 6 December CA.

5.2.5 The fourth problem with the *Pirelli* rule is that it results in different periods for persons engaged in comparable activities resulting in similar losses and the duration of liability bears no relation to culpability. The surveyor who advises his client to buy a defective building is liable from the purchase (*Secretary of State for the Environment* v *Essex Goodman & Suggitt* [1981] 1 WLR 1432). The architect who designs it and the builder who builds it become liable when physical damage occurs to the building (*Pirelli*), and the local authority which approves the plans becomes liable when the building becomes a danger to public health or safety (*Jones* v *Stroud DC* [1986] 1 WLR 1141).

5.2.6 In certain situations there is a right to recover for economic loss unconnected with physical damage: *Hedley Byrne & Co Ltd* v *Heller & Partners Ltd* [1964] AC 465, *Muirhead* v *Industrial Tank Specialities Ltd* [1986] 1 QB 507 and *Yuen Kun Yeu* v *AG of Hong Kong* [1988] AC 175. In these cases time runs in accordance with *Pirelli* when the damage occurs. Again, there are problems in identifying the damage and the date it occurs, and *Pirelli* offers no guidance in solving those problems. Indeed, the Court of Appeal appears to regard it as 'turning on special principles relating to its own peculiar subject matter': *D W Moore & Co Ltd* v *Ferrier* [1988] 1 WLR 267 at p 280. In nearly all cases of 'pure' economic loss the damage occurs when the negligent advice is acted on but there is no presumption to that effect and it is a question of fact in each case whether actual damage has been established and when: *Forster* v *Outred & Co* [1982] 1 WLR 86, *Melton* v *Walker & Stanger* (1981) 125 SJ 861, *Baker* v *Ollard & Bentley* (1982) 126 SJ 593 and *D W Moore & Co* v *Ferrier* [1988] 1 WLR 267. The decision in *Dove* v *Banhams Patent Locks Ltd* [1983] 1 WLR 1436 has been explained not as a case of pure economic loss but one related to property where some physical manifestation of the defect was required. Exceptionally, in *UBAF Ltd* v *European American Banking Corporation* [1984] QB 713 the Court of Appeal was not prepared to find that damage occurred when the advice was acted on. Where the damage can be prevented time does not run until it is too late to prevent it (*Midland Bank* v *Hett Stubbs & Kemp* [1979] Ch 384) and presumably in *Ross* v *Caunters* [1980] Ch 297 where wrong advice was given on executing a will, time did not run until the testator died. For surveyors' liability see *Secretary of State for the Environment* v *Essex Goodman & Suggitt* [1986] 1 WLR 1432 and *Kitney* v *Jones Lang & Wootton* (1988) 20 EG 88.

5.2.7 The result appears to be that even under *Pirelli* there is a distinction between pure economic loss and loss related to property. In the former the simple possibility of having to pay an unquantified sum in the future is sufficient to start time running while in the latter there must be some physical manifestation of the defect. In retrospect it seems unfortunate that the House of Lords did not draw the line between personal and financial injuries (where, despite Lord Fraser's analogy, there is a clear distinction of principle) instead of making a possibly unintended and certainly artificial distinction between different types of financial loss.

5.3 The alternative period

5.3.1 Sections 14A and 14B apply to any action for damages for negligence other than those which consist of or include claims for damages in respect of personal injuries. They apply only to actions for negligence and not to actions for nuisance or breach of statutory duty: contrast s 11. Subject to this they apply to all forms of negligence resulting in damage to property or economic loss and to actions commenced on or after 18 September 1986, unless the cause of action was already barred. The Law Reform Committee had contractual as well as tortious liability in mind (para 2.3 of its Report Cmnd 9390) and it seems negligent of the draftsman not to have indicated whether ss 14A and 14B apply to actions framed in contract as well as tort. In principle it would be odd if they did not but the reference in s 14A(2) to s 2 seems to indicate that the draftsman had only tort in mind.

5.3.2 Section 14A(3) provides that an action within the section is not to be brought outside the period specified in s 14A(4), ie either six years from the date on which the cause of action accrued or three years from a 'starting date' at which the plaintiff knew or ought to have known of the damage. If the three-year period expires first only the six-year period is relevant: Limitation Act 1980, ss 14A(1) and 14A(4)(b).

5.3.3 The six-year period runs from the date on which the cause of action accrued, ie the date on which the breach of contract occurred or the date on which the damage occurred in tort. The decision in *Pirelli* therefore continues to be material in cases of latent damage, not only for the past (to test whether the action was barred before 18 September 1986) but also for the future.

5.3.4 The three-year period runs from the earliest date on which the plaintiff (or any person in whom the cause of action was vested before him) first had both the knowledge required for bringing an action for damages in respect of the relevant damage and a right to bring such action. The constituent elements of knowledge set out in s 14 are repeated in s 14A but the drafting is slightly different. For time to run the plaintiff must have knowledge:

(a) of the material facts about the damage, ie such facts as would lead a reasonable person who had suffered such damage to consider it sufficiently serious to justify his instituting proceedings for damages against a defendant who did not dispute liability and was able to satisfy a judgment: Limitation Act 1980, ss 14A(6)(a) and (7) (compare for personal injuries ss 14(1)(a) and 14(2)); and

(b) of the other facts relevant to the current action mentioned in s 14A(8).

5.3.5 The other facts are:

(a) that the damage was attributable in whole or in part to the act or omission which is alleged to constitute negligence;

(b) the identity of the defendant; and

(c) in cases of vicarious liability, the identity of the person who committed the act or omission and the additional facts supporting the bringing of an action against the employer or other person responsible: Limitation Act 1980 s 14A(8), corresponding to ss 14(1)(b), (c) and (d) for personal injuries.

5.3.6 Cases on the 'date of knowledge' for the purposes of s 11(4) and s 14 of the Act will therefore be material for construing the corresponding provisions of s 14A. There is a similar provision that knowledge of the law is irrelevant: Limitation Act, s 14A(9) compared with s 14(1). Constructive knowledge is dealt with in s 14A(10) in terms similar to s 14(3) with the deletion of the reference to specifically medical advice. The plaintiff therefore is taken to know those facts reasonably observable or ascertainable by him as well as those facts which would have come to light if he had taken any expert advice which it was reasonable for him to take. However, he is not taken to know those facts which a reasonable expert adviser would have discovered but the plaintiff's expert did not discover.

5.4 The long-stop

5.4.1 Two major differences between cases of personal injury and other cases of negligent damage are that only the former have the discretionary period in s 33 and the latter are subject to a long-stop which prevents the action whether or not time has begun to run under the primary period.

5.4.2 The long-stop is contained in s 14(B) which provides in subsection (1) that an action for damages for negligence (other than one to which s 11 applies) shall not be brought after the expiration of fifteen years from the date (or if more than one from the last of the dates) on which there occurred any act or omission which is alleged to constitute negligence and to which the damage is alleged to be attributable in whole or in part. Section 14B(2) makes it clear that the long-stop applies whether or not the cause of action has accrued and whether or not the starting date for the three-year period has occurred. It does not apply to cases of deliberate concealment: Limitation Act 1980, s 32(5). Where the damage arises from an omission, the protection of the long-stop may be illusory: cf *Midland Bank* v *Hett Stubbs & Kemp* [1979] Ch 384.

5.4.3 The period for this purpose is therefore fifteen years from the date of the last breach of duty. The period is arbitrary and not suited to all cases. It applies to physical damage to property and professional negligence claims but not to personal injuries. It represents, in effect, a compromise between the interests of the general public and those of the building industry and the professions.

5.5 Successors

5.5.1 An owner of a defective chattel or building has a cause of action when damage occurs to the chattel or building and time begins to run against him from that date. If the damage is latent he may be able to dispose of it for its full value, and any loss will fall on the subsequent purchaser. Before the Latent Damage Act 1986 the better view was that the subsequent purchaser could not sue at all because he was not the owner when the damage occurred and the cause of action arose: *Sparham-Souter* v *Town and Country Developments (Essex) Ltd* [1976] QB 858 and *Perry* v *Tendring District Council* (1984) 3 Con LR 74. The contrary view that he could sue and time did not run until his date of purchase expressed in *Eames London Estates Ltd* v *North Herts District Council*

(1981) 259 EG 491 was disapproved in *Pirelli General Cable Works Ltd v Oscar Faber and Partners* [1983] 2 AC 1 at p 18.

5.5.2   The matter is now dealt with in s 3 of the Latent Damage Act by creating a statutory cause of action. Where a cause of action accrues to A in respect of negligence causing damage to his property and before A is aware of the material facts about the damage B acquires an interest in the property, a fresh cause of action accrues to B on the date when he acquires his interest: Latent Damage Act 1986, s 3(1). If A knows of his cause of action before he parts with his interest no new cause of action accrues to B. It is not clear whether the date of contract or of conveyance is the relevant date for this purpose, and the drafting of the section has been criticised as too wide by Professor Griew in the New Law Journal: (1986) 136 NLJ 1201.

5.5.3   Section 3 does not apply if the interest vests in B by operation of law, for example if B is A's executor, administrator or trustee in bankruptcy or if A is a company and an order is made vesting its property in B as liquidator: Latent Damage Act 1986, s 3(4). No extension for disability is available to B: Latent Damage Act 1986, s 3(3).

5.5.4   The new cause of action arises only if all previous owners (and any person with any interest in the property, including presumably a sitting tenant) were not aware of the material facts about the damage during the currency of their ownership. The material facts are such facts about the damage as would lead a reasonable owner to consider it sufficiently serious to justify his instituting proceedings for damages against a defendant who did not dispute liability and was able to satisfy a judgment: Latent Damage Act 1986, s 3(5), compare Limitation Act 1980, ss 14(2) and 14A(7). There is the same provision for constructive knowledge as in personal injury and other latent damage cases: Latent Damage Act 1986, s 3(6). Failure to have the property surveyed will not prevent the cause of action arising but it may start the three-year period running for the purchaser from the date of his purchase.

5.5.5   As the plaintiff with the new cause of action has acquired the property ex hypothesi before the facts concerning the damage have been discovered or become discoverable, the time limit for a s 3 action will be governed by the Limitation Act 1980, s 14A. The relevant periods will therefore be three years from discovery or discoverability, six years from the accrual of the cause of action and fifteen years from the negligent act or omission. Although s 3(1) of the Latent Damage Act 1986 provides that the new cause of action accrues on the date when the plaintiff acquires his interest, s 3(2) immediately reverses this for the purpose of limitation by providing that the new cause of action shall accrue on the date when the original cause of action accrued. This curious drafting preserves the

Pirelli rule that once time begins to run it runs against the current owner and all his successors: [1983] 2 AC at p 19.

5.5.6 A cause of action under s 3 arises only where an interest in damaged property is acquired after 18 September 1986, but it is immaterial when the original cause of action accrued unless it was already statute-barred on 18 September: Latent Damage Act 1986, ss 4(3) and 4(4). Presumably, the plaintiff in *Audsley* v *Leeds City Council* (1988) *The Times*, 2 June, acquired his interest before the Latent Damage Act came into force since no reference is made in the report to s 3, which would otherwise have been material.

Chapter 6

Land and mortgages

6.1 The periods

6.1.1 There are two main periods in the Limitation Act 1980 which are particularly relevant to land:

(*a*) a period of six years to recover arrears of rent or damages in respect of arrears of rent (Limitation Act 1980, s 19) or to recover arrears of interest payable in respect of any money secured by a mortgage or other charge or payable in respect of the proceeds of land or to recover damages in respect of such arrears (s 20(5)). This period applies even though the rent or interest is payable under a document executed under seal: s 8(2); and

(*b*) a period of twelve years to recover any land (Limitation Act 1980, s 15(1)), to redeem land in the possession of a mortgagee (s 16) or to recover any principal money secured by a mortgage or other charge or the proceeds of the sale of land (s 20(1)).

6.1.2 The time limit of twelve years to recover land is extended to thirty years where the plaintiff is the Crown or any spiritual or eleemosynary corporation sole: Limitation Act 1980, s 15(7) and para 10 of Schedule 1. Archbishops, bishops, vicars and some other holders of office in the Church of England are spiritual corporations sole. An eleemosynary charity is one established for the relief of poverty, age, sickness or other sorts of adversity (*Re Armitage* [1972] Ch 438) but it is doubtful whether eleemosynary corporations sole still exist in the age of the National Health Service. The thirty-year period does not apply to corporations aggregate such as the Church Commissioners or an Oxford college: *Ecclesiastical Commissioners* v *Rowe* (1880) 5 App Cas 736. Where the land is foreshore, ie the sea-bed below medium high-tide, the period is sixty years: para 11 of Schedule 1. All foreshore is prima facie owned by the Crown: *Fowley Marine (Emsworth) Ltd* v *Gafford* [1968] 2 QB 618. Where the land was Crown or Church land, a successor in title has twelve years from the accrual of his own cause of action or the period within which the Crown or Church could have sued whichever is the shorter: para 12 of Schedule 1.

6.2 Beginning of time

6.2.1 For rent and interest time begins to run when each instalment of rent or interest falls due: Limitation Act 1980, ss 19 and 20(5). A landlord or mortgagee whose title has not become barred can therefore always recover the last six years of rent or interest: *Barclays Bank* v *Walters* (1988) *The Times*, 20 October CA. There are special provisions for mortgage interest where a prior mortgagee has been in possession (s 20(6)) and where the mortgaged property includes a future interest or life insurance policy and the mortgage provides for interest to be added to capital: s 20(7).

6.2.2 Time runs from the accrual of the cause of action to the plaintiff (or his predecessor) in an action to recover land and the date on which the cause of action accrues is determined by the rules set out in Part I of Schedule 1 to the Act: Limitation Act 1980, ss 15(1) and (6).

6.2.3 For present interests there are four possibilities:
 (*a*) the owner was dispossessed, ie driven out of possession by another: *Rains* v *Buxton* (1880) 14 Ch D 537;
 (*b*) the owner has discontinued, ie abandoned, his possession: *Tecbild* v *Chamberlain* (1969) 20 P & CR 633;
 (*c*) the owner has failed to take possession under the will or on the intestacy of the previous owner; or
 (*d*) the owner has failed to take possession under a disposition made inter vivos by the previous owner.

6.2.4 These four situations are dealt with by paras 1, 2 and 3 of Schedule 1. In the first two cases the right of action is treated as accruing on the dispossession or discontinuance: para 1. In the last two cases, unless the previous owner had been dispossessed or discontinued his possession (in which case the previous rule applies) the right of action is treated as accruing on the death (for wills and intestacies) or on the date when the disposition took effect: paras 2 and 3. In no case is it necessary that the owner should be aware that he has been dispossessed or that another has taken possession: *Powell* v *McFarlane* (1977) 38 P & CR 452. A formal entry in the sense of a visit to vacant land may be sufficient to negative discontinuance: *Solling* v *Broughton* [1893] AC 556.

6.2.5 However, in every case it is essential that possession should have been taken by another, because otherwise the owner has no-one to bring an action against. The previous rules are therefore subject to para 8 of Schedule 1 which provides that where under the preceding provisions of the Schedule, any right of action is treated as accruing on a certain date and no person is in adverse possession on that date, the right of action is not to be treated as accruing unless and until adverse possession is taken of the land. 'Adverse possession' is defined unhelpfully, as the possession of some person in whose favour the period of limitation can run. This excludes at least persons who have the owner's permission (*Hughes* v *Griffin* [1969] 1 WLR 23) and persons in possession under a contract or trust (*Hyde* v *Pearce* [1982] 1 WLR 560) or by reason of some family relationship (*Keelan* v *Garvey* [1925] 1 IR).

6.2.6 Adverse possession is a matter of fact, depending on all the circumstances. The courts have been reluctant to find that possession has been taken where the acts relied on are comparatively trivial and the true owner has no immediate use for the land: *Leigh* v *Jack* (1879) 5 Ex D 264 and *Williams Brothers Direct Supply Ltd* v *Raftery* [1958] 1 QB 159. This approach was approved by the Law Reform Committee (1977 Cmnd 6923) but it did not approve of the development in *Wallis's Cayton Bay Holiday Camp Ltd* v *Shell Mex & BP Ltd* [1975] 1 QB 94 and *Gray* v *Wykeham-Martin & Goode* (1977) CA, Bar Library Transcript no 10A, where the Court of Appeal had explained the trivial acts approach as based on an implied licence. In *Treloar* v *Nute* [1976] 1 WLR 1295, a different Court of Appeal restated the law in traditional terms, and the Limitation Act 1980, para 8(4) of Schedule 1, now provides that it shall not be assumed by implication of law that a person's occupation is by permission merely because his occupation is not inconsistent with the owner's present or future enjoyment of the land. Trivial acts of trespass are therefore insufficient, not because they are not adverse but because they do not count as possession.

6.2.7 Adverse possession depends in the first instance on the relationship between the owner and the squatter (for example whether or not there is a licence) and in the second place on the acts done, the nature of the land, the intention of the owner and on the state of mind of the squatter: *Fowley Marine (Emsworth) Ltd* v *Gafford* [1968] 2 QB 618. The squatter must intend to occupy the land and exclude others but need not intend to acquire title: *Powell* v *Macfarlane* (1979) 38 P & CR 452, *Buckinghamshire CC* v *Moran*, (1989) *The Times,* 16 February CA and *Morrice* v *Evans*, (1989) *The Times*, 27 February CA. Where the true owner may have retained possession acts must be done which are inconsistent with the true owner's enjoyment of the land for the purposes for which he intends to use it (*Leigh* v *Jack* (1879) 5 Ex D 264) but where there are clear acts of ownership the plaintiff does not have to show that the owner was affected: *Treloar* v *Nute* [1976] 1 WLR and *Williams* v *Usherwood* (1983) 45 P & CR 235. Adverse possession does not have to be continuous from day to day (*Bligh* v *Martin* [1968] 1 WLR 804) and in some cases the nature of the land will permit only occasional acts: *West Bank Estates Ltd* v *Arthur* [1967] 1 AC 665, *Higgs* v *Nassauvian Ltd* [1975] AC 464 and *Red House Farms (Thorndon) Ltd* v *Catchpole* (1976) 244 EG 295. Where the land was open, fencing is strong evidence but it is not indispensable nor is it conclusive: *Littledale* v *Liverpool College* [1900] 1 Ch 19, *George Wimpey & Co Ltd* v *Sohn* [1967] Ch

487, *Basildon DC* v *Manning* (1976) 237 EG 879, *Williams* v *Usherwood* (1983) 45 P & CR 235 and *Boosey* v *Davis* (1988) 55 P & CR 83. The squatter's possession must always be exclusive (*Ocean Estates Ltd* v *Pinder* [1969] 2 AC 19) and if he cannot prove exclusive possession the owner is deemed to be in possession: *Powell* v *McFarlane* (1979) 38 P & CR 452.

6.2.8 If before the owner's right is barred the land ceases to be in adverse possession, time ceases to run and a fresh right of action accrues only when the land again comes into adverse possession: para 8(2) of Schedule 1. Therefore, if a squatter abandons possession during the twelve year period and after a lapse of time another takes possession, the owner has the full period of twelve years from the second entry. If, however, the first squatter is dispossessed by or gives up possession voluntarily to a second squatter, the two periods can be added together and the owner will be barred when time has run from the first entry: *Asher* v *Whitlock* (1865) LR 1 QB 1. The second squatter will not necessarily acquire a good title because if the first squatter was dispossessed time will not run against him until twelve years from the date of the second entry: *Perry* v *Clissold* [1907] AC 73. If the true owner obtains judgment against the squatter and does not enforce it, time runs again from the date of judgment: *BP Properties* v *Buckler* (1987) 55 P & CR 337. A mere demand for possession does not stop time running: *Mount Carmel Investments Ltd* v *Peter Thurlow Ltd* [1988] 1 WLR 1078.

6.3 Trusts and settled land

6.3.1 Until 1925 future interests in land were in general legal estates which were unaffected by anything which happened to a preceding interest. The 1925 property legislation converted all future estates into equitable interests and vested the legal estate in one or more trustees who were given exclusive powers to dispose of the land, leaving any equitable interests to subsist in the proceeds of any such disposition. It might have been more consistent with the policy of this legislation if equitable interests had been disregarded for the purposes of limitation and twelve years' adverse possession against the trustees had been effective to bar not only the trustees' estate but also all equitable interests in the land; any beneficiary who suffered loss from the trustees' action or inaction would be able to sue the trustees. This course was not followed.

6.3.2 The principle that time does not run against an owner of a future interest until the interest falls into possession was preserved by the Limitation Act 1939, s 6 and is now contained in para 4 of Schedule 1 to the Limitation Act 1980. Although the interest is equitable it is treated for the purposes of limitation as a legal estate: Limitation Act 1980, s 18(1). The legal title of trustees or statutory owners is not extinguished until all the beneficial interests have been barred (ss 18(2) and (3)) and they may bring actions on behalf of beneficiaries who have not been barred although their own cause of action would have been barred: s 18(4). This can lead to exceptionally long periods applying to land subject to a life interest, and this difficulty is only partially alleviated by the Limitation Act 1980, s 15(2). This provides, in effect, that when time has been running against the life tenant the period allowed to the remainderman shall be twelve years from the date on which the right of action accrued to the life tenant or six years from the date on which the right of action accrued to the remainderman, whichever is the longer period. A remainderman expectant upon an entail in possession is not entitled to the alternative six-year period if his interest could have been barred by the tenant in tail: Limitation Act 1980, s 15(3). He is treated as claiming through the tenant in tail in possession and both are barred at the same time: ss 15(1) and 38(5).

6.3.3 A trustee can never obtain title by adverse possession against his beneficiaries. No period of limitation prescribed by the Act applies to an action by a beneficiary under a trust to recover from the trustee trust property or the proceeds of trust property in the possession of the trustee or previously received by the trustee and converted to his use: Limitation Act 1980, s 21(1). The only exception to this rule applies to an honest and reasonable trustee who retains trust property as his share on a mistaken distribution. Although he is liable indefinitely to a disappointed beneficiary his liability after the limitation period has expired is limited to the excess over his own proper share: Limitation Act 1980, s 21(2).

6.3.4 A beneficiary who is not solely and absolutely entitled in equity can never obtain title against his trustee or against a co-beneficiary. His possession is treated as not being adverse and no right of action accrues to the trustees or other beneficiaries: Limitation Act 1980, para 9 of Schedule 1. Where a purchaser is in possession under an uncompleted contract, time will run in favour of a purchaser who has paid the purchase price because the vendor is a bare trustee and para 9 does not apply (*Bridges* v *Mees* [1957] Ch 475). However time will not run in favour of a purchaser who has not paid the price because he remains a licensee (*Hyde* v *Pearce* [1982] 1 WLR 560). Where the vendor is entitled to rescind, time does not run until he exercises that right: *Lakshmijit* v *Faiz Sherani* [1974] AC 605.

6.3.5 Since 1925 co-ownership of land has taken effect behind a trust for sale. Time will therefore not run in favour of one joint tenant or tenant in common against the other tenants or against the trustees: para 9 of Schedule 1 and *Re Landi* [1939] Ch 828. The position was different at common law (see *Paradise Beach Co Ltd* v *Price-Robinson* [1968] AC

1072, decided on the law of the Bahamas) and reforms intended to simplify conveyancing have affected substantive rights.

6.4 Leases and tenancies

6.4.1 A landlord will not be barred simply by dispossessing the tenant. Time does not normally run against a landlord until the lease expires and his right of action accrues: *Walter* v *Yalden* [1902] 2 KB 304 and Limitation Act 1980, para 4 of Schedule 1. Section 15(2) does not apply to terms of years and a reversioner on a lease has the full period of twelve years from the expiration of the term. Exceptionally, if a tenant who holds under a written lease pays a rent of at least £10 pa for twelve years to a person who wrongfully claims the reversion this will bar the landlord's rights altogether: Limitation Act 1980, para 6 of Schedule 1. In this case receipt of the rent is treated as adverse possession of the reversion (para 8(3)(*b*) of Schedule 1) and after twelve years the reversion will be extinguished. 'Wrongfully' includes a mistaken claim: *Williams* v *Pott* (1871) LR 12 Eq 149. The sum of £10 was increased from £1 pa in 1980 for future leases and is intended to exclude those leases where the rent was not worth collecting. Leases granted by the Crown are also excluded: Limitation Act 1980, para 6(2) of Schedule 1.

6.4.2 Time will not run against the landlord in favour of the tenant during the currency of the tenancy so as to affect the reversion. Failure to pay rent bars the landlord's claim to recover more than six years' arrears: Limitation Act 1980, s 19. It normally has no effect on the landlord's title. A right of re-entry during the term is a right to recover land (s 38(7)) and is therefore barred after twelve years, but a fresh right of action accrues when the lease expires. A new right of action also accrues whenever another breach is committed and if the breach is continuous, time continually begins to run again.

6.4.3 Time therefore effectively runs from the expiration of the lease or tenancy. In the case of a term of years this occurs when the term expires. In the case of a yearly or other periodic tenancy in writing, time runs when the tenancy is determined by notice or otherwise. If, however, there is no lease in writing and no single term is agreed, time runs from the end of the first year or other period of the tenancy or from the last receipt of rent: Limitation Act 1980, para 5 of Schedule 1. A rent-book is not a lease in writing for this purpose and the Rent Acts do not prevent time running: *Moses* v *Lovegrove* [1952] 2 QB 533. A tenant under an oral periodic tenancy can therefore bar his landlord's title by failing to pay rent: *Hayward* v *Chaloner* [1968] 1 QB 107 and *Jessamine Investment Co* v *Schwartz* [1978] QB 264. The Court of Appeal regretted the decision it was forced to make in *Hayward* v *Chaloner* and the Law Reform Committee recommended change but this recommendation was not implemented, apparently for fear that tenants would be discouraged from repairing.

6.4.4 The same rule used to apply to tenancies at will, which were notionally determined after one year from the creation of the tenancy, so that if the landlord took no action for thirteen years from the start of the tenancy his interest was extinguished: Limitation Act 1939, s 9(1). A tenant at will was therefore in a better position than a licensee in whose favour time could never run, and difficulty arose in distinguishing the two animals: *Cobb* v *Lane* [1952] 1 All ER 1199, *Hughes* v *Griffin* [1969] 1 WLR 23, *Heslop* v *Burns* [1974] 1 WLR 1241, *Palfrey* v *Palfrey* (1973) 229 EG 1593 and *Bellew* v *Bellew* (1982) IR 447. The distinction is now unnecessary for the purposes of limitation because s 9(1) was repealed by the Limitation Amendment Act 1980 and time does not run in favour of a tenant at will until his tenancy is actually determined: Limitation Act 1980, para 4 of Schedule 1. Entry to repair will not necessarily determine the tenancy: *Lynes* v *Smith* [1899] 1 QB 486.

6.4.5 If a tenant occupies neighbouring land during his tenancy, the encroachment will enure for the landlord's benefit, unless a different intention is shown: *Smirk* v *Lyndale Developments Ltd* [1975] Ch 317. If a tenant occupies other land belonging to the landlord during his tenancy, the land is presumed to be an extension of his tenancy and although the tenant may retain it during his tenancy he must surrender it when the tenancy ends, unless he has previously conveyed it to a third party and informed the landlord: *Smirk* v *Lyndale Developments Ltd* (supra). The tenant is also liable for dilapidations: *J F Perrott & Co* v *Cohen* [1951] 1 KB 705.

6.5 The effect of time

6.5.1 When the limitation period expires, both the right of action for the land and the previous owner's title are extinguished: Limitation Act 1980, s 17. Any right to rent or damages for trespass goes too: *Re Jolly* [1900] 2 Ch 616 and *Mount Carmel Investments Ltd* v *Peter Thurlow Ltd* [1988] 1 WLR 1078. The squatter holds a new estate of his own, founded on his adverse possession. If the title extinguished was the fee simple, the squatter will hold a fee simple. If the title extinguished was an equitable interest in possession, the squatter will have an independent legal estate of his own defeasible by any action brought by the remaindermen or the trustees.

6.5.2 In each case the squatter will hold subject to any third party rights which run with the land and have not been extinguished. As a squatter is not a purchaser for value, he is bound by all subsisting legal and equitable rights: *Re Nisbet and Potts' Contract* [1906] 1 Ch 386.

6.5.3 Where a squatter bars a tenant, the landlord's title is unaffected and he cannot eject the squatter unless some right of forfeiture has arisen. In *St Marylebone Property Co Ltd* v *Fairweather* [1963] AC 510, the House of Lords decided that if the dispossessed tenant surrendered his lease to the landlord after time had run against him the landlord acquired an immediate right of action to eject the squatter. The same applies if the former tenant acquires the freehold reversion: *Taylor* v *Twinberrow* [1930] 2 KB 16. This result is difficult to justify in logic (two plus nought makes three?) and puts the squatter entirely at the mercy of the person barred. The decision in the *St Marylebone* case has not been followed in Ireland (*Perry* v *Woodfarm Homes Ltd* [1975] IR 104) and the Law Reform Committee was evenly divided about changing the rule, eventually making no recommendation.

6.5.4 When a tenant has lost his title to a squatter he remains liable to the landlord on the covenants where there is privity of contract and possibly where there is privity of estate: *Spectrum Investment Co* v *Holmes* [1981] 1 WLR 221 but see *Re Field* [1918] 1 IR 140. The squatter is not personally liable on the covenants but if the lease is determinable on notice or contains a forfeiture clause the landlord can enforce those rights against the squatter (*Taylor* v *Twinberrow* [1930] 2 KB 16) and so compel him to perform the covenants. A squatter has no right to apply for relief against forfeiture: *Tickner* v *Buzzacott* [1965] Ch 426. Effectively therefore a squatter on leasehold property will normally have to pay the rent and so will become a periodic tenant at least.

6.5.5 In the case of rent and mortgage interest the Act bars the remedy but not the right. A landlord is not entitled to statute-barred arrears of rent on enfranchisement: *Re Howell's Application* [1972] Ch 509. But a mortgagor must as a condition of redeeming the mortgage pay all arrears of interest, however old (*Edmunds* v *Waugh* (1866) LR 1 Eq 418) and a mortgagee who realises his security is entitled to retain all arrears of interest: *Holmes* v *Cowcher* [1970] 1 WLR 834.

6.6 Mortgages and rentcharges

6.6.1 The mortgagee's right to sue for the principal money becomes barred after twelve years from the date when repayment became due under the mortgage: Limitation Act 1980, s 20(1). Where the charge is to secure a bank overdraft payable on demand, time runs from the demand: *Lloyds Bank* v *Margolis* [1954] 1 WLR 644. The mortgagee's right to foreclose and to sue for possession are barred after twelve years from the date when he became entitled to possession: Limitation Act 1980, ss 15(1) and 20(4). This may or may not be the same date as the date for repayment. A mortgagee's most effective remedy is to take possession and sell in which case he can keep even statute-barred debts.

In principle the mortgagee is entitled to possession before the ink is dry on the mortgage (*Four-Maids Ltd* v *Dudley Marshall (Properties) Ltd* [1957] Ch 317) but his right to possession may be affected by provisions in the mortgage deed postponing possession until default is made or creating a tenancy or licence for the mortgagor. Any tenancy at will is no longer automatically terminated after a year and the decisions in *Kibble* v *Fairthorne* [1895] 1 Ch 219 and *Parnell* v *Roche* [1927] 2 Ch 142 may no longer be good law insofar as they rely on particular sections of the Real Property Limitation Acts. It is primarily a question of construction of the terms of the mortgage, and after the period for bringing an action for possession has expired the mortgagee's title is extinguished: Limitation Act 1980, s 17. Where the mortgage is of personal property, the same rules apply unless the mortgagee was in possession of the mortgaged property (in which case his right to foreclose does not accrue until he ceases to be in possession) or the property comprises any future interest or extant life insurance policy (in which case the right does not accrue until the interest or policy falls in): Limitation Act 1980, ss 20(2) and 20(3).

6.6.2 The mortgagor's right to redeem is barred if the mortgagee remains in possession of the mortgaged land for twelve years without any written acknowledgement or payment on account of principal or interest: Limitation Act 1980, s 16. Receipt of rents while in possession does not count as a payment although the mortgagee must account for them: *Harlock* v *Ashberry* (1882) 19 Ch D 539. The mortgagor's title is then extinguished: s 17. The rights of a second mortgagee may be extinguished under these sections (*Young* v *Clarey* [1948] Ch 191) and he then ceases to be entitled to redeem the first mortgage: *Cotterell* v *Price* [1960] 1 WLR 1097. No specific period applies to the redemption of personalty (*Weld* v *Petre* [1929] 1 Ch 33) but in the case of a mixed fund the twelve year period applies: *Charter* v *Watson* [1899] 1 Ch 175.

6.6.3 A mortgagee cannot sue for more than six years' arrears of interest: Limitation Act 1980, s 20(5). However, a mortgagee who sells may retain all arrears of interest and a mortgagor who redeems must pay all arrears of interest: *Holmes* v *Cowcher* [1970] 1 WLR 834. If the first mortgagee sells, the second mortgagee is entitled to all his arrears of interest out of any surplus proceeds, unless the mortgage itself is barred: *Re Thomson's Mortgage Trusts* [1920] 1 Ch 508 and *Young* v *Clarey* [1948] Ch 191.

6.6.4 Rentcharges have been of declining importance since the Rentcharges Act 1977 prohibited the creation of new rent charges after 21 August 1977, with certain limited exceptions. Contrary to the rule for rent under leases, non-payment does bar a rentcharge and any ancillary power of re-entry: *Sykes* v *Williams* [1933] Ch 285. In a case of a rentcharge in possession, time runs from the last payment of rent: Limitation Act 1980, s 38(8). If no rent is paid for twelve years the rent charge is extinguished: para 8(3)(*a*) of Schedule 1. If rent is paid to the wrong owner for twelve years, the previous owner's claim is extinguished and the wrong owner becomes entitled to enforce it: Limitation Act 1980, ss 15(1), 17 and 38(1). The Act does not apply to annuities charged on land abroad: *Pitt* v *Lord Dacre* (1876) 3 Ch D 295.

6.7 Registered land

6.7.1 The same principles apply to registered land as apply to non-registered land save that the registered proprietor retains the legal estate but holds it on trust for the squatter until he applies to be registered as proprietor (Land Registration Act 1925, s 75(1)). The *St Marylebone* decision does not apply: *Spectrum Investment Co* v *Holmes* [1981] 1 WLR 211 but see 1982 Conv 201. If the squatter's estate is registered, he holds it by a 'parliamentary conveyance' unlike unregistered land. If it is not registered, it still prevails as an overriding interest: Land Registration Act 1925, s 70(1)(*f*). Any person claiming to have acquired title under the Limitation Act 1980 can apply to be registered as proprietor: Land Registration Act 1980, s 75(2).

6.8 Exceptions

6.8.1 Land for the purposes of limitation does not include easements and profits for which separate provision is made by way of prescription: Limitation Act 1980, s 38(1) and Prescription Act 1832. It does include mines and minerals but nothing in the Act affects the Crown's right to gold or silver mines and no period of limitation applies to a coal mine: Limitation Act 1980, s 37(6), and the Coal Industry Nationalisation Act 1946, s 49(3).

Chapter 7

Trusts estates and equity

7.1 Trusts

7.1.1 There are effectively three rules for trustees:

(a) time does not run in respect of any fraud of fraudulent breach of trust to which the trustee was a party or privy;

(b) time does not run in an action to recover from the trustee trust property or the proceeds thereof in the possession of the trustee or previously received by the trustee and converted to his use; and

(c) otherwise an action to recover trust property or in respect of a breach of trust shall not be brought more than six years after the right of action accrued: Limitation Act 1980, s 21.

7.1.2 These rules apply to personal representatives as well as trustees and to constructive as well as express trustees: Limitation Act 1980 s 38(1), incorporating the definition of trustee in s 68(17) of the Trustee Act 1925. It is immaterial whether or not the trustee is also a beneficiary. For this purpose trustee may include a fiduciary agent (*Soar* v *Ashwell* (1893) 2 QB 390), a solicitor who receives money for investment or manages his client's affairs generally (*Burdick* v *Garrick* (1870) LR 5 Ch 233), a director of a company, duly appointed or de facto (*Tintin Exploration Syndicate Ltd* v *Sandys* (1947) 177 LT 412 and *Selangor United Rubber Estates* v *Cradock (No 3)* [1968] 1 WLR 1555) an auditor of a company (*GL Baker Ltd* v *Medway Building & Supplies Ltd* [1958] 1 WLR 1216) and a mortgagee who has realized his security (*Thorne* v *Heard* [1895] AC 495), but not a trustee in bankruptcy (*Re Cornish* [1896] 1 QB 99) nor the liquidator of a company (*Re Windsor Steam Coal Co Ltd* [1928] Ch 609) nor (probably) an executor de son tort (1974 Conv NS 177) and not a commercial agent (*Henry* v *Hammond* [1913] 2 KB 515), nor a banker vis-a-vis the customer.

7.1.3 In the first two cases trustees and recipients from a trustee, other than bona fide purchasers for value, remain liable indefinitely: *Barnes* v *Addy* (1874) LR 9 Ch 244. The receipt of trust property can be notional so that the concept extends to property which the trustees ought to

48

have received: *Re Howlett* [1949] Ch 767. The rule does not apply where the fraud is committed by the trustees' agent or solicitor: *Thorne v Heard* [1895] AC 495. The claim can be defeated by laches or acquiesence: *Re Jarvis* [1958] 1 WLR 815. Indefinite liability probably applies even when there is no pre-existing trust relationship and the trusteeship arises out of the act complained of: *Shephard v Cartwright* [1955] AC 431 at p 450, but see *Taylor v Davies* [1920] AC 636 and *Clarkson v Davies* [1923] AC 100.

7.1.4 There is a minor statutory exception to the second rule. Where a trustee in good faith distributes trust property among all those whom he reasonably believes to be entitled, including himself, a person who claims more than six years after the distribution cannot recover more from the trustee than the trustee would have had to pay if all the beneficiaries had been sued in time: Limitation Act 1980, s 21(2). Thus, if a trustee has distributed one-third of the trust property to himself and one-third to each of two other beneficiaries in ignorance of the existence of a fourth, he is liable to the fourth outside the six-year period only for the difference between one-third and one-quarter i.e. one-twelfth.

7.1.5 The six-year period applies to an action by a beneficiary to recover trust property or in respect of any breach of trust: Limitation Act 1980, s 21(3). It does not apply to an action by the Attorney-General to enforce a charitable trust because there is no relevant beneficiary: *AG v Cocke* [1988] Ch 414. A purchase by a trustee of trust property is not a breach of trust for this purpose and the six-year period does not apply: *Tito v Waddell (No 2)* [1977] Ch 106. Nor does it apply where the recipient is aware of the breach of trust and himself becomes a trustee *(Re Eyre-Williams* [1923] 2 Ch 533) but otherwise it does apply to actions against wrongly paid beneficiaries or strangers: *Re Blake* [1932] 1 Ch 54. Time runs from the date of breach, whether the beneficiary is aware of it or not *(Re Somerset* [1894] 1 Ch 231) but if his interest is reversionary time does not run until it falls into possession: Limitation Act 1980, s 21(3). An interest does not fall into possession when an invalid advance is made: *Re Pauling's Settlement Trust (No 1)* [1964] Ch 303. A beneficiary who is barred under this provision cannot benefit from proceedings brought by one who is not: Limitation Act 1980, s 21(4) and *Re Somerset* [1894] 1 Ch 231. The six-year period applies equally to a claim for administration of the trusts: *Re Page* [1893] 1 Ch 304 and *Re Richardson* [1920] 1 Ch 423.

7.2 Estates

7.2.1 The death of a debtor or tortfeasor does not affect the running of time and the creditor or person injured has six years from the date when his cause of action accrued to sue the estate: *Rhodes* v *Smethhurst* (1840) 6 M & W 351. Time continues to run even if the creditor becomes the debtor's executor: *Bowring-Hanbury's Trustee* v *Bowring-Hanbury* [1943] Ch 104. An order for administration by the Court will stop time running against debts not already barred: *Re Greaves* (1881) 18 Ch D 551.

7.2.2 Similarly, the death of the creditor has no effect on the running of time. Where the debtor becomes the creditor's executor the debt was extinguished at common law but equity intervened and made him accountable to the estate: *Re Greg* [1921] 2 Ch 243. Where the debtor becomes the creditor's administrator, the same result is achieved by s 21A of the Administration of Estates Act 1925, reversing the rule in *Seagram* v *Knight* (1867) LR 2 Ch 628, that liability was suspended during the period of administration.

7.2.3 One duty of the personal representative is to pay debts of the estate with due diligence having regard to the assets in hand: *Re Tankard* [1942] Ch 69. If the assets of the estate are distributed without satisfying the creditors, the creditor has a new cause of action against the personal representative personally. The claim is probably tortious rather than contractual: *Lacons* v *Warmoll* [1907] 2 KB 350. In either case there is six years from the date of the breach: *Re Gale* (1883) 22 Ch D 820. A creditor is not a beneficiary for the purpose of the extended time limits in what is now s 21 of the Limitation Act 1980: *Re Blow* [1914] 1 Ch 233.

7.2.4 If the debtor charges his estate or a particular part of it with the payment of his debt the creditor has twelve years from the date when his right to receive the money accrued in which to enforce the charge: Limitation Act 1980, s 20(1). A general direction to pay debts does not create a trust but may create a charge: *Scott* v *Jones* (1838) 4 Cl & F 382, *Re Stephens* (1889) 43 Ch D 39, *Re Ball's Estate* [1909] 1 Ch 791 and *Re Raggi* [1913] 2 Ch 206.

7.2.5 For beneficiaries the general rules are:
  (a) no action in respect of any claim to the personal estate of a deceased person or to any share in such estate (whether under a will or on intestacy) shall be brought after twelve years from the date on which the right to receive the share accrued: Limitation Act 1980, s 22(a);
  (b) no claim to recover land can be made more than twelve years after the date on which the right of action accrued: Limitation Act 1980, s 15(1); and
  (c) no action to recover arrears of interest in respect of any legacy or damages in respect of such arrears shall be brought after six

years from the date on which the interest became due: Limitation
Act 1980, s 22(*b*).

7.2.6 These periods are all effectively subject to s 21(1)(*b*), so that no
time runs against a personal representative to recover trust property
in his possession or previously converted to his use: ss 21(1) and 22.
Paying the wrong beneficiary is not converting trust property to one's
own use: *Re Timmis* [1902] 1 Ch 176 and *Re Sharp* [1906] 1 Ch 793.
Sections 21(3) and 22 are probably mutually exclusive and whether the
period is six or twelve years will depend on whether the personal
representative has become a trustee by completing administration: *Re
Swain* [1891] 3 Ch 233, *Re Timmis* [1902] 1 Ch 176, *Re Richardson* [1920]
1 Ch 423 and *Re Oliver* [1927] 2 Ch 323. The twelve-year period applies
not only to actions against the personal representatives but also to actions
against other beneficiaries who have been overpaid and against strangers
who have been wrongly paid: *Ministry of Health* v *Simpson* [1951] AC
251.

7.2.7 The right to receive property is not the same as the right to sue
for it and in the case of an immediate legacy time runs from the death:
Hornsey Local Board v *Monarch Investment Building Society* (1889) 24
QBD 1. However, no right accrues until the present representative has
funds to satisfy the claim and if assets fall into the estate after death
the residuary legatees or next-of-kin have twelve years from the date
when the assets fall into possession: *Re Johnson* (1884) 29 Ch D 964.
The right to receive a contingent legacy accrues when the contingency
is satisfied: *Rudd* v *Rudd* [1895] 1 IR 15.

7.3 Equity

7.3.1 The Limitation Act 1980, s 36(1) provides that the time limits
under ss 2, 4A, 5, 7, 8, 9 and 24 of the Act shall not apply to any
claim for specific performance of a contract or for an injunction or
for other equitable relief. The reason for this exemption is to preserve
flexibility in the grant of equitable remedies. A party seeking specific
performance must act with reasonable diligence, but what is reasonable
diligence will vary with the subject-matter of the contract and other
circumstances, and there may be cases where the failure to seek relief
within the statutory period is fully justifiable. As to interlocutory
injunctions, if a party has not acted promptly in complaining of the
infringement, there are grounds for believing that the infringement is
not disastrous and he will not suffer serious damage if he waits until
trial. At the trial, so long as the plaintiff's legal cause of action is not
barred, he will normally be granted his most effective remedy, whether
that be an injunction or damages. It is difficult to envisage circumstances
in which an injuction would be granted although the claim for damages

was barred, but specific performances of contracts have been ordered long after the contractual date for completion: *Williams* v *Greatrex* [1957] 1 WLR 31.

7.3.2 Section 36(1) preserves the practice of the Courts of Chancery to apply the statutory period by analogy. With some exceptions (eg *Holmes* v *Cowcher* [1970] 1 WLR 834) equity followed the law in matters of limitation and where the equitable remedy corresponded to a common-law remedy equity applied the corresponding common-law limitation period: *Smith* v *Clay* (1767) 3 Bro CC 639, *Friend* v *Young* [1897] 2 Ch 421 and *Bulli Coal Mining Co* v *Osborne* [1899] AC 351. The Limitation Act 1980 now covers most claims, so that the scope for applying the statute by analogy is very limited.

7.3.3 As to equitable defences, the Limitation Act 1980, s 36(2), provides that nothing in the Act shall affect any equitable jurisdiction to refuse relief on the ground of acquiescence or otherwise. Acquiescence can mean either standing by and doing nothing while one's rights are being infringed or, after learning of an infringement, behaving in a matter which makes any subsequent attempt to complain inequitable. Acquiescence in the first sense is a defence distinct from and independent of limitation: *Ramsden* v *Dyson* (1866) LR 1 HL 129 and *De Bussche* v *Alt* (1878) 8 Ch D 286. The strict rules laid down by Fry, J in *Willmott* v *Barber* (1880) 15 Ch D 96 for this defence are no longer in fashion and the test seems to be whether or not the defendant's behaviour is 'unconscionable': *Crabb* v *Arun DC* [1976] Ch 179, *Taylor's Fashions Ltd* v *Liverpool Victorian Trustees Co* [1982] QB 133 and *Habib Bank Ltd* v *Habib Bank AG Zurich* [1981] 1 WLR 1265. Acquiescence in the second sense is an element in laches.

7.3.4 The other equitable ground for refusing relief is laches, ie inexcusable delay which has prejudiced the other side: *Tottenham Hotspur Football Co* v *Princegrove Publishers Ltd* [1974] 1 WLR 113. In deciding whether or not laches should cost the plaintiff his remedy, the court has to look at the conduct and position of both parties: *Lindsay Petroleum Oil Co* v *Hurd* (1874) LR 5 PC 221, approved in *Erlanger* v *New Sombrero Phosphate Co* (1878) 3 App Cas 1218. Delay alone is insufficient: *Re Eustace* [1912] 1 Ch 561. It is essential that lapse of time should have made it unjust to grant relief: *Re Jarvis* [1958] 1 WLR 815 and *Re Bailey Hay & Co Ltd* [1971] 1 WLR 1357. It is also essential that the plaintiff knew or ought to have known of his rights: *Re Howlett* [1949] Ch 767. A defendant cannot rely on laches if it is his conduct that has led to the delay: *Gowa* v *AG* [1985] 1 WLR 1003.

7.3.5 Where there is an express statutory period for the claim there is no room for the doctrine of laches: *Re Pauling's Settlement Trusts (No 1)* [1964] Ch 303. Similarly, where an equitable remedy is claimed in respect of a legal right and the statutory period for enforcing that right has not expired, laches is no defence: *Archbold* v *Scully* (1861) 9 HL Cas 360, *Fulwood* v *Fulwood* (1878) 9 Ch D 176 and *Re Baker* (1881) 20 Ch D 230. Where an equitable claim is analogous to a legal claim subject to a statutory period, equity will apply the period by analogy: *Knox* v *Gye* (1872) LR 5 HL 656. Therefore, only in the case of purely equitable claims, such as rescission or rectification does laches apply without reference to any particular period: *Turner* v *Collins* (1871) LR 7 Ch 329 and *Allcard* v *Skinner* (1887) 36 Ch D 145.

Chapter 8

Special periods

8.1 Certain causes of action receive or used to receive special treatment in the Limitation Acts.

8.2 Accounts

8.2.1 An action for an account cannot be brought after the expiration of the time limit applicable to the claim which is the basis of the duty to account: Limitation Act 1980, s 23. This provision replaces a six-year period which was criticized in *Tito* v *Waddell (No 2)* [1977] Ch 106. The drafting of this section was found wanting in *AG* v *Cocke* [1988] Ch 414 on the ground that the duty to account arises out of a fiduciary relationship and not any particular breach of duty. The claim therefore often has no applicable time limit.

8.2.2 During a partnership time is no bar to one partner's claim for an account: *Miller* v *Miller* (1869) LR 8 Eq 499. Time does begin to run from the death of a partner (*Knox* v *Gye* (1872) LR 5 HL 656) or the determination of the partnership from any other cause (*Noyes* v *Crawley* (1878) 10 Ch D 31) but it does not run between the survivors if they continue in partnership: *Betjemann* v *Betjemann* [1895] 2 Ch 474.

8.3 Admiralty matters

8.3.1 Since 1 August 1980 admiralty cases are governed by the same general periods as other actions. Section 2(6) of the Limitation Act 1939, which excluded admiralty actions enforceable in rem, was repealed by the Limitation Amendment Act 1980 and not replaced in the Limitation Act 1980. Particular Acts relating to shipping have their own limitation periods.

8.4 Advowsons

8.4.1 There is no longer any period of limitation applicable to advowsons. The 100-year period in s 25 of the Limitation Act 1980 was repealed by the Patronage (Benefices) Measure 1986 as from 1 January 1989. There is now a register of patrons kept by the registrar of each diocese.

8.5 Arbitration

8.5.1 The Limitation Act 1980 and all other Acts relating to limitation of actions apply to arbitrations as they apply to High Court actions: Limitation Act 1980, s 34. Therefore, the arbitrator must give effect to any limitation period appropriate to the subject-matter of the arbitration, provided that the statute is relied on. The accrual of the claim which is being arbitrated corresponds to the accrual of the cause of action in litigation: *Pegler* v *Railway Executive* [1948] AC 332. It is not necessary for the parties to fail to agree (*West Riding of Yorkshire CC* v *Huddersfield Corporation* [1957] 1 QB 540) and a *Scott* v *Avery* clause does not operate to prevent time running: Limitation Act 1980, s 34(2). The parties can contract for a shorter period (*H Ford & Co Ltd* v *Compagnie Furness (France)* [1922] 2 KB 797) but the court can extend the time on the ground of undue hardship: Arbitration Act 1950, s 27. 'Undue hardship' is liberally construed: *Liberian Shipping Corporation* v *A King & Sons* [1967] 2 QB 86.

8.5.2 Section 34(3) defines the commencement of the arbitration, ie the date at which time ceases to run, as the date when one side gives to the other side notice requiring him to appoint an arbitrator or to agree to the appointment of an arbitrator or (where there is a specified arbitrator) notice requiring him to submit the dispute to the specified arbitrator. A letter requesting proposals to settle or alternatively 'name your arbitrators' is sufficient for this purpose: *Nea Agrex SA* v *Baltic Shipping Co Ltd* [1976] QB 933.

8.5.3 When the award is made, the rights of the parties merge in the award which may be enforced by action or, with leave of the court, as a judgment. The application for leave to enforce is itself an action and therefore the same period applies in either case. If the submission was not under seal the period is six years (Limitation Act 1980, s 7) and time runs from the date of the failure to honour the award: *Agromet Motoimport* v *Maulden Engineering Co Ltd* [1985] 1 WLR 762. If the submission was under seal, the period is twelve years (Limitation Act 1980, s 8) and time probably runs from the same date. If there was no submission (eg a statutory arbitration) the period is six years (Limitation Act 1980, s 7) and time runs from the making of the award: *Turner* v *Midland Railway* [1911] 1 KB 832.

8.6 Consumer protection

8.6.1 The Consumer Protection Act 1987, which implements the EC's Directive on Product Liability, received the Royal Assent on 15 May 1987 and came into force on 1 March 1988. The Act imposes strict liability on manufacturers and others for unsafe products (other than buildings) which cause personal injury or damage to other property. The Act also introduces a new section 11A into the Limitation Act 1980 to govern the period in which the new statutory cause of action may be brought. Finally, it makes consequential amendments to ss 12, 14, 28, 32 and 33. The period applies only to the statutory cause of action and not to any alternative common-law action.

8.6.2 The basic period is three years which runs from whichever date is later — that at which the cause of action accrued or the date at which the plaintiff acquired knowledge of the relevant facts: Limitation Act 1980, s 11A(3). The date on which the cause of action accrues is not defined, so that in accordance with *Pirelli General Cable Works Ltd* v *Oscar Faber & Partners* [1983] 2 AC 1, it is the date when the defect causes personal injury or damage to other property. The date of knowledge is defined by s 14(1A) of the Limitation Act 1980 in a manner which corresponds to the date of knowledge for the purposes of personal injury claims. The same provision as to constructive knowledge applies: Limitation Act 1980 s 14(3).

8.6.3 The court has jurisdiction to disapply s 11A of the Act unless the claim is for damage to property only: Limitation Act 1980, s 33(1A)(*b*). All claims under the Consumer Protection Act 1987 are subject to a ten-year long-stop period from the relevant time: Limitation Act 1980, s 11A(4). The relevant time is defined in s 4(2) of the Consumer Protection Act 1987 and depends on whether the defendant is a person facing primary liability (the manufacturer, importer or 'own-brander') or a person facing secondary liability (the supplier). In most cases the period probably begins when the producer first markets the product in question, which may be long before the plaintiff acquired his particular item. The ten-year period overrides the ordinary three-year period (as well as any extension under s 28 for disability) and cannot be extended by the court under s 33: Limitation Act 1980, s 33(1A)(*a*). It operates to extinguish the right of action whether or not the right has accrued: Limitation Act 1980, s 11A(3). This has important consequences for contribution: Civil Liability (Contribution) Act 1978, s 1(3).

8.6.4 Where death occurs as a result of a defective product the principles applicable to claims under the Law Reform (Miscellaneous Provisions) Act 1934 and the Fatal Accidents Act 1976 are with one exception the same whether the plaintiffs rely on common-law or claim under the Consumer Protection Act 1987. The one exception is that the ten-year long-stop applies to all claims under the 1987 Act. If the death occurred within the limitation period, it is possible that the long-stop does not apply to a Fatal Accidents Act claim: Limitation Act 1980, s 12(2).

8.6.5 The problem of persons who acquire property damaged by a defective product before the damage is discovered is dealt with by ss 5(5)–(7) of the Consumer Protection Act 1987. In contrast to s 3 of the Latent Damage Act 1986, which creates a separate cause of action, s 5 of the Consumer Protection Act 1987 provides that for the purpose of determining who has suffered damage the damage shall be treated as occurring at the earliest time when a person with an interest in the property had knowledge of the material facts. This avoids the problem (which arose in *Perry* v *Tendring DC* (1985) 3 Con LR 74) of the need for an assignment of the cause of action.

8.7 Contribution and indemnity

8.7.1 Under s 1 of the Civil Liability (Contribution) Act 1978 any person liable in respect of damage suffered by another person may recover contribution from any other person liable in respect of the same damage. As from 1 January 1979 this replaced the more limited provisions of s 6 of the Law Reform (Married Women and Tortfeasors) Act 1935. The limitation period under both Acts is two years from the date when the right to contribution accrued: Limitation Act 1980, s 10(1) and Limitation Act 1963, s 4(1), saved for this purpose by Limitation Act 1980, para 1 of Schedule 2.

8.7.2 Under the 1935 Act problems arose when different limitation periods applied to different persons liable in respect of the same damage: *George Wimpey & Co Ltd* v *BOAC* [1955] AC 169. These problems are now resolved by s 1(3) of the Civil Liability (Contribution) Act 1978 which provides that it is immaterial that the contributor's liability to the plaintiff is barred by limitation unless the effect is (as under the Consumer Protection Act 1987) to extinguish the right as well as the remedy. It is also immaterial that the defendant's liability to the plaintiff would have been barred at the time he makes his claim for contribution, provided that the liability has been established by judgment or compromise: Civil Liability (Contribution) Act 1978, s 1(2).

8.7.3 Time for claiming contribution runs from the date provided in ss 10(3) or 10(4) of the Limitation Act 1980. If the person claiming contribution is held liable in civil proceedings or arbitration, time runs from the date when judgment is given or from the date of the award. If, in any other case, the claimant admits liability or agrees to make a payment to any of the persons who suffered the damage in respect of which contribution is claimed, time runs from the first date on which the amount to be paid is agreed. Where a payment into court is made, the relevant date is the date of acceptance.

8.7.4 The right to contribution between co-sureties is equitable and not statutory. The period is six years and the right accrues when the liability to the principal creditor is established: *Wolmershausen* v *Gullick* [1893] 2 Ch 514. The same applies to contribution between trustees: *Robinson* v *Harkin* [1896] 2 Ch 415.

8.7.5 Similarly, there is no special provision for persons claiming an indemnity under a contract, express or implied. The period is the contractual one of six years and time runs from the date when the primary liability is established and ascertained: *R & H Green & Silley Weir Ltd* v *British Railways Board* [1985] 1 WLR 570 and *Telfair Shipping Corp* v *Inersea Carriers SA* [1985] 1 WLR 553. The same applies to a recourse action under the Hague-Visby Rules: *The Andros* [1987] 1 WLR 1213.

8.8 Judgments

8.8.1 Section 24(1) of the Limitation Act 1980 provides that an action shall not be brought on a judgment after the expiration of six years from the date on which it became enforceable. This section applies only to a judgment obtained in England or Wales. The period for suing on a foreign judgment is also six years, because such a claim is a simple contract debt in England: *Dupleix* v *De Roven* (1705) 2 Vern 540. A justices' warrant for possession is a judgment for this purpose: *Mills* v *Allen* [1953] 2 QB 341.

8.8.2 In fact actions on a judgment are a rarity and they will be dismissed as an abuse if there is any other way of obtaining satisfaction: *Pritchett* v *English and Colonial Syndicate* [1899] 2 QB 428. The date on which a judgment becomes enforceable is, subject to its terms, the date on which it is pronounced: RSC Ord 42, r 3 and *Holtby* v *Hodgson* (1889) 24 QBD 103.

8.8.3 In the case of foreign judgments the period runs in contract from the date of the breach of the implied obligation to observe it. In *Berliner Industriebank AG* v *Jost* [1971] 2 QB 463, the Court of Appeal held that a foreign 'ascertainment' in bankruptcy proceedings counted as a judgment despite a stay of execution and that time ran accordingly.

8.8.4 An action on a judgment must be distinguished from the enforcement of a judgment (*W T Lamb & Sons* v *Rider* [1948] 2 KB 331 and *Easton* v *Brown* [1981] 3 All ER 278) although 'action' includes any proceeding in a court of law (s 38(1) Limitation Act 1980) and an application for a distress warrant to enforce arrears of rates is an action: *China* v *Harrow UDC* 1954 1 QB 178. After six years leave is required to enforce a judgment by fi fa etc: RSC Ord 46, r 2(1) CCR Ord 26, r 5. When the period for suing on a judgment was twelve years, leave would not be granted when that period had expired (*Lougher* v *Donovan* [1948] 2 All ER 11) and now that it is six years it is doubtful whether leave can ever properly be granted under RSC Ord 46, r 2(1)(*a*).

8.9 Specialties

8.9.1 An action on a specialty shall not be brought after the expiration of twelve years from the date on which the cause of action accrued: Limitation Act 1980, s 8(1). The cause of action accrues on the breach of the obligation in question.

8.9.2 'Specialty' includes a bond, a contract under seal, a covenant, a judgment and a statute (*Royal Trust Co* v *AG for Alberta* [1930] AC 144) but judgments and moneys due under statute are dealt with separately. Actions for non-pecuniary relief in which an obligation under statute forms part of the cause of action are governed by s 8(1): *Collin* v *Duke of Westminster* [1985] QB 581. Dividends are recoverable as simple contract debts and not by an action on a specialty: *Re Compania de Electricidad de la Provincia de Buenos Aires Ltd* [1980] Ch 146.

8.9.3 Any shorter period of limitation prescribed by the Act overrides s 8(1): Limitation Act 1980 s 8(2). Therefore, although actions on a judgment or to recover money due under statute are actions on a specialty (*Cork & Bandon Railway Co* v *Goode* (1853) 13 CB 826) they are governed by a six-year period: *Central Electricity Board* v *Halifax Corporation* [1963] AC 785. Similarly, arrears of rent or mortgage interest, even though payable under a covenant under seal, are recoverable only for the last six years: Limitation Act 1980, ss 19 and 20(5).

8.10 Statutes

8.10.1 An action to recover any sum recoverable by virtue of any enactment (except the Civil Liability (Contribution) Act 1978) shall not be brought after the expiration of six years from the date on which the cause of action accrued: Limitation Act 1980, s 9. If the enactment itself provides a period, that period prevails: Limitation Act 1980, s 39. The Rent Acts do not provide a period for recovery of unlawful premiums: *Temple* v *Lewis* [1954] 1 QB 23.

8.10.2 The cause of action accrues when any money becomes payable even though the sum cannot yet be quantified: *Yorkshire Electricity Board* v *British Telecommunications Plc* [1986] 1 WLR 1029. Individual statutes sometimes provide a date when the cause of action is deemed to accrue, eg Defective Premises Act 1972 s 1(5).

8.10.3 An action is prima facie within this section if there would be no cause of action without the statute (*Pratt* v *Cook, Son & Company (St Paul's) Ltd* [1940] AC 437) but an action for damages for breach of statutory duty, as distinct from one to recover money payable under statute, is treated as an action in tort. An action for non-pecuniary relief is an action on a specialty to which the period of twelve years under s 8 applies: *Collin* v *Duke of Westminster* [1985] QB 581. There is no longer any distinction between bringing an action on a statute and suing in respect of a cause of action given by a statute. Provided the action is to recover money, both are within s 9: *Central Electricity Board* v *Halifax Corporation* [1963] AC 785.

Chapter 9

Disability, fraud and mistake

9.1 Scope

9.1.1 The Limitation Act 1980 contains provisions extending or excluding the ordinary time limits in cases of disability, acknowledgment, part payment, fraud, concealment and mistake. The discretionary extensions of time under ss 32A and 33 are dealt with in Chapters 3 and 4 in the context of libel and personal injuries. There is another obligatory extension of time for enemies and prisoners in the Limitation (Enemies and War Prisoners) Act 1945, dealt with in para **9.5** below.

9.1.2 Part I of the Limitation Act 1980 which lays down the primary periods is expressly made subject to Part II which contains the provisions for extension: Limitation Act 1980, s 1(2). Nevertheless, there are exceptions to the rule that Part II always operates to extend the period. Claims for contribution may be postponed by disability or fraud but are not affected by acknowledgment or part payment: Limitation Act 1980, s 10(5). Actions under the Fatal Accidents Act 1976 are affected by disability but not by acknowledgment, part payment, fraud, mistake or concealment: Limitation Act 1980, s 12(3).

9.2 Disability

9.2.1 Time does not run against a plaintiff who is under a disability at the time of the accrual of his cause of action: Limitation Act 1980, s 28(1). A person is under a disability if he is an infant or of unsound mind: Limitation Act 1980, s 38(2). An infant is a person under 18 years: Family Law Reform Act 1969, s 1. It is no longer necessary to inquire whether he is in the custody of a parent (as in *Todd* v *Davison* [1972] AC 392) as this qualification (which applied only to personal injury claims) was abolished in 1975. A person is of unsound mind if by reason of mental disorder he is incapable of managing and administering his property and affairs: Limitation Act 1980, s 38(3) and see *Kirby* v *Leather* [1965] 2 QB 367. A person is conclusively presumed to be of unsound mind while he is liable to be detained or subject to guardianship under the Mental Health Act 1983 or is receiving in-patient treatment in a hospital or mental nursing-home immediately after being liable to be detained under the Mental Health Act 1983: Limitation Act 1980, s 38(4). Under s 31(3) of the Limitation Act 1939 the fact of detention was conclusive evidence and the change in wording may have revived the catch-22 situation in *Harnett* v *Fisher* [1927] AC 573.

9.2.2 The general rule is that if at the time the cause of action accrued the person to whom it accrued was under a disability, the action may be brought at any time within the period of six years from the cesser of the disability or the person's death, whichever first occurs: Limitation Act 1980, s 28(1). The extension applies only when a disability exists when the cause of action accrues. There is no extension for subsequent disabilities (*Parnell* v *Roche* [1927] 2 Ch 142) but if the cause of action accrues to an infant who becomes insane before he reaches eighteen, time does not run until he recovers: *Borrows* v *Ellison* (1871) LR 6 Ex 128. It is essential that the person to whom the right first accrued should be then under a disability: Limitation Act 1980, s 28(2). Once the section has begun to operate, there is no further extension if the right passes to another person under disability on the first person's death: Limitation Act 1980, s 28(3).

9.2.3 Where there are shorter periods of limitation those periods apply in lieu of the six-year period. Thus, in contribution and defamation cases the periods are two and three years respectively from the cesser of the disability: Limitation Act 1980, ss 28(5) and 28(4A). In personal injuries cases the period is three years from the cesser of the disability: s 28(6). In Fatal Accidents Act claims the test is first whether the deceased was barred (Limitation Act 1980, s 12(1)) and then whether the dependant is barred (s 12(2)). Disability can apply to both tests but the dependant's disability will not preserve the action if the deceased himself was barred, taking into account any disability extension: Limitation Act 1980, s 12(3).

9.2.4 In cases of latent damage s 28 applies with the full six-year period if the plaintiff would otherwise rely on the period of six years from the date of accrual of the cause of action. In this case the long-stop of fifteen years does not apply. On the other hand, if the relevant period is three years from the date of knowledge, the extension allowed for disability is three years from the cesser of disability or death and the long-stop of fifteen years does apply: Limitation Act 1980, s 28A. This is an exceptional case where disability occurring after the accrual of the cause of action may postpone time.

9.2.5 For actions to recover land or money charged on land there is a long-stop of thirty years. No extension for disability allows such an action to be brought more than thirty years after the date on which the right of action first accrued: Limitation Act 1980, s 28(4). Where the right of action accrues on the last payment of rent, the disability must be in existence at that date: *Owen* v *De Beauvoir* (1847) 16 M & W 547.

9.3 Acknowledgments and part payments

9.3.1 After the Limitation Act 1623 the courts, assuming the 'task of decorously disregarding an Act of Parliament' (*Spencer* v *Hemmerde* [1922] 2 AC 507 at p 519), evolved a principle that an acknowledgment of a right of action or a payment in respect of a debt had the effect of starting time running again. The rules are now statutory and contained in ss 29-31 of the Limitation Act 1980.

9.3.2 What amounts to an acknowledgment is deliberately not defined. 'The decisions on the exact meaning and effect of the words employed by generations of shifty debtors are irreconcilable' and the words of one debtor are of little assistance in interpreting those of another: *Spencer* v *Hemmerde* [1922] 2 AC 507 per Lord Sumner at p 534. The acknowledgment must be made by the proper person or his agent, be in writing and signed by the maker and made to the person (or his agent) whose title or claim is being acknowledged: Limitation Act 1980, s 30. An Inland Revenue affidavit signed by the executor is not a sufficient acknowledgment of a debt owed by the testator because it is not made to the creditor: *Bowring-Hanbury's Trustee* v *Bowring-Hanbury* [1943] Ch 104. Solicitors can be a mortgagor's agent for the purpose of making an acknowledgment: *Wright* v *Pepin* [1954] 1 WLR 635. Auditors of a company certifying accounts as required by statute are not the company's agents for an acknowledgment: *Re Transplanters (Holding Co) Ltd* [1958] 1 WLR 822. A man cannot give an acknowledgment to himself (*Ledingham* v *Bermejo Estancia Co Ltd* [1947] 1 All ER 749) nor can he as a director of a debtor company when he is required to sign by the Companies Act: *Re Transplanters (Holding Co) Ltd* (supra), but see *Re Gee & Co (Woolwich) Ltd* [1975] Ch 52.

9.3.3 Where the claim is to recover land or to foreclose on any property, the acknowledgment must be given by the person in possession of the land or other property: Limitation Act 1980, s 29(2). Where the claim is to redeem land of which the mortgagee is in possession, the acknowledgment must be given by the morgagee in possession: s 29(4). Where the right is to a debt or other liquidated pecuniary claim, the acknowledgment must be made by the person liable or accountable for the claim: s 29(5).

9.3.4 The acknowledgment need not imply a promise to pay (*Moodie* v *Bannister* (1859) 4 Drew 432) but a letter admitting part of the liability is not an acknowledgment of the disputed balance: *Surendra Overseas Ltd* v *Government of Sri Lanka* [1977] 1 WLR 565. A balance sheet signed by directors and presented to a creditor at a company meeting can be a sufficient acknowledgment (*Jones* v *Bellgrove Properties* [1949] 2 KB 700) but only if it is an acknowledgment of an existing liability: *Consolidated Agencies Ltd* v *Bertram Ltd* [1965] AC 470, *Re Gee & Co (Woolwich) Ltd* [1975] Ch 52, *Re Overmark Smith Warden Ltd* [1982] 1 WLR 1195 and *Stage Club* v *Millers Hotels Proprietary* (1987) 150 CLR 535. Nor are company accounts an acknowledgment to a creditor who did not receive a copy: *Re Compania de Electricidad de la Provincia de Buenos Aires Ltd* [1980] Ch 146.

9.3.5 A letter from a squatter offering to purchase the land can be an acknowledgment even if the writer does not know the identity of the owner: *Edginton* v *Clark* [1964] 1 QB 367. An acknowledgment of a debt need not quantify the amount but must at least admit that something is (not might be) owing: *Good* v *Parry* [1963] 2 QB 418, *Dungate* v *Dungate* [1965] 1 WLR 1477 and *Kamouh* v *Associated Electrical Industries International Ltd* [1980] QB 199. An admission of a claim to unliquidated damages has no effect on the running of time, but a claim for quantum meruit is a liquidated pecuniary claim: *Amantilla* v *Telefusion* (1987) 9 Con LR 139. Pleadings in a foreign action admitting certain facts but denying liability are not a sufficient acknowledgment: *Re Flynn deceased (no 2)* [1969] 2 Ch 403.

9.3.6 A payment of principal or interest by the person in possession of the mortgaged property or personally liable for the debt will have the same effect on a foreclosure action as an acknowledgment, and the receipt by a mortgagee in possession of any sum in respect of principal or interest will have the same effect on a redemption action: Limitation Act 1980, ss 29(3) and 29(4). A payment in respect of any debt or other liquidated pecuniary claim or any claim to the personal estate of a deceased person will also have the same effect as an acknowledgment: s 29(5). A payment of the balance said to be due is not a payment in respect of the disputed and unpaid moneys: *Surendra Overseas Ltd* v *Government of Sri Lanka* [1977] 1 WLR 565. On the other hand a payment generally on account is a payment in respect of the whole sum due at the time: *Re Footman Bower & Co Ltd* [1961] Ch 443. Part payment of rent does not extend the time for claiming the remainder due: Limitation Act 1980, s 29(6). The payment need not be in money (*Re Wilson* [1937] Ch 675) and no money need actually pass: *Maber* v *Maber* (1867) LR 2 Ex 153.

9.3.7 In actions to recover land and to foreclose an acknowledgment or payment in respect of the mortgage debt binds all persons in possession thereafter and has the effect of making time run from the date of the acknowledgment or payment: Limitation Act 1980, ss 29(2), (3) and 31(1), (2). In redemption actions an acknowledgment or receipt by a sole mortgagee binds him and all his successors and starts a new period of twelve years: Limitation Act 1980, s 29(4). An acknowledgment or receipt by one of several mortagees does not bind any other mortgagee or his successors but an acknowledgment given to one of several mortgagors benefits them all: Limitation Act 1980, ss 31(3) and (5).

9.3.8 In all cases to recover land, to foreclose or to redeem an acknowledgment or payment outside the statutory period have no effect since the right has already been extinguished by s 17 of the Limitation Act 1980: *Sanders* v *Sanders* (1881) 19 Ch D 373 and *Nicholson* v *England* [1926] 2 KB 93.

9.3.9 Where the claim is for a debt or other liquidated pecuniary claim, an acknowledgment binds the person making it and his successors but not any other person, whereas a payment binds all persons liable: Limitation Act 1980, ss 31(6) and (7). An acknowledgment or payment by one of several personal representatives binds the deceased's estate: s 31(8) but as to trustees see *Astbury* v *Astbury* [1898] 2 Ch 111. In either case the right is treated for limitation purposes as having accrued at the date of the acknowledgment or payment: s 29(5).

9.3.10 In the case of debts, liquidated pecuniary claims and claims to the personal estate of a deceased the substantive right is not extinguished by the limitation period but a right once barred will not be revived by any acknowledgment or payment outside the period: Limitation Act 1980, s 29(7). The law was different before 1 August 1980 and was changed by the Limitation Amendment Act 1980. The period may be repeatedly extended by further acknowledgments or payments within the current period, but not so as to extend the period for claiming any arrears of rent or interest: Limitation Act 1980, ss 29(6) and (7). Payment of rent or mortgage interest therefore has the effect of extending the time for recovery of the land or the principal sum.

9.4 Fraud, concealment and mistake

9.4.1 Section 32 of the Limitation Act 1980 replaced s 26 of the Limitation Act 1939 which was criticized by the Law Reform Committee (Cmnd 6923) as misleading. They observed that despite its title and actual wording it was not limited to fraud in the common-law sense and it covered recklessness as well as cases of active concealment.

9.4.2 Section 32 now covers three situations:
  (*a*) where the action is based on the fraud of the defendant;
  (*b*) where any fact relevant to the plaintiff's right of action has been deliberately concealed by the defendant; or
  (*c*) where the action is for relief from the consequences of a mistake.
In these situations time does not begin to run until the plaintiff has discovered the fraud, concealment or mistake or could with reasonable

diligence have discovered it. References to the defendant include the defendant's agent, any person through whom the defendant claims and that person's agent: Limitation Act 1980, s 32(1). A builder can be the developer's agent for this purpose: *Applegate* v *Moss* [1971] 1 QB 406. It is essential that the fraud should be committed by the defendant or his agent or someone through whom he claims: *Re McCallum* [1901] 1 Ch 143.

9.4.3 For the action to be based on the fraud of the defendant the fraud must be an essential part of the cause of action (*Beaman* v *ARTS Ltd* [1949] 1 KB 550). The situation covers fraudulent torts (eg *GL Baker Ltd* v *Medway Building & Supplies Ltd* [1958] 1 WLR 1216) and fraudulent breaches of trust (*Eddis* v *Chichester Constable* [1969] 2 Ch 345). Before the amendments in 1980 fraud was construed as unconscionable conduct (*Shaw* v *Shaw* [1954] 2 QB 429, *Kitchen* v *RAF Association* [1958] 1 WLR 563 and *King* v *Victor Parsons & Co* [1972] 1 WLR 801) but this construction may no longer hold good after the introduction of a specific reference to deliberate concealment. Forged transfers are a nullity and time does not run at all: *Welch* v *Bank of England* [1955] Ch 508.

9.4.4 Deliberate concealment includes deliberate commission of a breach of duty in circumstances in which it is unlikely to be discovered for some time: Limitation Act 1980, s 32(2). It is essential that facts relevant to the right of action should be concealed; it is not sufficient to conceal evidence which is required to prove those facts: *Frisby* v *Theodore Goddard & Co* (1984) *The Times*, 7 March. It is sufficient if a builder deliberately uses the wrong bricks (*Clark* v *Woor* 1965 1 WLR 650) but not if the defendant is unaware that he has committed a wrong: *Wood* v *Jones* (1889) 61 LT 551, *Re Coole* [1920] 2 Ch 536, *Bartlett* v *Barclays Trust Co* [1980] Ch 515 and *William Hill Organisation Ltd* v *Bernard Sunley & Sons Ltd* (1983) 22 Build LR 1 but see *Westlake* v *Bracknell DC* (1987) 282 EG 868. 'Deliberate' presumably means intentional and the decision in *King* v *Victor Parsons & Co* [1972] 1 WLR 801 may no longer be good law insofar as it extends to reckless conduct. It would seem that the concealment must occur before the cause of action accrues, because s 32(1) does not in terms suspend time once it has begun to run (*Tito* v *Waddell (no 2)* [1977] Ch 106), but the act of concealment may in itself give rise to a further cause of action: *Kitchen* v *RAF Association* [1958] 1 WLR 563 and *UBAF Ltd* v *European American Banking Corporation* [1984] QB 713.

9.4.5 For mistake to operate it is not enough that the cause of action should be concealed by a mistake or that the plaintiff should be mistaken as to his rights. He must plead a cause of action in which mistake is an essential ingredient: *Phillips-Higgins* v *Harper* [1954] 1 QB 411. Proceedings at common law or in equity to recover money paid or property transferred as a result of a mistake are within the paragraph: *Re Diplock* [1948] Ch 465 affirmed sub nom *Ministry of Health* v *Simpson* [1951] AC 251.

9.4.6 Time in each of these cases runs from the date when the plaintiff discovered the fraud concealment or mistake or could with reasonable diligence have discovered it. For the meaning of reasonable diligence see *Willis* v *Earl Howe* [1893] 2 Ch 545 and *Peco Arts Inc* v *Hazlitt Gallery Ltd* [1983] 1 WLR 1315. The express reference to the defendant's agent in s 32(1) makes it doubtful whether the reference to the plaintiff includes the plaintiff's agent. In personal injuries cases where time does not run until the date of knowledge it will rarely be necessary to rely on s 32, but there may be circumstances where the plaintiff discovers the relevant facts (so as to set time running under s 11(4)) before he discovers that they have been deliberately concealed from him (so as to set time running under s 32(1)). Section 32 does not apply to an action under the Fatal Accidents Act 1976: Limitation Act 1980, s 12(3).

9.4.7 The long-stop of thirty years for actions to recover land applies only to disabilities and not to extensions under s 32: Limitation Act 1980, s 28(4). The long-stop of ten years for actions under the Consumer Protection Act 1987 does apply where time is extended under s 32: and overrides any extension under s 32: Limitation Act 1980, s 32(4A). In latent damage claims however, s 32(1)(*b*) overrides the fifteen-year long-stop and a six-year period runs either from when the damage occurred or from when the concealment was or should have been discovered, whichever is the later date: Limitation Act 1980, s 32(5). This has been justified on the ground of preventing persons taking advantage of their own wrong but it impairs significantly the impact of the long-stop.

9.4.8 The extension in s 32 does not apply if the property in question has been bought for valuable consideration by an innocent third party since the fraud, concealment or mistake occurred. In that case an action to recover the property or its value (see *Eddis* v *Chichester Constable* [1969] 2 Ch 345 at p 357) or to enforce any charge against or to set aside any transaction affecting the property cannot be brought if it would (apart from s 32) be statute-barred: s 32(3). An innocent third party is defined in s 32(4) as a person who: in the case of fraud or concealment was not a party to the fraud or concealment and did not at the time of purchase know or have reason to believe that the fraud or concealment had taken place; and in the case of mistake did not at the time of purchase know or have reason to believe that the mistake had been made. In this context 'reason to believe' probably requires that the person should actually hold the belief and that he knows facts which would induce a reasonable person to hold that belief: cf *Nakkuda Ali* v *Jayaratne* [1951] AC 66. The benefit of this proviso does not extend to persons purchasing through agents who have notice: *Vane* v *Vane* (1873) LR 8 Ch 383.

9.5 Enemies and prisoners of war

9.5.1 At common law an alien enemy could not sue but he could be sued. A person in prison in any part of the world can in theory sue or be sued. In a time of war, therefore, time runs both for and against prisoners of war but only for an alien enemy and not against him. If a cause of action accrued before the war time would continue to run in any event.

9.5.2 The position is now governed by the Limitation (Enemies and War Prisoners) Act 1945 which suspends the running of time while any necessary party to the action is an enemy or is detained in enemy territory or remains in enemy territory after detention: ss 1(1) and 2(3). The Act does not revive claims which are barred before the necessary party is detained or becomes an enemy, but if it does apply time is extended to at least one year from the date when the person ceased to be an enemy or to be detained or to be resident in enemy teritory: s 1(1). Two or more periods of suspension are treated as one continuous period without interval: s 1(3).

9.5.3 'Enemy' is defined by reference to the Trading with the Enemy Act 1939. This does not include enemy nationals as such but does include individuals resident in and persons incorporated or trading in enemy territory: Trading with the Enemy Act 1939, s 2(1), *Re Hatch* [1948] Ch 592 and *Vamvakas* v *Custodian of Enemy Property* [1952] 2 QB 183. 'Enemy territory' is defined to include areas under the sovereignty of or occupied by a Power with whom Her Majesty is at war as well as other areas designated by the Secretary of State: Limitation (Enemies and War Prisoners) Act 1945 s 2(1). Because this definition differs from that of alien enemy at common law it is possible for a person to be able to sue at common law but for no period of limitation to be running against him: *Societe Dunkerquoise de Remorquage* v *Owners of the Atlantic Scout* [1950], p 266. France ceased to be 'enemy territory' on 6 May 1953.

Chapter 10

Procedure

10.1 Pleading and proof

10.1.1 Despite the recurring words 'an action shall not be brought' the Limitation Act must be pleaded if it is to be relied on: *Dismore v Milton* [1938] 3 All ER 762 and RSC Ord 18, r 8(1) which now applies to foreign limitation periods. The Court will not strike out a statement of claim which is clearly out of time under Ord 18, r 19(1)(*a*) on the ground that it discloses no cause of action but it may do so under r 19(1)(*b*) or (*d*) on the ground that it is vexatious or an abuse if it is clearly bound to fail: *Riches v DPP* [1973] 1 WLR 1019 and *Ronex Properties Ltd v John Laing Construction Ltd* [1983] QB 398.

10.1.2 Once the statute has been pleaded it is for the plaintiff to show that it does not operate to bar his claim: *Darley Main Colliery v Mitchell* (1886) 11 App Cas 127 and *Cartledge v E Jopling & Sons Ltd* [1963] AC 758. The plaintiff has to show that his cause of action accrued on a given day within the appropriate period. When that stage is reached the evidential burden passes to the defendant to prove that the given day or selected period is incorrect: *London Congregational Union Inc v Harriss & Harriss* [1988] 1 All ER 15. As to proof of damages see *Clarkson v Modern Foundries Ltd* [1957] 1 WLR 1210.

10.1.3 Where the defendant has deliberately or carelessly failed to plead the Act, it is open to him to apply for leave to amend. The practice used to be that an amendment would be allowed if it could be made without injustice to the other side and there was no injustice if the other side could be compensated in costs: *Clarapede & Co v Commercial Union Association* (1883) 32 WR 262 and *GL Baker Ltd v Medway Building Supplies Ltd* [1958] 1 WLR 1216. However, in *Ketteman v Hansel Properties* [1987] AC 189, the House of Lords held by a majority that if a defence of limitation was not pleaded because it was overlooked by the defendant's lawyers until a very late stage the defendant should usually have to bear the consequences and look to his lawyers for compensation.

10.1.4 Where the plaintiff intends to rely on any extension of time or on the discretion in s 33 of the Limitation Act 1980 he should plead in the Statement of Claim all facts and matters relied on and where appropriate include in the prayer for relief a claim for a direction under s 33: *Busch* v *Stevens* [1963] 1 QB 1. If he fails to do this or if it is clear that s 33 could not apply, the defendant can apply to have the action dismissed under Ord 18, r 19: *Walkley* v *Precision Forgings Ltd* [1979] 1 WLR 606. After the close of pleadings either party may apply to have the limitation defence tried as a seperate issue. Such applications are common practice as they may save the expense and trouble of a full hearing: *Walkley* (supra) and in the Court of Appeal [1978] 1 WLR 1228. A Master in the High Court has the power to make the direction under s 33 but a registrar in the County Court does not: RSC Ord 32, r 9A and *Firman* v *Ellis* [1978] QB 886. It is unusual for issues under s 11, 14 or 33 of the Limitation Act 1980 to be decided prior to discovery: *Harris* v *Newcastle-upon-Tyne Health Authority* (1989) 1 WLR 96.

10.2 New claims in pending actions

10.2.1 Once an action has begun the plaintiff may wish to add new parties or to extend the scope of the existing action. A defendant may wish to counterclaim against the plaintiff or to claim against a co-defendant or a third party. These possibilities raise problems of both substantive and procedural law which are now governed by s 35 of the Limitation Act 1980.

10.2.2 A claim by way of set-off or counterclaim against an existing party is treated as a separate action commenced on the same date as the original action (or third party proceedings if the claim is made in the course of third party proceedings): Limitation Act 1980, s 35(1)(*b*). This replaces s 28 of the Limitation Act 1939 and has the effect of preventing a plaintiff from avoiding a set-off or counterclaim by a careful choice of the dates to issue and serve his writ, but see *The Brede* [1974] QB 233 where a special period applied to freight. A party who has not previously made any claim in the action needs no leave to make a counterclaim or raise a set-off even if time has expired between the issue of the writ and the making of the counterclaim: Limitation Act 1980, s 35(3).

10.2.3 A claim against a new party other than a claim to add a new defendant to an existing claim is called 'third party proceedings' and the claim is also treated as a separate action but in this case commenced on the date when the third party proceedings are commenced: Limitation Act 1980, s 35(1)(*a*). This resolves an uncertainty in the 1939 Act which was the subject of dispute. Subject to rules of court a litigant does not need leave to make a claim against a third (or fourth or fifth) party but time does not begin to run until he makes his claim. The commencement of third party proceedings is not defined but it is probably the date of issue of the third party notice or, where leave is required, the date on which the ex parte affidavit is lodged with the court: RSC Ord 16, r 2. In cases under the Civil Liability (Contribution) Act 1978, time will ex hypothesi not have run but in all other cases the claimant must bring his claim within the relevant limitation period which may be the same as for the plaintiff's claim.

10.2.4 Where the claim is against an existing party but is not by way of set-off or counterclaim, eg a claim against a co-defendant, the Law Reform Committee probably intended it to be treated as third party proceedings: para 5.2 of the Final Report on Limitation of Actions (Cmnd 6923). However s 35 of the Limitation Act 1980 is so drafted as to make such a claim relate back to the commencement of the action; it remains, however, a 'new claim' so that if the relevant limitation period has expired before it is made the person making the claim must apply under s 33, if applicable: *Kennett* v *Brown* [1988] 1 WLR 582.

10.2.5 Where a new party or a new cause of action is added, the claim is again treated as a separate action and if the separate action arises in the original action it is treated as having been commenced at the issue of the writ: Limitation Act 1980, ss 35(1)(*b*) and 35(2). This differs from the law under the 1939 Act where it was eventually decided that an amendment to add a defendant did not take effect until the service of the amended writ: *Ketteman* v *Hansel Properties Ltd* [1987] AC 189. There is therefore no relation back where the action was commenced before 1 August 1980 or where for some other reason (for example if the period of limitation that applies is one prescribed by some other Act) the Limitation Act 1980 does not apply.

10.2.6 Where there is relation back the existing defendant (in the case of a new cause of action) or the added defendant will have lost his limitation defence if time expired between the issue of the writ and the making of the amendment. Consequently, the amendment will be allowed only in four strictly defined situations and in each of these, except the first, the validity of the limitation defence must be decided when the amendment is made. After the amendment or joinder it will be too late to raise the defence of limitation and an order must be sought either disallowing the amendment (for example under RSC Ord 20, r 4) or revoking the joinder (under Ord 15, r 6(2)). There is no longer any discretion to allow joinder on terms excluding relation back (as in *Liptons Cash Registers and Business Equipment Ltd* v *Hugin (GB) Ltd* [1982] 1 All ER 595) and s 35 is mandatory and exclusive. The four situations where leave can be given are as follows.

10.2.7 The first is where the plaintiff proposes to rely on the discretion to disapply in s 33: Limitation Act 1980, s 35(3) and RSC Ord 15, r 6(5)(*b*). In this case the correct procedure is to give leave to join and allow the application to be made later under s 33: *Kennett* v *Brown* [1988] 1 WLR 582. In all cases except this one the limitation period must be current at the issue of the writ: RSC Ord 15, r 6(5)(*a*) and Ord 20, r 5(2).

10.2.8 The second, which applies only to new causes of action, is where the cause of action arises out of the same facts or substantially the same facts as are already in issue on any claim previously made: Limitation Act 1980, s 35(5)(*a*) and RSC Ord 20, rr 5(2) and 5(5). Rule 5(2) existed before the Limitation Act 1980 and its validity was unsuccessfully challenged in *Rodriguez* v *Parker* [1967] 1 QB 116 and *Mitchell* v *Harris Engineering Co Ltd* [1967] 2 QB 703. The effect of s 35(5) is to confirm the pre-existing rule and to make clear that it is exhaustive, thus resolving the doubts expressed in *Brickfield Properties Ltd* v *Newton* [1971] 1 WLR 862. Section 35(5)(*a*) is very restrictive and in effect no new cause of action will be allowed to be raised unless substantially all of the facts necessary to support it are already pleaded: *Fannon* v *Backhouse* (1987) *The Times,* 22 August CA.

10.2.9 The third, which applies to substitution of parties only, is where a new party is substituted for a party whose name was given in the original claim by mistake for the new party: Limitation Act 1980 ss 35(5)(*b*) and 35(6)(*a*) and RSC Ord 20, rr 5(2) and 5(3), It is not always easy, even for the Court of Appeal, to distinguish between a mistake in name and a mistake in identity: *Evans Constructions Co Ltd* v *Charrington & Co Ltd* [1983] QB 810; *Thistle Hotels Ltd* v *Sir Robert McAlpine & Sons Ltd* (1989) *The Times,* 7 April CA and compare *Beardmore Motors Ltd* v *Birch Bros Properties Ltd* [1959] Ch 298. The mistake must be a genuine mistake and not misleading or such as to cause any reasonable doubt: Ord 20,r 5(3).

10.2.10 The fourth, which applies to joinder or substitution of parties only, is where the new party is a necessary party to the original action in the sense that a claim made in the original action cannot be determined unless he is added or substituted: Limitation Act 1980, ss 35(5)(*b*) and 35(6)(*b*) and RSC Ord 15, rr 6(5)(*a*) and 6(*b*). An example is the case of an equitable assignee who needs to join the legal assignor: *Performing Right Society Ltd* v *London Theatre of Varieties Ltd* [1924] AC 1 and *Central Insurance Co Ltd* v *Seacalf Shipping Corpn* [1983] 2 Lloyd's Rep 25. A comprehensive list of the relevant situations is contained in RSC Ord 15, r 6(6). The same rules apply in the County Court: CCR Ord 15, r 1(1) and (2).

10.2.11 An amendment to the capacity in which the plaintiff sues may be allowed even though he did not have that capacity at the issue of the writ and even after time has expired for suing in that capacity:

Limitation Act 1980, s 35(7) and RSC Ord 20, r 5(4). This enables a widow who sues as a defendant under the Fatal Accidents Act to amend to claim as administratrix on behalf of the estate if she subsequently obtains letters of administration even though an administrator's title dates only from the grant. Another example is *Robinson v Unicos Property Corporation Ltd* [1962] 1 WLR 520.

10.3 Want of prosecution

10.3.1 The law of limitation is concerned with time elapsed before writ. A court asked to dismiss an action for want of prosecution is concerned with time elapsed since writ. The two, however, interact and the limitation rules affect the circumstances in which an action can be struck out for want of prosecution.

10.3.2 In principle an action will be dismissed if there has been either a deliberate disobedience to a particular order of the Court or an inordinate and inexcusable delay affecting the likelihood of a fair trial or causing some other prejudice to the defendant: *Allen v Sir Alfred McAlpine & Sons Ltd* [1968] 2 QB 229. In *Birkett v James* [1978] AC 297 the House of Lords decided that if an action was dismissed for want of prosecution the court had no power, save in exceptional circumstances, to prevent a second action during the limitation period. Dismissing the first action would therefore only cause further delay and expense. The same principle applies to cases of laches: *Joyce v Joyce* [1978] 1 WLR 1170. In disobedience cases the court can stay a second action (compare *Janov v Morris* [1981] 1 WLR 1389 and *Bailey v Bailey* [1983] 1 WLR 1129), and there are exceptional circumstances where the first action will be dismissed even though the plaintiff is not out of time for bringing a second action: *Wright v Morris* (1988) *The Times,* 31 October. The principle of *Birkett v James* does not apply to an inquiry as to damages but the party resisting the inquiry must show prejudice as well as delay: *Nichols Advanced Vehicles Systems Inc v Rees* (1985) 129 SJ 401. Even after the limitation period has expired, an application to strike out will not succeed if the defendant has encouraged the plaintiff to believe that no such application would be made: *Simpson v Smith* (1989) *The Times,* 19 January CA.

10.3.3 Where a writ has been issued within the limitation period and that period has expired at the time of the application to dismiss, there is no possibility of issuing another writ and relying on the discretion in s 33: *Walkley v Precision Forgings Ltd* [1979] 1 WLR 606. On the other hand, where the plaintiff is entitled to an extension on the ground of disability and the extended period has not expired the first action will not be struck out: *Tolley v Morris* [1979] 1 WLR 592. Dicta in *Biss v Lambeth Area Health Authority* [1978] 1 WLR 382 suggests that this does not apply where the primary period is based on the date of knowledge but these dicta may be 'far too sweeping': *Tolley* v *Morris* (supra) at p 600.

10.3.4 In considering whether to strike out, the Court is entitled to consider the totality of the delay (*William C Parker* v *FJ Ham & Son Ltd* [1972] 1 WLR 1583) but there must be prejudice resulting from post-writ delay because the statutes of limitation ex hypothesi allow the delay up to issue of the writ: *Birkett* v *James* [1978] AC 219. The action will not be struck out if a fair trial remains possible and the defendant has not suffered real prejudice: *Department of Transport* v *Chios Smaller (Transport) Ltd* [1989] 2 WLR 578. However, prejudice is not to be found solely in the death or disappearance of witnesses or their fading memories or in the loss or destruction of records. There is much prejudice to a defendant in having an action hanging over his head indefinitely: *Biss* v *Lambeth Area Health Authority* [1978] 1 WLR 382 at p 389 but see *Engil Trust Co Ltd* v *Pigott-Brown* [1985] 3 All ER 119 and *Department of Transport* v *Chios Smaller (Transport) Ltd* (supra) at p 587. There is no power to dismiss an arbitration for want of prosecution: *Allied Marine Transport Ltd* v *Vale do Rio Don Navegacao SA* [1985] 1 WLR 925.

10.4 Renewal of writs

10.4.1 A writ is valid in the first instance for one year but may be extended by order of the court: RSC Ord 6, r 8. Before *Kleinwort Benson Ltd* v *Barbrak Ltd* [1987] AC 597, the practice was not to renew a writ so as to deprive a defendant of the accrued benefit of a limitation period unless there were 'exceptional circumstances': *Heaven* v *Road and Rail Wagons Ltd* [1965] 2 QB 355 approved in *Chappell* v *Cooper* [1980] 1 WLR 958. The *Kleinwort Benson* decision leaves open the possibility of renewal in cases where there is 'good reason', eg where there has been a clear agreement to defer service, where the defendant has been evading service or where he has been guilty of some sharp practice. The balance of hardship is a relevant factor (*Jones* v *Jones* [1970] 2 QB 576) but the discretion does not necessarily fall to be exercised in the same way as the discretion under s 33 of the Limitation Act 1980: *Waddon* v *Whitecroft Scovell Ltd* [1988] 1 WLR 309. The same rules apply to an originating summons: RSC Ord 7, r 6 and *Re Chittenden* [1970] 1 WLR 1618.

Appendix 1

Limitation Act 1980

(1980 c 58)

ARRANGEMENT OF SECTIONS

PART I

ORDINARY TIME LIMITS FOR DIFFERENT CLASSES OF ACTION

Time limits under Part I subject to extension or exclusion under Part II

PART II

EXTENSION OR EXCLUSION OF ORDINARY TIME LIMITS

Disability

An Act to consolidate the Limitation Acts 1939 to 1980

[13 November 1980]

Northern Ireland. With a minor exception this Act does not apply; see s 41(4)
post.

APPENDIX 1

Part I

Ordinary Time Limits for Different Classes of Action

Time limits under Part I subject to extension or exclusion under Part II

1 Time limits under Part I subject to extension or exclusion under Part II

(1) This Part of this Act gives the ordinary time limits for bringing actions of the various classes mentioned in the following provisions of this Part.

(2) The ordinary time limits given in this Part of this Act are subject to extension or exclusion in accordance with the provisions of Part II of this Act.

Actions founded on tort

2 Time limit for actions founded on tort

An action founded on tort shall not be brought after the expiration of six years from the date on which the cause of action accrued.

3 Time limit in case of successive conversions and extinction of title of owner of converted goods

(1) Where any cause in respect of the conversion of a chattel has accrued to any person and, before he recovers possession of the chattel, a further conversion takes place, no action shall be brought in respect of the further conversion after the expiration of six years from the accrual of the cause of action in respect of the original conversion.

(2) Where any such cause of action has accrued to any person and the period prescribed for bringing that action has expired and he has not during that period recovered possession of the chattel, the title of that person to the chattel shall be extinguished.

4 Special time limit in case of theft

(1) The right of any person from whom a chattel is stolen to bring an action in respect of the theft shall not be subject to the time limits under sections 2 and 3(1) of this Act, but if his title to the chattel is extinguished under section 3(2) of this Act he may not bring an action in respect of a theft preceding the loss of his title, unless the theft in question preceded the conversion from which time began to run for the purposes of section 3(2).

(2) Subsection (1) above shall apply to any conversion related to the theft of a chattel as it applies to the theft of a chattel; and, except as provided below, every conversion following the theft of a chattel before the person from whom it is stolen recovers possession of it shall be regarded for the purposes of this section as related to the theft.

If anyone purchases the stolen chattel in good faith neither the purchase nor any conversion following it shall be regarded as related to the theft.

(3) Any cause of action accruing in respect of the theft or any conversion related to the theft of a chattel to any person from whom the chattel is stolen shall be disregarded for the purpose of applying section 3(1) or (2) of this Act to his case.

(4) Where in any action brought in respect of the conversion of a chattel it is proved that the chattel was stolen from the plaintiff or anyone through whom he claims it shall be presumed that any conversion following the theft is related to the theft unless the contrary is shown.

(5) In this section 'theft' includes—

> (a) any conduct outside England and Wales which would be theft if committed in England and Wales; and
> (b) obtaining any chattel (in England and Wales or elsewhere) in the circumstances described in section 15(1) of the Theft Act 1968 (obtaining by deception) or by blackmail within the meaning of section 21 of that Act;

and references in this section to a chattel being 'stolen' shall be constructed accordingly.

[4A Time limit for actions for libel or slander

The time limit under section 2 of this Act shall not apply to an action for libel or slander, but no such action shall be brought after the expiration of three years from the date on which the cause of action accrued.]

Actions founded on simple contract

5 Time limit for actions founded on simple contract

An action founded on simple contract shall not be brought after the expiration of six years from the date on which the cause of action accrued.

6 Special time limit for actions in respect of certain loans

(1) Subject to subsection (3) below, section 5 of this Act shall not bar the right of action on a contract of loan to which this section applies.

(2) This section applies to any contract of loan which—

> (a) does not provide for repayment of the debt on or before a fixed or determinable date; and
> (b) does not effectively (whether or not it purports to do so) make the obligation to repay the debt conditional on a demand for repayment made by or on behalf of the creditor or on any other matter;

except where in connection with taking the loan the debtor enters into any collateral obligation to pay the amount of the debt or any part of it (as, for example, by delivering a promissory note as security for the debt) on terms which would exclude the application of this section to the contract of loan if they applied directly to repayment of the debt.

(3) Where a demand in writing for repayment of the debt under a contract of loan to which this section applies is made by or on behalf of the creditor (or, where there are joint creditors, by or on behalf of any one of them) section 5 of this Act shall thereupon apply as if the cause of action to recover the debt had accrued on the date on which the demand was made.

(4) In this section 'promissory note' has the same meaning as in the Bills of Exchange Act 1882.

7 Time limit for actions to enforce certain awards

An action to enforce an award, where the submission is not by an instrument under seal, shall not be brought after the expiration of six years from the date on which the cause of action accrued.

General rule for actions on a specialty

8 Time limit for actions on a specialty

(1) An action upon a specialty shall not be brought after the expiration of twelve years from the date on which the cause of action accrued.

(2) Subsection (1) above shall not affect any action for which a shorter period of limitation is prescribed by any other provision of this Act.

Actions for sums recoverable by statute

9 Time limit for actions for sums recoverable by statute

(1) An action to recover any sum recoverable by virtue of any enactment shall not be brought after the expiration of six years from the date on which the cause of action accrued.

(2) Subsection (1) above shall not affect any action to which section 10 of this Act applies.

10 Special time limit for claiming contribution

(1) Where under section 1 of the Civil Liability (Contribution) Act 1978 any person becomes entitled to a right to recover contribution in respect of any damage from any other person, no action to recover contribution by virtue of that right shall be brought after the expiration of two years from the date on which that right accrued.

(2) For the purposes of this section the date on which a right to recover contribution in respect of any damage accrues to any person (referred to below in this section as 'the relevant date') shall be ascertained as provided in subsections (3) and (4) below.

(3) If the person in question is held liable in respect of that damage—

    (*a*) by a judgment given in any civil proceedings; or
    (*b*) by an award made on any arbitration;

the relevant date shall be the date on which the judgment is given, or the date of the award (as the case may be).

For the purposes of this subsection no account shall be taken of any judgment or award given or made on appeal in so far as it varies the amount of damages awarded against the person in question.

(4) If, in any case not within subsection (3) above, the person in question makes or agrees to make any payment to one or more persons in compensation for that damage (whether he admits any liability in respect of the damage or not), the relevant date shall be the earliest date on which the amount to be paid by him is agreed between him (or his representative) and the person (or each of the persons, as the case may be) to whom the payment is to be made.

(5) An action to recover contribution shall be one to which sections 28, 32 and 35 of this Act apply, but otherwise Parts II and III of this Act (except sections 34, 37 and 38) shall not apply for the purposes of this section.

Actions in respect of wrongs causing personal injuries or death

11 Special time limit for actions in respect of personal injuries

(1) This section applies to any action for damages for negligence, nuisance or breach of duty (whether the duty exists by virtue of a contract or of provision made by or under a statute or independently of any contract or any such provision) where the damages claimed by the plaintiff for the negligence, nuisance or breach of duty consist of or include damages in respect of personal injuries to the plaintiff or any other person.

(2) None of the time limits given in the preceding provisions of this Act shall apply to an action to which this section applies.

(3) An action to which this section applies shall not be brought after the expiration of the period applicable in accordance with subsection (4) or (5) below.

(4) Except where subsection (5) below applies, the period applicable is three years from—

    (*a*) the date on which the cause of action accrued; or
    (*b*) the date of knowledge (if later) of the person injured.

(5) If the person injured dies before the expiration of the period mentioned in subsection (4) above, the period applicable as respects the cause of action surviving for the benefit of his estate by virtue of section 1 of the Law Reform (Miscellaneous Provisions) Act 1934 shall be three years from—

    (*a*) the date of death; or
    (*b*) the date of the personal representative's knowledge;

whichever is the later.

(6) For the purposes of this section 'personal representative' includes any person who is or has been a personal representative of the deceased, including an executor who has not proved the will (whether or not he has renounced probate) but not anyone appointed only as a special personal representative

in relation to settled land; and regard shall be had to any knowledge acquired by any such person while a personal representative or previously.

(7) If there is more than one persona! representative, and their dates of knowledge are different, subsection (5)(*b*) above shall be read as referring to the earliest of those dates.

11A Actions in respect of defective products

(1) This section shall apply to an action for damages by virtue of any provision of Part 1 of the Consumer Protection Act 1987.

(2) None of the time limits given in the preceding provisions of this Act shall apply to an action to which this section applies.

(3) An action to which this section applies shall not be brought after the expiration of the period of ten years from the relevant time, within the meaning of section 4 of the said Act of 1987; and this subsection shall operate to extinguish a right of action and shall do so whether or not that right of action had accrued, or time under the following provisions of this Act had begun to run, at the end of the said period of ten years.

(4) Subject to subsection (5) below, an action to which this section applies in which the damages claimed by the plaintiff consist of or include damages in respect of personal injuries to the plaintiff or any other person or loss of or damage to any property, shall not be brought after the expiration of the period of three years from whichever is the later of —

> (*a*)   the date on which the cause of action accrued; and
> (*b*)   the date of knowledge of the injured person or, in the case of loss of or damage to property, the date of knowledge of the plaintiff or (if earlier) of any person in whom his cause of action was previously vested.

(5) If in a case where the damages claimed by the plaintiff consist of or include damages in respect of personal injuries to the plaintiff or any other person the injured person died before the expiration of the period mentioned in subsection (4) above, that subsection shall have effect as respects the cause of action surviving for the benefit of his estate by virtue of section 1 of the Law Reform (Miscellaneous Provisions) Act 1934 as if for the reference to that period there were substituted a reference to the period of three years from whichever is the later of—

> (*a*)   the date of death; and
> (*b*)   the date of the personal representative's knowledge.

(6) For the purposes of this section 'personal representative' includes any person who is or has been a personal representative of the deceased, including an executor who has not proved the will (whether or not he has renounced probate) but not anyone appointed only as a special personal representative in relation to settled land; and regard shall be had to any knowledge acquired by any such person while a personal representative or previously.

(7) If there is more than one personal representative and their dates of

knowledge are different, subsection (5)(*b*) above shall be read as referring to the earliest of those dates.

(8) Expressions used in this section or section 14 of this Act and in Part I of the Consumer Protection Act 1987 have the same meanings in this section or that section as in that Part; and section 1(1) of that Act (Part I to be construed as enacted for the purpose of complying with the product liability Directive) shall apply for the purpose of construing this section and the following provisions of this Act so far as they relate to an action by virtue of any provision of that Part as it applies for the purpose of construing that Part.

12 Special time limit for actions under Fatal Accidents legislation

(1) An action under the Fatal Accidents Act 1976 shall not be brought if the death occurred when the person injured could no longer maintain an action and recover damages in respect of the injury (whether because of a time limit in this Act or in any other Act, or for any other reason).

Where any such action by the injured person would have been barred by the time limit in section 11 of this Act, no account shall be taken of the possibility of that time limit being overridden under section 33 of this Act.

(2) None of the time limits given in the preceding provisions of this Act shall apply to an action under the Fatal Accidents Act 1976, but no such action shall be brought after the expiration of three years from—

(*a*) the date of death; or
(*b*) the date of knowledge of the person for whose benefit the action is brought;

whichever is the later.

(3) An action under the Fatal Accidents Act 1976 shall be one to which sections 28, 33 and 35 of this Act apply, and the application to any such action of the time limit under subsection (2) above shall be subject to section 39; but otherwise Parts II and III of this Act shall not apply to any such action.

13 Operation of time limit under section 12 in relation to different dependants

(1) Where there is more than one person for whose benefit an action under the Fatal Accidents Act 1976 is brought, section 12(2)(*b*) of this Act shall be applied separately to each of them.

(2) Subject to subsection (3) below, if by virtue of subsection (1) above the action would be outside the time limit given by section 12(2) as regards one or more, but not all, of the persons for whose benefit it is brought, the court shall direct that any person as regards whom the action would be outside that limit shall be excluded from those for whom the action is brought.

(3) The court shall not give such a direction if it is shown that if the action were brought exclusively for the benefit of the person in question it would not be defeated by a defence of limitation (whether in consequence of section 28 of this Act or an agreement between the parties not to raise the defence, or otherwise).

**14 Definition of date of knowledge for purposes of sections 11
and 12**

(1) In sections 11 and 12 of this Act references to a person's date of knowledge
are references to the date on which he first had knowledge of the following
facts—

  (a) that the injury in question was significant; and
  (b) that the injury was attributable in whole or in part to the act or
       omission which is alleged to constitute negligence, nuisance or breach
       of duty; and
  (c) the identity of the defendant; and
  (d) if it is alleged that the act or omission was that of a person other
       than the defendant, the identity of that person and the additional
       facts supporting the bringing of an action against the defendant;

and knowledge that any acts or omissions did or did not, as a matter of law,
involve negligence, nuisance or breach of duty is irrelevant.

(1A) In section 11A of this Act and in section 12 of this Act so far as that
section applies to an action by virtue of section 6(1)(a) of the Consumer Protection
Act 1987 (death caused by defective product) references to a person's date of
knowledge are references to the date on which he first had knowledge of the
following facts—

  (a) such facts about the damage caused by the defect as would lead
       a reasonable person who had suffered such damage to consider it
       sufficiently serious to justify his instituting proceedings for damages
       against a defendant who did not dispute liability and was able to
       satisfy a judgment; and
  (b) that the damage was wholly or partly attributable to the facts and
       circumstances alleged to constitute the defect; and
  (c) the identity of the defendant;

but in determining the date on which a person first had such knowledge there
shall be disregarded both the extent (if any) of that person's knowledge on any
date of whether particular facts or circumstances would or would not, as a
matter of law, constitute a defect and, in a case relating to loss of or damage
to property, any knowledge which that person had on a date on which he had
no right of action by virtue of Part I of that Act in respect of the loss or damage.

(2) For the purposes of this section an injury is significant if the person whose
date of knowledge is in question would reasonably have considered it sufficiently
serious to justify his instituting proceedings for damages against a defendant
who did not dispute liability and was able to satisfy a judgment.

(3) For the purposes of this section a person's knowledge includes knowledge
which he might reasonably have been expected to acquire—

  (a) from facts observable or ascertainable by him; or
  (b) from facts observable by him with the help of medical or other
       appropriate expert advice which it is reasonable for him to seek;

but a person shall not be fixed under this subsection with knowledge of a fact ascertainable only with the help of expert advice so long as he has taken all reasonable steps to obtain (and, where appropriate, to act on) that advice.

Actions in respect of latent damage not involving
personal injuries

14A Special time limit for negligence actions where facts relevant to cause of action are not known at date of accrual

(1) This section applies to any action for damages for negligence, other than one to which section 11 of this Act applies, where the starting date for reckoning the period of limitation under subsection (4)(*b*) below falls after the date on which the cause of action accrued.

(2) Section 2 of this Act shall not apply to an action to which this section applies.

(3) An action to which this section applies shall not be brought after the expiration of the period applicable in accordance with subsection (4) below.

(4) That period is either—

 (*a*) six years from the date on which the cause of action accrued; or
 (*b*) three years from the starting date as defined by subsection (5) below, if that period expires later than the period mentioned in paragraph (*a*) above.

(5) For the purposes of this section, the starting date for reckoning the period of limitation under subsection (4)(*b*) above is the earliest date on which the plaintiff or any person in whom the cause of action was vested before him first had both the knowledge required for bringing an action for damages in respect of the relevant damage and a right to bring such an action.

(6) In subsection (5) above 'the knowledge required for bringing an action for damages in respect of the relevant damage' means knowledge both—

 (*a*) of the material facts about the damage in respect of which damages are claimed; and
 (*b*) of the other facts relevant to the current action mentioned in subsection (8) below.

(7) For the purposes of subsection (6)(*a*) above, the material facts about the damage are such facts about the damage as would lead a reasonable person who had suffered such damage to consider it sufficiently serious to justify his instituting proceedings for damages against a defendant who did not dispute liability and was able to satisfy a judgment.

(8) The other facts referred to in subsection (6)(*b*) above are—

 (*a*) that the damage was attributable in whole or in part to the act or omission which is alleged to constitute negligence; and
 (*b*) the identity of the defendant; and
 (*c*) if it is alleged that the act or omission was that of a person other

than the defendant, the identity of that person and the additional facts supporting the bringing of an action against the defendant.

(9) Knowledge that any acts or omissions did or did not, as a matter of law, involve negligence is irrelevant for the purposes of subsection (5) above.

(10) For the purposes of this section a person's knowledge includes knowledge which he might reasonably have been expected to acquire—

(a) from facts observable or ascertainable by him; or

(b) from facts ascertainable by him with the help of appropriate expert advice which it is reasonable for him to seek;

but a person shall not be taken by virtue of this subsection to have knowledge of a fact ascertainable only with the help of expert advice so long as he has taken all reasonable steps to obtain (and, where appropriate, to act on) that advice.

14B Overriding time limit for negligence actions not involving personal injuries

(1) An action for damages for negligence, other than one to which section 11 of this Act applies, shall not be brought after the expiration of fifteen years from the date (or, if more than one, for the last of the dates) on which there occurred any act or omission—

(a) which is alleged to constitute negligence; and

(b) to which the damage in respect of which damages are claimed is alleged to be attributable (in whole or in part).

(2) This section bars the right of action in a case to which subsection (1) above applies notwithstanding that—

(a) the cause of action has not yet accrued; or

(b) where section 14A of this Act applies to the action, the date which is for the purposes of that section the starting date for reckoning the period mentioned in subsection (4)(b) of that section has not yet occurred;

before the end of the period of limitation prescribed by this section.

Actions to recover land and rent

15 Time limit for actions to recover land

(1) No action shall be brought by any person to recover any land after the expiration of twelve years from the date on which the right of action accrued to him or, if it first accrued to some person through whom he claims, to that person.

(2) Subject to the following provisions of this section, where—

(a) the estate or interest claimed was an estate or interest in reversion or remainder or any other future estate or interest and the right of action to recover the land accrued on the date on which the estate or interest fell into possession by the determination of the preceding estate or interest; and

(b) the person entitled to the preceding estate or interest (not being a term of years absolute) was not in possession of the land on that date;

no action shall be brought by the person entitled to the succeeding estate or interest after the expiration of twelve years from the date on which the right of action accrued to the person entitled to the preceding estate or interest or six years from the date on which the right of action accrued to the person entitled to the succeeding estate or interest, whichever period last expires.

(3) Subsection (2) above shall not apply to any estate or interest which falls into possession on the determination of an entailed interest and which might have been barred by the person entitled to the entailed interest.

(4) No person shall bring an action to recover any estate or interest in land under an assurance taking effect after the right of action to recover the land had accrued to the person by whom the assurance was made or some person through whom he claimed or some person entitled to a preceding estate or interest, unless the action is brought within the period during which the person by whom the assurance was made could have brought such an action.

(5) Where any person is entitled to any estate or interest in land in possession and, while so entitled, is also entitled to any future estate or interest in that land, and his right to recover the estate or interest in possession is barred under this Act, no action shall be brought by that person, or by any person claiming through him, in respect of the future estate or interest, unless in the meantime possession of the land has been recovered by a person entitled to an intermediate estate or interest.

(6) Part I of Schedule 1 to this Act contains provisions for determining the date of accrual of rights of action to recover land in the cases there mentioned.

(7) Part II of that Schedule contains provisions modifying the provisions of this section in their application to actions brought by, or by a person claiming through, the Crown or any spiritual or eleemosynary corporation sole.

16 Time limit for redemption actions

When a mortgagee of land has been in possession of any of the mortgaged land for a period of twelve years, no action to redeem the land of which the mortgagee has been so in possession shall be brought after the end of that period by the mortgagor or any person claiming through him.

17 Extinction of title to land after expiration of time limit

Subject to—

(a) section 18 of this Act; and
(b) section 75 of the Land Registration Act 1925;

at the expiration of the period prescribed by this Act for any person to bring an action to recover land (including a redemption action) the title of that person to the land shall be extinguished.

18 Settled land and land held on trust

(1) Subject to section 21(1) and (2) of this Act, the provisions of this Act shall apply to equitable interests in land, including interests in the proceeds of the sale of land held upon trust for sale, as they apply to legal estates.

Accordingly a right of action to recover the land shall, for the purposes of this Act but not otherwise, be treated as accruing to a person entitled in possession to such an equitable interest in the like manner and circumstances, and on the same date, as it would accrue if his interest were a legal estate in the land (and any relevant provision of Part I of Schedule 1 to this Act shall apply in any such case accordingly).

(2) Where the period prescribed by this Act has expired for the bringing of an action to recover land by a tenant for life or a statutory owner of settled land—

> (a) his legal estate shall not be extinguished if and so long as the right of action to recover the land of any person entitled to a beneficial interest in the land either has not accrued or has not been barred by this Act; and
>
> (b) the legal estate shall accordingly remain vested in the tenant for life or statutory owner and shall devolve in accordance with the Settled Land Act 1925;

but if and when every such right of action has been barred by this Act, his legal estate shall be extinguished.

(3) Where any land is held upon trust (including a trust for sale) and the period prescribed by this Act has expired for the bringing of an action to recover the land by the trustees, the estate of the trustees shall not be extinguished if and so long as the right of action to recover the land of any person entitled to a beneficial interest in the land or in the proceeds of sale either has not accrued or has not been barred by this Act; but if and when every such right of action has been so barred the estate of the trustees shall be extinguished.

(4) Where—

> (a) any settled land is vested in a statutory owner; or
>
> (b) any land is held upon trust (including a trust for sale);

an action to recover the land may be brought by the statutory owner or trustees on behalf of any person entitled to a beneficial interest in possession in the land or in the proceeds of sale whose right of action has not been barred by this Act, notwithstanding that the right of action of the statutory owner or trustees would apart from this provision have been barred by this Act.

19 Time limit for actions to recover rent

No action shall be brought, or distress made, to recover arrears of rent, or damages in respect of arrears of rent, after the expiration of six years from the date on which the arrears became due.

Actions to recover money secured by a mortgage or charge or to recover proceeds of the sale of land

20 Time limit for actions to recover money secured by a mortgage or charge or to recover proceeds of the sale of land

(1) No action shall be brought to recover—

(*a*) any principal sum of money secured by a mortgage or other charge on property (whether real or personal); or

(*b*) proceeds of the sale of land;

after the expiration of twelve years from the date on which the right to receive the money accrued.

(2) No foreclosure action in respect of mortgaged personal property shall be brought after the expiration of twelve years from the date on which the right to foreclose accrued.

But if the mortgagee was in possession of the mortgaged property after that date, the right to foreclose on the property which was in his possession shall not be treated as having accrued for the purposes of this subsection until the date on which his possession discontinued.

(3) The right to receive any principal sum of money secured by a mortgage or other charge and the right to foreclose on the property subject to the mortgage or charge shall not be treated as accruing so long as that property comprises any future interest or any life insurance policy which has not matured or been determined.

(4) Nothing in this section shall apply to a foreclosure action in respect of mortgaged land, but the provisions of this Act relating to actions to recover land shall apply to such an action.

(5) Subject to subsections (6) and (7) below, no action to recover arrears of interest payable in respect of any sum of money secured by a mortgage or other charge or payable in respect of proceeds of the sale of land, or to recover damages in respect of such arrears shall be brought after the expiration of six years from the date on which the interest became due.

(6) Where—

(*a*) a prior mortgagee or other incumbrancer has been in possession of the property charged; and

(*b*) an action is brought within one year of the discontinuance of that possession by the subsequent incumbrancer;

the subsequent incumbrancer may recover by that action all the arrears of interest which fell due during the period of possession by the prior incumbrancer or damages in respect of those arrears, notwithstanding that the period exceeded six years.

(7) Where—

(*a*) the property subject to the mortgage or charge comprises any future interest or life insurance policy; and (*b*) it is a term of the mortgage or charge that arrears of interest shall be treated as part of the principal sum of money secured by the mortgage or charge;

interest shall not be treated as becoming due before the right to recover the principal sum of money has accrued or is treated as having accrued.

Actions in respect of trust property or the personal estate of deceased persons

21 Time limit for actions in respect of trust property

(1) No period of limitation prescribed by this Act shall apply to an action by a beneficiary under a trust, being an action—

(*a*) in respect of any fraud or fraudulent breach of trust to which the trustee was a party or privy; or

(*b*) to recover from the trustee trust property or the proceeds of trust property in the possession of the trustee, or previously received by the trustee and converted to his use.

(2) Where a trustee who is also a beneficiary under the trust receives or retains trust property or its proceeds as his share on a distribution of trust property under the trust, his liability in any action brought by virtue of subsection (1)(*b*) above to recover that property or its proceeds after the expiraton of the period of limitation prescribed by this Act for bringing an action to recover trust property shall be limited to the excess over his proper share.

This subsection only applies if the trustee acted honestly and reasonably in making the distribution.

(3) Subject to the preceding provisions of this section, an action by a beneficiary to recover trust property or in respect of any breach of trust, not being an action for which a period of limitation is prescribed by any other provision of this Act, shall not be brought after the expiration of six years from the date on which the right of action accrued.

For the purposes of this subsection, the right of action shall not be treated as having accrued to any beneficiary entitled to a future interest in the trust property until the interest fell into possession.

(4) No beneficiary as against whom there would be a good defence under this Act shall derive any greater or other benefit from a judgment or order obtained by any other beneficiary than he could have obtained if he had brought the action and this Act had been pleaded in defence.

22 Time limit for actions claiming personal estate of a deceased person

Subject to section 21(1) and (2) of this Act—

(*a*) no action in respect of any claim to the personal estate of a deceased person or to any share or interest in any such estate (whether under a will or on intestacy) shall be brought after the expiration of twelve years from the date on which the right to receive the share or interest accrued; and (*b*) no action to recover arrears of interest in respect of any legacy, or damages in respect of such arrears, shall be brought after the expiration of six years from the date on which the interest became due.

Actions for an account

23   Time limit in respect of actions for an account

An action for an account shall not be brought after the expiration of any time limit under this Act which is applicable to the claim which is the basis of the duty to account.

Miscellaneous and supplemental

24   Time limit for actions to enforce judgments

(1) An action shall not be brought upon any judgment after the expiration of six years from the date on which the judgment became enforceable.

(2) No arrears of interest in respect of any judgment debt shall be recovered after the expiration of six years from the date on which the interest became due.

25   Time limit for actions to enforce advowsons and extinction of title to advowsons

[Repealed (provinces of Canterbury and York) (1.1.89) by Patronage (Benefices) Measure 1986].

26   Administration to date back to death

For the purposes of the provisions of this Act relating to actions for the recovery of land and advowsons an administrator of the estate of a deceased person shall be treated as claiming as if there had been no interval of time between the death of the deceased person and the grant of the letters of administration.

27   Cure of defective disentailing assurance

(1) This section applies where—

(*a*) a person entitled in remainder to an entailed interest in any land makes an assurance of his interest which fails to bar the issue in tail or the estates and interests taking effect on the determination of the entailed interest, or fails to bar those estates and interests only; and

(*b*) any person takes possession of the land by virtue of the assurance.

(2) If the person taking possession of the land by virtue of the assurance, or any other person whatsoever (other than a person entitled to possession by virtue of the settlement) is in possession of the land for a period of twelve years from the commencement of the time when the assurance could have operated as an effective bar, the assurance shall thereupon operate, and be treated as

having always operated, to bar the issue in tail and the estates and interests taking effect on the determination of the entailed interest.

(3) The reference in subsection (2) above to the time when the assurance could have operated as an effective bar is a reference to the time at which the assurance, if it had then been executed by the person entitled to the entailed interest, would have operated, without the consent of any other person, to bar the issue in tail and the estates and interests taking effect on the determination of the entailed interest.

Part II

Extension or Exclusion of Ordinary Time Limits

Disability

28 Extension of limitation period in case of disability

(1) Subject to the following provisions of this section, if on the date when any right of action accrued for which a period of limitation is prescribed by this Act, the person to whom it accrued was under a disability, the action may be brought at any time before the expiration of six years from the date when he ceased to be under a disability or died (whichever first occurred) notwithstanding that the period of limitation has expired.

(2) This section shall not affect any case where the right of action first accrued to some person (not under a disability) through whom the person under a disability claims.

(3) When a right of action which has accrued to a person under a disability accrues, on the death of that person while still under a disability, to another person under a disability, no further extension of time shall be allowed by reason of the disability of the second person.

(4) No action to recover land or money charged on land shall be brought by virtue of this section by any person after the expiration of thirty years from the date on which the right of action accrued to that person or some person through whom he claims.

[(4A) If the action is one to which section 4A of this Act applies, subsection (1) above shall have effect as if for the words from 'at any time' to 'occurred)' there were substituted the words 'by him at any time before the expiration of three years from the date when he ceased to be under a disability.]

(5) If the action is one to which section 10 of this Act applies, subsection (1) above shall have effect as if for the words 'six years' there were substituted the words 'two years'.

(6) If the action is one to which section 11 or 12(2) of this Act applies, subsection (1) above shall have effect as if for the words 'six years' there were substituted the words 'three years'.

(7) If the action is one to which section 11A of this Act applies or one by

virtue of section 6(1)(*a*) of the Consumer Protection Act 1987 (death caused by defective product), subsection (1) above—

(*a*) shall not apply to the time limit prescribed by subsection (3) of the said section 11A or to that time limit as applied by virtue of section 12(1) of this Act; and

(*b*) in relation to any other time limit prescribed by this Act shall have effect as if for the words 'six years' there were substituted the words 'three years'.

28A Extension for cases where the limitation period is the period under section 14A(4)(*b*)

(1) Subject to subsection (2) below, if in the case of any action for which a period of limitation is prescribed by section 14A of this Act—

(*a*) the period applicable in accordance with subsection (4) of that section is the period mentioned in paragraph (b) of that subsection;

(*b*) on the date which is for the purposes of that section the starting date for reckoning that period the person by reference to whose knowledge that date fell to be determined under subsection (5) of that section was under a disability; and

(*c*) section 28 of this Act does not apply to the action;

the action may be brought at any time before the expiration of three years from the date when he ceased to be under a disability or died (whichever first occurred) notwithstanding that the period mentioned above has expired.

(2) An action may not be brought by virtue of subsection (1) above after the end of the period of limitation prescribed by section 14B of this Act.

Acknowledgment and part payment

29 Fresh accrual of action on acknowledgment or part payment

(1) Subsections (2) and (3) below apply where any right of action (including a foreclosure action) to recover land or an advowson or any right of a mortgagee of personal property to bring a foreclosure action in respect of the property has accrued.

(2) If the person in possession of the land, benefice or personal property in question acknowledges the title of the person to whom the right of action has accrued—

(*a*) the right shall be treated as having accrued on and not before the date of the acknowledgment; and

(*b*) in the case of a right of action to recover land which has accrued to a person entitled to an estate or interest taking effect on the determination of an entailed interest against whom time is running under section 27 of this Act, section 27 shall thereupon cease to apply to the land.

(3) In the case of a foreclosure or other action by a mortgagee, if the person in possession of the land, benefice or personal property in question or the person

liable for the mortgage debt makes any payment in respect of the debt (whether of principal or interest) the right shall be treated as having accrued on and not before the date of the payment.

(4) Where a mortgagee is by virtue of the mortgage in possession of any mortgaged land and either—

> (a) receives any sum in respect of the principal or interest of the mortgage debt; or
>
> (b) acknowledges the title of the mortgagor, or his equity of redemption;

an action to redeem the land in his possession may be brought at any time before the expiration of twelve years from the date of the payment or acknowledgment.

(5) Subject to subsection (6) below, where any right of action has accrued to recover—

> (a) any debt or other liquidated pecuniary claim; or
>
> (b) any claim to the personal estate of a deceased person or to any share or interest in any such estate;

and the person liable or accountable for the claim acknowledges the claim or makes any payment in respect of it the right shall be treated as having accrued on and not before the date of the acknowledgment or payment.

(6) A payment of a part of the rent or interest due at any time shall not extend the period for claiming the remainder then due, but any payment of interest shall be treated as payment in respect of the principal debt.

(7) Subject to subsection (6) above, a current period of limitation may be repeatedly extended under this section by further acknowledgments or payments, but a right of action, once barred by this Act shall not be revived by any subsequent acknowledgment or payment.

30 Formal provisions as to acknowledgments and part payments

(1) To be effective for the purposes of section 29 of this Act, an acknowledgment must be in writing and signed by the person making it.

(2) For the purposes of section 29, any acknowledgment or payment—

> (a) may be made by the agent of the person by whom it is required to be made under that section; and
>
> (b) shall be made to the person, or to an agent of the person, whose title or claim is being acknowledged or, as the case may be, in respect of whose claim the payment is being made.

31 Effect of acknowledgment or part payment on persons other than the maker or recipient

(1) An acknowledgment of the title to any land, benefice, or mortgaged

personally by any person in possession of it shall bind all other persons in possession during the ensuing period of limitation.

(2) A payment in respect of a mortgage debt by the mortgagor or any other person liable for the debt, or by any person in possession of the mortgaged property, shall, so far as any right of the mortgagee to foreclose or otherwise to recover the property is concerned, bind all other persons in possession of the mortgaged property during the ensuing period of limitation.

(3) Where two or more mortgagees are by virtue of the mortgage in possession of the mortgaged land, an acknowledgment of the mortgagor's title or of his equity of redemption by one of the mortgagees shall only bind him and his successors and shall not bind any other mortgagee or his successors.

(4) Where in a case within subsection (3) above the mortgagee by whom the acknowledgment is given is entitled to a part of the mortgaged land and not to any ascertained part of the mortgage debt the mortgagor shall be entitled to redeem that part of the land on payment, with interest, of the part of the mortgage debt which bears the same proportion to the whole of the debt as the value of the part of the land bears to the whole of the mortgaged land.

(5) Where there are two or more mortgagors, and the title or equity of redemption of one of the mortgagors is acknowledged as mentioned above in this section, the acknowledgment shall be treated as having been made to all the mortgagors.

(6) An acknowledgment of any debt or other liquidated pecuniary claim shall bind the acknowledgor and his successors but not any other person.

(7) A payment made in respect of any debt or other liquidated pecuniary claim shall bind all persons liable in respect of the debt or claim.

(8) An acknowledgment by one of several personal representatives of any claim to the personal estate of a deceased person or to any share or interest in any such estate, or a payment by one of several personal representatives in respect of any such claim, shall bind the estate of the deceased person.

(9) In this section 'successor', in relation to any mortgagee or person liable in respect of any debt or claim, means his personal representatives and any other person on whom the rights under the mortgage or, as the case may be, the liability in respect of the debt or claim devolve (whether on death or bankruptcy or the disposition of property or the determination of a limited estate or interest in settled property or otherwise).

Fraud, concealment and mistake

32 Postponement of limitation period in case of fraud, concealment or mistake

(1) Subject to subsection (3) below, where in the case of any action for which a period of limitation is prescribed by this Act, either—

 (*a*) the action is based upon the fraud of the defendant; or
 (*b*) any fact relevant to the plaintiff's right of action has been deliberately concealed from him by the defendant; or

(c) the action is for relief from the consequences of a mistake;

the period of limitation shall not begin to run until the plaintiff has discovered the fraud, concealment or mistake (as the case may be) or could with reasonable diligence have discovered it.

References in this subsection to the defendant include references to the defendant's agent and to any person through whom the defendant claims and his agent.

(2) For the purposes of subsection (1) above, deliberate commission of a breach of duty in circumstances in which it is unlikely to be discovered for some time amounts to deliberate concealment of the facts involved in that breach of duty.

(3) Nothing in this section shall enable any action—

(a) to recover, or recover the value of, any property; or
(b) to enforce any charge against, or set aside any transaction affecting, any property;

to be brought against the purchaser of the property or any person claiming through him in any case where the property has been purchased for valuable consideration by an innocent third party since the fraud or concealment or (as the case may be) the transaction in which the mistake was made took place.

(4) A purchaser is an innocent third party for the purposes of this section—

(a) in the case of fraud or concealment of any fact relevant to the plaintiff's right of action, if he was not a party to the fraud or (as the case may be) to the concealment of that fact and did not at the time of the purchase know or have reason to believe that the fraud or concealment had taken place; and
(b) in the case of mistake, if he did not at the time of the purchase know or have reason to believe that the mistake had been made.

(4A) Subsection (1) above shall not apply in relation to the time limit prescribed by section 11A(3) of this Act or in relation to that time limit as applied by virtue of section 12(1) of this Act.

(5) Sections 14A and 14B of this Act shall not apply to any action to which subsection (1)(b) above applies (and accordingly the period of limitation referred to in that subsection, in any case to which either of those sections would otherwise apply, is the period applicable under section 2 of this Act).

[Discretionary extension of time limit for actions for libel or slander]

[32A Discretionary extension of time limit for actions for libel or slander

Where a person to whom a cause of action for libel or slander has accrued has not brought such an action within the period of three years mentioned in section 4A of this Act (or, where applicable, the period allowed by section 28(1) as modified by section 28(4A)) because all or any of the facts relevant to that cause of action did not become known to him until after the expiration of that period, such an action—

(a) may be brought by him at any time before the expiration of one year from the earliest date on which he knew all the facts relevant to that cause of action; but

(b)   shall not be so brought without the leave of the High Court.]

Discretionary exclusion of time limit for actions in respect of personal injuries or death

33 Discretionary exclusion of time limit for actions in respect of personal injuries or death

(1) If it appears to the court that it would be equitable to allow an action to proceed having regard to the degree to which—

(a)   the provisions of section 11 or 12 of this Act prejudice the plaintiff or any person whom he represents; and

(b)   any decision of the court under this subsection would prejudice the defendant or any person whom he represents;

the court may direct that those provisions shall not apply to the action, or shall not apply to any specified cause of action to which the action relates.

[(1A) The court shall not under this section disapply—

(a)   subsection (3) of section 11A; or

(b)   where the damages claimed by the plaintiff are confined to damages for loss of or damage to any property, any other provision in its application to an action by virtue of Part 1 of the Consumer Protection Act 1987.]

(2) The court shall not under this section disapply section 12(1) except where the reason why the person injured could no longer maintain an action was because of the time limit in section 11.

If, for example, the person injured could at his death no longer maintain an action under the Fatal Accidents Act 1976 because of the time limit in Article 29 in Schedule 1 to the Carriage by Air Act 1961, the court has no power to direct that section 12(1) shall not apply.

(3) In acting under this section the court shall have regard to all the circumstances of the case and in particular to—

(a)   the length of, and the reasons for, the delay on the part of the plaintiff;

(b)   the extent to which, having regard to the delay, the evidence adduced or likely to be adduced by the plaintiff or the defendant is or is likely to be less cogent than if the action had been brought within the time allowed by section 11 or (as the case may be) by section 12;

(c)   the conduct of the defendant after the cause of action arose, including the extent (if any) to which he responded to requests reasonably made by the plaintiff for information or inspection for the purpose of ascertaining facts which were or might be relevant to the plaintiff's cause of action against the defendant;

(d)   the duration of any disability of the plaintiff arising after the date of the accrual of the cause of action;

(*e*) the extent to which the plaintiff acted promptly and reasonably once he knew whether or not the act or omission of the defendant, to which the injury was attributable, might be capable at that time of giving rise to an action for damages;

(*f*) the steps, if any, taken by the plintiff to obtain medical, legal or other expert advice and the nature of any such advice he may have received.

(4) In a case where the person injured died when, because of section 11, he could no longer maintain an action and recover damages in respect of the injury, the court shall have regard in particular to the length of, and the reasons for, the delay on the part of the deceased.

(5) In a case under subsection (4) above, or any other case where the time limit, or one of the time limits, depends on the date of knowledge of a person other than the plaintiff, subsection (3) above shall have effect with appropriate modifications, and shall have effect in particular as if references to the plaintiff included references to any person whose date of knowledge is or was relevant in determining a time limit.

(6) A direction by the court disapplying the provisions of section 12(1) shall operate to disapply the provisions to the same effect in section 1(1) of the Fatal Accidents Act 1976.

(7) In this section 'the court' means the court in which the action has been brought.

(8) References in this section to section 11 include references to that section as extended by any of the preceding provisions of this Part of this Act or by any provision of Part III of this Act.

Part III

Miscellaneous and General

34 Application of Act and other limitation enactments to arbitrations

(1) This Act and any other limitation enactment shall apply to arbitrations as they apply to actions in the High Court.

(2) Notwithstanding any term in an arbitration agreement to the effect that no cause of action shall accrue in respect of any matter required by the agreement to be referred until an award is made under the agreement, the cause of action shall, for the purposes of this Act and any other limitation enactment (whether in their application to arbitrations or to other proceedings), be deemed to have accrued in respect of any such matter at the time when it would have accrued but for that term in the agreement.

(3) For the purposes of this Act and of any other limitation enactment an arbitration shall be treated as being commenced—

(*a*) when one party to the arbitration serves on the other party or parties a notice requiring him or them to appoint an arbitrator or to agree to the appointment of an arbitrator; or (*b*) where the arbitration agreement provides that the reference shall be to a person named or designated in the agreement, when one party to the arbitration serves on the other party or parties a notice requiring him or them to submit the dispute to the person so named or designated.

(4) Any such notice may be served either—

(*a*) by delivering it to the person on whom it is to be served; or

(*b*) by leaving it at the usual or last-known place of abode in England and Wales of that person; or;

(*c*) by sending it by post in a registered letter addressed to that person at his usual or last-known place of abode in England and Wales;

as well as in any other manner provided in the arbitration agreement.

(5) Where the High Court—

(*a*) orders that an award be set aside; or

(*b*) orders, after the commencement of an arbitration, that the arbitration agreement shall cease to have effect with respect to the dispute referred;

the court may further order that the period between the commencement of the arbitration and the date of the order of the court shall be excluded in computing the time prescribed by this Act or by any other limitation enactment for the commencement of proceedings (including arbitration) with respect to the dispute referred.

(6) This section shall apply to an arbitration under an Act of Parliament as well as to an arbitration pursuant to an arbitration agreement.

Subsections (3) and (4) above shall have effect, in relation to an arbitration under an Act, as if for the references to the arbitration agreement there were substituted references to such of the provisions of the Act or of any order, scheme, rules, regulations or byelaws made under the Act as relate to the arbitration.

(7) In this section—

(*a*) 'arbitration', 'arbitration agreement' and 'award' have the same meanings as in Part I of the Arbitration Act 1950; and

(*b*) references to any other limitation enactment are references to any other enactment relating to the limitation of actions, whether passed before or after the passing of this Act.

35 New claims in pending actions: rules of court

(1) For the purposes of this Act, any new claim made in the course of any action shall be deemed to be a separate action and to have been commenced—

(*a*) in the case of a new claim made in or by way of third party proceedings, on the date on which those proceedings were commenced; and (*b*) in the case of any other new claim, on the same date as the original action.

(2) In this section a new claim means any claim by way of set-off or counterclaim, and any claim involving either—

    (*a*) the addition or substitution of a new cause of action; or
    (*b*) the addition or substitution of a new party;

and 'third party proceedings' means any proceedings brought in the course of any action by any party to the action against a person not previously a party to the action, other than proceedings brought by joining any such person as defendant to any claim already made in the original action by the party bringing the proceedings.

(3) Except as provided by section 33 of this Act or by rules of court, neither the High Court nor any county court shall allow a new claim within subsection (1)*(b)* above, other than an original set-off or counterclaim, to be made in the course of any action after the expiry of any time limit under this Act which would affect a new action to enforce that claim.

For the purposes of this subsection, a claim is an original set-off or an original counterclaim if it is a claim made by way of set-off or (as the case may be) by way of counterclaim by a party who has not previously made any claim in the action.

(4) Rules of court may provide for allowing a new claim to which subsection (3) above applies to be made as there mentioned, but only if the conditions specified in subsection (5) below are satisified, and subject to any further restrictions the rules may impose.

(5) The conditions referred to in subsection (4) above are the following—

    (*a*) in the case of a claim involving a new cause of action, if the new cause of action arises out of the same facts or substantially the same facts as are already in issue on any claim previously made in the original action; and
    (*b*) in the case of a claim involving a new party, if the addition or substitution of the new party is necessary for the determination of the original action.

(6) The addition or substitution of a new party shall not be regarded for the purposes of subsection (5)*(b)* above as necessary for the determination of the original action unless either—

    (*a*) the new party is substituted for a party whose name was given in any claim made in the original action in mistake for the new party's name; or
    (*b*) any claim already made in the original action cannot be maintained by or against an existing party unless the new party is joined or substituted as plaintiff or defendant in that action.

(7) Subject to subsection (4) above, rules of cout may provide for allowing a party to any action to claim relief in a new capacity in respect of a new

cause of action notwithstanding that he had no title to make that claim at the date of the commencement of the action.

This subsection shall not be taken as prejudicing the power of rules of court to provide for allowing a party to claim relief in a new capacity without adding or substituting a new cause of action.

(8) Subsections (3) to (7) above shall apply in relation to a new claim made in the course of third party proceedings as if those proceedings were the original action, and subject to such other modifications as may be prescribed by rules of court in any case or class of case.

(9) [Repealed by the Supreme Court Act 1981.]

36 Equitable jurisdiction and remedies

(1) The following time limits under this Act, that is to say—

- (a) the time limit under section 2 for actions founded on tort;
- [(aa) the time limit under section 4A for actions for libel or slander;]
- (b) the time limit under section 5 for actions founded on simple contract;
- (c) the time limit under section 7 for actions to enforce awards where the submission is not by an instrument under seal;
- (d) the time limit under section 8 for actions on a speciality;
- (e) the time limit under section 9 for actions to recover a sum recoverable by virtue of any enactment; and
- (f) the time limit under section 24 for actions to enforce a judgment;

shall not apply to any claim for specific performance of a contract or for an injunction or for other equitable relief, except in so far as any such time limit may be applied by the court by analogy in like manner as the corresponding time limit under any enactment repealed by the Limitation Act 1939 was applied before 1st July 1940.

(2) Nothing in this Act shall affect any equitable jurisdiction to refuse relief on the ground of acquiescence or otherwise.

37 Application to the Crown and the Duke of Cornwall

(1) Except as otherwise expressly provided in this Act, and without prejudice to section 39, this Act shall apply to proceedings by or against the Crown in like manner as it applies to proceedings between subjects.

(2) Notwithstanding subsection (1) above, this Act shall not apply to—

- (a) any proceedings by the Crown for the recovery of any tax or duty or interest on any tax or duty;
- (b) any forfeiture proceedings under the customs and excise Acts (within the meaning of the Customs and Excise Management Act 1979); or
- (c) any proceedings in respect of the forfeiture of a ship.

In this subsection 'duty' includes any debt due to Her Majesty under section

16 of the Tithe Act 1936, and 'ship' includes every description of vessel used in navigation not propelled by oars.

(3) For the purposes of this section, proceedings by or against the Crown include—

    (a) proceedings by or against Her Majesty in right of the Duchy of Lancaster;

    (b) proceedings by or against any Government department or any officer of the Crown as such or any person acting on behalf of the Crown; and

    (c) proceedings by or against the Duke of Cornwall.

(4) For the purposes of the provisions of this Act relating to actions for the recovery of land and advowsons, references to the Crown shall include references to Her Majesty in right of the Duchy of Lancaster; and those provisions shall apply to lands and advowsons forming part of the possessions of the Duchy of Cornwall as if for the references to the Crown there were substituted references to the Duke of Cornwall as defined in the Duchy of Cornwall Management Act 1863.

(5) For the purposes of this Act a proceeding by petition of right (in any case where any such proceeding lies, by virtue of any saving in section 40 of the Crown Proceedings Act 1947, notwithstanding the general abolition by that Act of proceedings by way of petition of right) shall be treated as being commenced on the date on which the petition is presented.

(6) Nothing in this Act shall affect the prerogative right of Her Majesty (whether in right of the Crown or of the Duchy of Lancaster) or of the Duke of Cornwall to any gold or silver mine.

38 Interpretation

(1) In this Act, unless the context otherwise requires—

'action' includes any proceeding in a court of law, including an ecclesiastical court;

'land' includes corporeal hereditaments, tithes and rentcharges and any legal or equitable estate or interest therein, including an interest in the proceeds of the sale of land held upon trust for sale, but except as provided above in this definition does not include any incorporeal hereditament;

'personal estate' and 'personal property' do not include chattels real;

'personal injuries' includes any disease and any impairment of a person's physical or mental condition, and 'injury' and cognate expressions shall be construed accordingly;

'rent' includes a rentcharge and a rentservice;

'rentcharge' means any annuity or periodical sum of money charged upon or payable out of land, except a rent service or interest on a mortgage on land;

'settled land', 'statutory owner' and 'tenant for life' have the same meanings respectively as in the Settled Land Act 1925;

'trust' and 'trustee' have the same meanings as in the Trustee Act 1925; and

'trust for sale' has the same meaning as in the Law of Property Act 1925.

(2) For the purposes of this Act a person shall be treated as under a disability while he is an infant, or of unsound mind.

(3) For the purposes of subsection (2) above a person is of unsound mind if he is a person who, by reason of mental disorder within the meaning of the [Mental Health Act 1983], is incapable of managing and administering his property and affairs.

(4) Without prejudice to the generality of subsection (3) above, a person shall be conclusively presumed for the purposes of subsection (2) above to be of unsound mind—

> (a) while he is liable to be detained or subject to guardianship under [the Mental Health Act 1983 (otherwise than by virtue of section 35 or 89)]; and
>
> (b) while he is receiving treatment as an in-patient in any hospital within the meaning of the Mental Health Act 1983 or mental nursing home within the meaning of the Nursing Homes Act 1975 without being liable to be detained under the said Act of 1983 (otherwise than by virtue of section 35 or 89), being treatment which follows without any interval a period during which he was liable to be detained or subject to guardianship under the Mental Health Act 1959, or the said Act of 1983 (otherwise than by virtue of section 35 or 89) or by virtue of any enactment repealed or excluded by the Mental Health Act 1959[7]

(5) Subject to subsection (6) below, a person shall be treated as claiming through another person if he became entitled by, through, under, or by the act of that other person to the right claimed, and any person whose estate or interest might have been barred by a person entitled to an entailed interest in possession shall be treated as claiming through the person so entitled.

(6) A person becoming entitled to any estate or interest by virtue of a special power of appointment shall not be treated as claiming through the appointor.

(7) References in this Act to a right of action to recover land shall include references to a right to enter into possession of the land or, in the case of rentcharges and tithes, to distrain for arrears of rent or tithe, and references to the bringing of such an action shall include references to the making of such an entry or distress.

(8) References in this Act to the possession of land shall, in the case of tithes and rentcharges, be construed as references to the receipt of the tithe or rent, and references to the date of dispossession or discontinuance of possession of land shall, in the case of rentcharges, be construed as references to the date of the last receipt of rent.

(9) References in Part II of this Act to a right of action shall include references to—

> (a) a cause of action;
>
> (b) a right to receive money secured by a mortgage or charge on any property;
>
> (c) a right to recover proceeds of the sale of land; and

(*d*) a right to receive a share or interest in the personal estate of a deceased person.

(10) References in Part II to the date of the accrual of a right of action shall be construed—

(*a*) in the case of an action upon a judgment, as references to the date on which the judgment became enforceable; and

(*b*) in the case of an action to recover arrears of rent or interest, or damages in respect of arrears of rent or interest, as references to the date on which the rent or interest became due.

39 Saving for other limitation enactments

This Act shall not apply to any action or arbitration for which a period of limitation is prescribed by or under any other enactment (whether passed before or after the passing of this Act) or to any action or arbitration to which the Crown is a party and for which, if it were between subjects, a period of limitation would be prescribed by or under any such other enactment.

40 Transitional provisions, amendments and repeals

(1) Schedule 2 to this Act, which contains transitional provisions, shall have effect.

(2) The enactments specified in Schedule 3 to this Act shall have effect subject to the amendments specified in that Schedule, being amendments consequential on the provisions of this Act; but the amendment of any enactment by that Schedule shall not be taken as prejudicing the operation of section 17(2) of the Interpretation Act 1978 (effect of repeals).

(3) The enactments specified in Schedule 4 to this Act are hereby repealed to the extent specified in column 3 of that Schedule.

41 Short title, commencement and extent

(1) This Act may be cited as the Limitation Act 1980.

(2) This Act, except section 35, shall come into force on 1st May 1981.

(3) Section 35 of this Act shall come into force on 1st May 1981 to the extent (if any) that the section substituted for section 28 of the Limitation Act 1939 by section 8 of the Limitation Amendment Act 1980 is in force immediately before that date; but otherwise section 35 shall come into force on such day as the Lord Chancellor may by order made by statutory instrument appoint, and different days may be appointed for different purposes of that section (including its application in relation to different courts or proceedings).

(4) The repeal by this Act of section 14(1) of the Limitation Act 1963 and the corresponding saving in paragraph 2 of Schedule 2 to this Act shall extend to Northern Ireland, but otherwise this Act does not extend to Scotland or to Northern Ireland.

SCHEDULES

SCHEDULE 1

Section 15(6), (7)

PROVISIONS WITH RESPECT TO ACTIONS TO RECOVER LAND

PART I

ACCRUAL OF RIGHTS OF ACTION TO RECOVER LAND

Accrual of right of action in case of present interests in land

1. Where the person bringing an action to recover land, or some person through whom he claims, has been in possession of the land, and has while entitled to the land been dispossessed or discontinued his possession, the right of action shall be treated as having accrued on the date of the dispossession or discontinuance.

2. Where any person brings an action to recover any land of a deceased person (whether under a will or on intestacy) and the deceased person—

(a) was on the date of his death in possession of the land or, in the case of a rentcharge created by will or taking effect upon his death, in possession of the land charged; and

(b) was the last person entitled to the land to be in possession of it;

the right of action shall be treated as having accrued on the date of his death.

(3) Where any person brings an action to recover land, being an estate or interest in possession assured otherwise than by will to him, or to some person through whom he claims, and—

(a) the person making the assurance was on the date when the assurance took effect in possession of the land or, in the case of a rentcharge created by the assurance, in possession of the land charged; and

(b) no person has been in possession of the land by virtue of the assurance;

the right of action shall be treated as having accrued on the date when the assurance took effect.

Accrual of right of action in case of future interests

4. The right of action to recover any land shall, in a case where—

(a) the estate or interest claimed was an estate or interest in reversion or remainder or any other future estate or interest; and

(b) no person has taken possession of the land by virtue of the estate or interest claimed;

be treated as having accrued on the date on which the estate or interest fell into possession by the determination of the preceding estate or interest.

5.—(1) Subject to sub-paragraph (2) below, a tenancy from year to year or other period, without a lease in writing, shall for the purposes of this Act be treated as being determined at the expiration of the first year or other period; and accordingly the right of action of the person entitled to the land subject to the tenancy shall be treated as having accrued at the date on which in accordance with this sub-paragraph the tenancy is determined.

(2) Where any rent has subsequently been received in respect of the tenancy, the right of action shall be treated as having accrued on the date of the last receipt of rent.

6.—(1)   Where—

   (a)   any person is in possession of land by virtue of a lease in writing by which a rent of not less than ten pounds a year is reserved; and

   (b)   the rent is received by some person wrongfully claiming to be entitled to the land in reversion immediately expectant on the determination of the lease; and

   (c)   no rent is subsequently received by the person rightfully so entitled;

the right of action to recover the land of the person rightfully so entitled shall be treated as having accrued on the date when the rent was first received by the person wrongfully claiming to be so entitled and not on the date of the determination of the lease.

(2) Sub-paragraph (1) above shall not apply to any lease granted by the Crown.

Accrual of right of action in case of forfeiture or breach of condition

7.—(1) Subject to sub-paragraph (2) below, a right of action to recover land by virtue of a forfeiture or breach of condition shall be treated as having accrued on the date on which the forfeiture was incurred or the condition broken.

(2) If any such right has acrued to a person entitled to an estate or interest in reversion or remainder and the land was not recovered by virtue of that right, the right of action to recover the land shall not be treated as having accrued to that person until his estate or interest fell into possession, as if no such forfeiture or breach of condition had occurred.

Right of action not to accrue or continue unless there is adverse possession

8.—(1) No right of action to recover land shall be treated as accruing unless the land is in the possession of some person in whose favour the period of limitation can run (referred to below in this paragraph as 'adverse possession'); and where under the preceding provisions of this Schedule any such right of action is treated as accruing on a certain date and no person is in adverse possession on that date, the right of action shall not be treated as accruing unless and until adverse possession is taken of the land.

(2) Where a right of action to recover land has accrued and after its accrual, before the right is barred, the land ceases to be in adverse possession, the right of action shall no longer be treated as having accrued and no fresh right of action shall be treated as accruing unless and until the land is again taken into adverse possession.

(3) For the purposes of this paragraph—

(a) possession of any land subject to a rentcharge by a person (other than the person entitled to the rentcharge) who does not pay the rent shall be treated as adverse possession of the rentcharge; and

(b) receipt of rent under a lease by a person wrongfully claiming to be entitled to the land in reversion immediately expectant on the determination of the lease shall be treated as adverse possession of the land.

(4) For the purpose of determining whether a person occupying any land is in adverse possession of the land it shall not be assumed by implication of law that his occupation is by permission of the person entitled to the land merely by virtue of the fact that his occupation is not inconsistent with the latter's present or future enjoyment of the land.

This provision shall not be taken as prejudicing a finding to the effect that a person's occupation of any land is by implied permission of the person entitled to the land in any case where such a finding is justified on the actual facts of the case.

Possession of beneficiary not adverse to others interested in settled land or land held on trust for sale

9. Where any settled land or any land held on trust for sale is in the possession of a person entitled to a beneficial interest in the land or in the proceeds of sale (not being a person solely or absolutely entitled to the land or the proceeds), no right of action to recover the land shall be treated for the purposes of this Act as accruing during that possession to any person in whom the land is vested as tenant for life, statutory owner or trustee, or to any other person entitled to a beneficial interest in the land or the proceeds of sale.

PART II

MODIFICATIONS OF SECTION 15 WHERE CROWN OR CERTAIN CORPORATIONS SOLE ARE INVOLVED

10. Subject to paragraph 11 below, section 15(1) of this Act shall apply to the bringing of an action to recover any land by the Crown or by any spiritual or eleemosynary corporation sole with the substitution for the reference to twelve years of a reference to thirty years.

11.—(1) An action to recover foreshore may be brought by the Crown at any time before the expiration of sixty years from the date mentioned in section 15(1) of this Act.

(2) Where any right of action to recover land which has ceased to be foreshore but remains in the ownership of the Crown accrued when the land was foreshore, the action may be brought at any time before the expiration of

(a) sixty years from the date of accrual of the right of action; or

(b) thirty years from the date when the land ceased to be foreshore;

whichever period first expires.

(3) In this paragraph 'foreshore' means the shore and bed of the sea and

of any tidal water, below the line of the medium high tide between the spring tides and the neap tides.

12. Notwithstanding section 15(1) of this Act, where in the case of any action brought by a person other than the Crown or a spiritual or eleemosynary corporation sole the right of action first accrued to the Crown or any such corporation sole through whom the person in question claims, the action may be brought at any time before the expiration of—

(*a*) the period during which the action could have been brought by the Crown or the corporation sole; or

(*b*) twelve years from the date on which the right of action accrued to some person other than the Crown or the corporation sole;

whichever period first expires.

13. Section 15(2) of this Act shall apply in any case where the Crown or a spiritual or eleemosynary corporation sole is entitled to the succeeding estate or interest with the substitution—

(*a*) for the reference to twelve years of a reference to thirty years; and

(*b*) for the reference to six years of a reference to twelve years.

SCHEDULE 2

Section 40(1)

TRANSITIONAL PROVISIONS

1. Nothing in this Act shall affect the operation of section 4 of the Limitation Act 1963, as it had effect immediately before 1 January 1979 (being the date on which the Civil Liability (Contribution) Act 1978 came into force), in relation to any case where the damage in question occurred before that date.

2. The amendment made by section 14(1) of the Limitation Act 1963 in section 5 of the Limitation (Enemies and War Prisoners) Act 1945 (which provides that section 5 shall have effect as if for the words 'in force in Northern Ireland at the date of the passing of this Act' there were substituted the words 'for the time being in force in Northern Ireland') shall continue to have effect notwithstanding the repeal by this Act of section 14(1).

3. It is hereby declared that a decision taken at any time by a court to grant, or not to grant, leave under Part I of the Limitation Act 1963 (which, so far as it related to leave, was repealed by the Limitation Act 1975) does not affect the determination of any question in proceedings under any provision of this Act which corresponds to a provision of the Limitation Act 1975, but in such proceedings account may be taken of evidence admitted in proceedings under Part I of the Limitation Act 1963.

4.—(1) In section 33(6) of this Act the reference to section 1(1) of the Fatal Accidents Act 1976 shall be construed as including a reference to section 1 of the Fatal Accidents Act 1846.

(2) Any other reference in that section, or in section 12 or 13 of this Act to the Fatal Accidents Act 1976 shall be construed as including a reference to the Fatal Accidents Act 1846.

5. Nothwithstanding anything in section 29(7) of this Act or in the repeals made by this Act, the Limitation Act 1939 shall continue to have effect in relation to any acknowledgment or payment made before the coming into force of section 6 of the Limitation Amendment Act 1980 (which amended section 23 of the Limitation Act 1939 and made certain repeals in sections 23 and 25 of that Act so as to prevent the revival by acknowledgment or part payment of a right of action barred by that Act) as it had effect immediately before section 6 came into force.

6. Section 28 of the Limitation Act 1939 (provisions as to set-off or counterclaim) shall continue to apply (as originally enacted) to any claim by way of set-off or counterclaim made in an action to which section 35 of this Act does not apply, but as if the reference in section 28 to that Act were a reference to this Act; and, in relation to any such action, references in this Act to section 35 of this Act shall be construed as references to section 28 as it applies by virtue of this paragraph.

7. Section 37(2)(c)of this Act shall be treated for the purposes of the Hovercraft Act 1968 as if it were contained in an Act passed before that Act.

8. In relation to a lease granted before the coming into force of section 3(2) of the Limitation Amendment Act 1980 (which substituted 'ten pounds a year' for 'twenty shillings' in section 9(3) of the Limitation Act 1939), paragraph 6(1)(a) of Schedule 1 to this Act shall have effect as if for the words 'ten pounds a year' there were substituted the words 'twenty shillings'.

9.—(1) Nothing in any provision of this Act shall—

   (a) enable any action to be brought which was barred by this Act or (as the case may be) by the Limitation Act 1939 before the relevant date; or
   (b) affect any action or arbitration commenced before that date or the title to any property which is the subject of any such action or arbitration.

(2) In sub-paragraph (1) above 'the relevant date' means—

   (a) in relation to section 35 of this Act, the date on which that section comes into force in relation to actions of the description in question or, if section 8 of the Limitation Amendment Act 1980 (which substituted the provisions reproduced in section 35 for section 28 of the Limitation Act 1939) is in force immediately before 1st May 1981 in relation to actions of that description, the date on which section 8 came into force in relation to actions of that description; and
   (b) in relation to any other provision of this Act, 1st August 1980 (being the date of coming into force of the remaining provisions of the Limitation Amendment Act 1980, apart from section 8)

(*Sch 3, para 1 amends the Land Registration Act 1925, s 83(11), Vol 37, title* Real Property (Pt 2); *para 2 provides that in s 21A of the Administration of Estates Act 1925, Vol 17, title* Executors and Administrators *the reference in subsection (2) to the Limitation Act 1939 shall be construed as including a reference to this Act; para 3 amends the Limitation (Enemies and War Prisoners) Act 1945, s 2(1) ante; para 4 amends the Charitable Trusts (Validation) Act 1954, s 3(4), Vol 5, title* Charities; *para 5 amends the Carriage by Air Act 1961, s 5(3), Vol 4, title* Aviation; *para 6 amends the Carriage of Goods by Road Act 1965, s 7(2)(a), Vol 38, title* Road Traffic; *para 7 amends the Agriculture Act 1967, Sch 3 para 7(6), Vol 1 title* Agriculture (Pt 1)*; para 8 amends the Mines and Quarries (Tips) Act 1969, Sch 3, para 6(2), Vol 29, title* Mines, Minerals and Quarries; *para 9 amends the Law of Property Act 1969, s 25(5), Vol 37, title* Real Property (Pt 1); *para 10 amends the Animals Act 1971, s 10, Vol 2, title* Animals; *para 11 amends the Deposit of Poisonous Waste Act 1972, s 2(4) (repealed); s 12 amends the Control of Pollution Act 1974, s 88(4)(c), Vol 35, title* Public Health.)

SCHEDULE 4

Section 40(3)

ENACTMENTS REPEALED

Chapter	Short title	Extent of Repeal
2 & 3 Geo 6 c 21	The Limitation Act 1939	The whole Act.
7 & 8 Eliz 2 c 72	The Mental Health Act 1959	In Schedule 7, Part I, the entry relating to the Limitation Act 1939.
1963 c 47	The Limitation Act 1963	Sections 4 and 5. Section 7(7). Section 14(1). Sections 15 and 16.
1975 c 54	The Limitation Act 1975	The whole Act.
1976 c 30	The Fatal Accidents Act 1976	In Schedule 1, paragraph 3.
1978 c 47	The Civil Liability (Contribution) Act 1978	In Schedule 1, paragraph 6.
1980 c 24	The Limitation Amendment Act 1980	Sections 1 to 9. Sections 11 to 13. Section 14(2) to (4). Schedules 1 and 2.

Limitation (Enemies and War Prisoners) Act 1945

(8 & 9 Geo 6 c 16)

An Act to provide for suspending the operation of certain statutes of limitation in relation to proceedings affecting persons who have been enemies or have been detained in enemy territory

[28 March 1945]

Northern Ireland. This Act applies; see s 5 post.

1 Suspension of limitation period where party was an enemy or detained in enemy territory

(1) If at any time before the expiration of the period prescribed by any statute of limitation for the bringing of any action any person who would have been a necessary party to that action if it had then been brought was an enemy or was detained in enemy territory, the said period shall be deemed not to have run while the said person was an enemy or was so detained, and shall in no case expire before the end of twelve months from the date when he ceased to be an enemy or to be so detained, or from the date of the passing of this Act, whichever is the later:

Provided that, where any person was only an enemy as respects a business carried on in enemy territory, this section shall only apply, so far as that person is concerned, to actions arising in the course of that business.

(2) If it is proved in any action that any person was resident or carried on business or was detained in enemy territory at any time, he shall for the purposes of this Act be presumed to have continued to be resident or to carry on business or to be detained, as the case may be, in that territory until it ceased to be enemy territory, unless it is proved that he ceased to be resident or to carry on business or to be detained in that territory at an earlier date.

(3) If two or more periods have occurred in which any person who would have been such a necessary party as aforesaid was an enemy or was detained in enemy territory, those periods shall be treated for the purposes of this Act as one continuous such period beginning with the beginning of the first period and ending with the end of the last period.

2 Interpretation

(1) In this Act the following expressions have the meanings hereby respectively assigned to them, that is to say:—

'action' means civil proceedings before any court or tribunal and includes arbitration proceedings;

'enemy' means any person who is, or is deemed to be, an enemy for any of the purposes of the Trading with the Enemy Act 1939, except that in ascertaining whether a person is such an enemy the expression 'enemy territory' in section two of the said Act shall have the meaning assigned to that expression by this section;

'enemy territory' means:—

(*a*) any area which is enemy territory as defined by subsection (1) of section fifteen of the Trading with the Enemy Act 1939;

(*b*) any area in relation to which the provisions of the said Act apply, by virtue of an order made under subsection (1A) of the said section fifteen, as they apply in relation to enemy territory as so defined; and

(*c*) any area which, by virtue of regulation six or regulation seven of the Defence (Trading with the Enemy) Regulations 1940, or any order made thereunder, is treated for any of the purposes of the said Act as enemy territory as so defined or such territory as is referred to in the last foregoing paragraph;

'statute of limitation' means any of the following enactments, that is to say,—

[the Limitation Act 1980],

subsection three of section two of the Fatal Accidents Act 1976,

section four of the Employers' Liability Act 1880,

section ten of the Copyright Act 1911,

section eight of the Maritime Conventions Act 1911,

Rule 6 of Article III of the Schedule to the Carriage of Goods by Sea Act 1971,

section one of the Law Reform (Miscellaneous Provisions) Act 1934,

[section 13(2) of the Matrimonial Causes Act 1973 and paragraph 11(3) of Schedule 1 to that Act]

[subsection (1) of section four of the Limitation Act 1963],

[section 3(2) of the Nullity of Marriage Act 1971],

[and, in a case to which section 1(1) of the Foreign Limitation Periods Act 1984 applies, so much of the law of any country outside England and Wales as applies by virtue of that Act].

(2) References in this Act to any person who would have been a necessary party to an action shall be construed as including references to any person who would have been such a necessary party but for the provisions of section seven of the Trading with the Enemy Act 1939, or any order made thereunder.

(3) References in this Act to the period during which any person was detained in enemy territory shall be construed as including references to any period

immediately following the period of such detention during which that person remained in enemy territory.

(4) Subsection (2) of section fifteen of the Trading with the Enemy Act 1939 (which provides that a certificate of a Secretary of State shall, for the purposes of proceedings under or arising out of that Act, be conclusive evidence of certain matters affecting the definition of 'enemy territory') shall apply for the purposes of any action to which this Act relates.

(5) References in this Act to any enactment or to any Defence Regulation shall be construed as referring to that enactment or Regulation as amended by any subsequent enactment or Defence Regulation.

3 Application to the Crown

This Act shall apply to proceedings to which the Crown is a party, including proceedings to which His Majesty is a party in right of the Duchy of Lancaster and proceedings in respect of property belonging to the Duchy of Cornwall.

4 (*Applies to Scotland only*)

5 Application to Northern Ireland

In the application of this Act to Northern Ireland, the expression 'statute of limitation' means any enactment (whether of the Irish Parliament or of the Parliament of the United Kingdom or of the Parliament of Northern Ireland) [for the time being in force in Northern Ireland] under which a period is prescribed as the period within which any action to which such enactment relates is required to be brought, but does not include any enactment prescribing a period within which any criminal proceedings, or any proceedings to recover any penalty imposed as a punishment for a criminal offence, or any proceedings before a court of summary jurisdiction must be brought.

6 Short title and date of operation

(1) This Act may be cited as the Limitation (Enemies and War Prisoners) Act 1945.

(2) [Repealed by the Statute Law Revision Act 1950]

Appendix 3

Foreign Limitation Periods Act 1984

(1984 c 16)

An Act to provide for any law relating to the limitation of actions to be treated, for the purposes of cases in which effect is given to foreign law or to determinations by foreign courts, as a matter of substance rather than as a matter of procedure   [24 May 1984]

Commencement. This Act was brought into force on 1 October 1985 by the Foreign Limitation Periods Act 1984 (Commencement) Order 1985, SI 1985/1276, made under s 7(2) post.

Northern Ireland. This Act does not apply; see s 7(4) post.

1 Application of foreign limitation law

(1) Subject to the following provisions of this Act, where in any action or proceedings in a court in England and Wales the law of any other country falls (in accordance with rules of private international law applicable by any such court) to be taken into account in the determination of any matter—

(*a*) the law of that other country relating to limitation shall apply in respect of that matter for the purposes of the action or proceedings; and

(*b*) except where that matter falls within subsection (2) below, the law of England and Wales relating to limitation shall not so apply.

(2) A matter falls within this subsection if it is a matter in the determination of which both the law of England and Wales and the law of some other country fall to be taken into account.

(3) The law of England and Wales shall determine for the purposes of any law applicable by virtue of subsection (1)(*a*) above whether, and the time at which, proceedings have been commenced in respect of any matter; and, accordingly, section 35 of the Limitation Act 1980 (new claims in pending proceedings) shall apply in relation to time limits applicable by virtue of subsection (1)(*a*) above as it applies in relation to time limits under that Act.

(4) A court in England and Wales, in exercising in pursuance of subsection (1)(*a*) above any discretion conferred by the law of any other country, shall so far as practicable exercise that discretion in the manner in which it is exercised in comparable cases by the courts of that other country.

(5) In this section 'law', in relation to any country, shall not include rules of private international law applicable by the courts of that country or, in the case of England and Wales, this Act.

2 Exceptions to s 1

(1) In any case in which the application of section 1 above would to any extent conflict (whether under subsection (2) below or otherwise) with public policy, that section shall not apply to the extent that its application would so conflict.

(2) The application of section 1 above in relation to any action or proceedings shall conflict with public policy to the extent that its application would cause undue hardship to a person who is, or might be made, a party to the action or proceedings.

(3) Where, under a law applicable by virue of section 1(1)(*a*) above for the purposes of any action or proceedings, a limitation period is or may be extended or interrupted in respect of the absence of a party to the action or proceedings from any specified jurisdiction or country, so much of that law as provides for the extension or interruption shall be disregarded for those purposes.

(4) [Amends s 2(1) Limitation (Enemies and War Prisoners) Act 1945]

3 Foreign judgments on limitation points

Where a court in any country outside England and Wales has determined any matter wholly or partly by reference to the law of that or any other country (including England and Wales) relating to limitation, then, for the purposes of the law relating to the effect to be given in England and Wales to that determination, that court shall, to the extent that it has so determined the matter, be deemed to have determined it on its merits.

4 Meaning of law relating to limitation

(1) Subject to subsection (3) below, references in this Act to the law of any country (including England and Wales) relating to limitation shall, in relation to any matter, be construed as references to so much of the relevant law of that country as (in any manner) makes provision with respect to a limitation period applicable to the bringing of proceedings in respect of that matter in the courts of that country and shall include—

    (a) references to so much of that law as relates to, and to the effect of, the application, extension, reduction or interruption of that period; and

    (b) a reference, where under that law there is no limitation period which is so applicable, to the rule that such proceedings may be brought within an indefinite period.

(2) In subsection (1) above 'relevant law', in relation to any country, means the procedural and substantive law applicable, apart from any rules of private international law, by the courts of that country.

(3) References in this Act to the law of England and Wales relating to limitation shall not include the rules by virtue of which a court may, in the exercise of any discretion, refuse equitable relief on the grounds of acquiescence or otherwise; but, in applying those rules to a case in relation to which the law of any country outside England and Wales is applicable by virtue of section 1(1)(a) above (not being a law that provides for a limitation period that has expired), a court in England and Wales shall have regard, in particular, to the provisions of the law that is so applicable.

5 Application of Act to arbitrations

The references to any other limitation enactment in section 34 of the Limitation Act 1980 (application of limitation enactments to arbitration) include references to sections 1, 2 and 4 of this Act; and, accordingly, in subsection (5) of the said section 34, the reference to the time prescribed by a limitation enactment has effect for the purposes of any case to which section 1 above applies as a reference to the limitation period (if any) applicable by virtue of section 1 above.

6 Application to Crown

(1) This Act applies in relation to any action or proceedings by or against the Crown as it applies in relation to actions and proceedings to which the Crown is not a party.

(2) For the purposes of this section references to an action or proceedings by or against the Crown include references to—

    (a) any action or proceedings by or against Her Majesty in right of the Duchy of Lancaster;

    (b) any action or proceedings by or against any Government department or any officer of the Crown as such or any person acting on behalf of the Crown;

    (c) any action or proceedings by or against the Duke of Cornwall.

7 Short title, commencement, transitional provision and extent

(1) This Act may be cited as the Foreign Limitation Periods Act 1984.

(2) This Act shall come into force on such day as the Lord Chancellor may by order made by statutory instrument appoint.

(3) Nothing in this Act shall—

    (*a*) affect any action, proceedings or arbitration commenced in England and Wales before the day appointed under subsection (2) above; or

    (*b*) apply in relation to any matter if the limitation period which, apart from this Act, would have been applied in respect of that matter in England and Wales expired before that day.

(4) This Act extends to England and Wales only.

Appendix 4

The Latent Damage Act 1986
(1986 c 37)

ARRANGEMENT OF SECTIONS

An Act to amend the law about limitation of actions in relation to actions for damages for negligence not involving personal injuries; and to provide for a person taking an interest in property to have, in certain circumstances, a cause of action in respect of negligent damage to the property occurring before he takes that interest   **[18 July 1986]**

Time limits for negligence actions in respect of latent damage not involving personal injuries

1 [Amends the Limitation Act 1980 by inserting ss 14A and 14B]

2 [Contains consequential amendments to the Limitation Act 1980]

Accrual of cause of action to successive owners in respect of latent damage to property

3 Accrual of cause of action to successive owners in respect of latent damage to property

(1) Subject to the following provisions of this section, where—

(a) a cause of action ('the original cause of action') has accrued to any person in respect of any negligence to which damage to any property in which he has an interest is attributable (in whole or in part); and

(b) another person acquires an interest in that property after the date on which the original cause of action accrued but before the material facts about the damage have become known to any person who, at the time when he first has knowledge of those facts, has any interest in the property;

a fresh cause of action in respect of that negligence shall accrue to that other person on the date on which he acquires his interest in the property.

(2) A cause of action accruing to any person by virtue of subsection (1) above—

(a) shall be treated as if based on breach of a duty of care at common law owed to the person to whom it accrues; and

(b) shall be treated for the purposes of section 14A of the 1980 Act (special time limit for negligence actions where facts relevant to cause of action are not known at date of accrual) as having accrued on the date on which the original cause of action accrued.

(3) Section 28 of the 1980 Act (extension of limitation period in case of disability) shall not apply in relation to any such cause of action.

(4) Subsection (1) above shall not apply in any case where the person acquiring an interest in the damaged property is either—

(a) a person in whom the original cause of action vests by operation of law; of

(b) a person in whom the interest in that property vests by virtue of any order made by a court under section 538 of the Companies Act 1985 (vesting of company property in liquidator).

(5) For the purposes of subsection (1)(b) above, the material facts about the damage are such facts about the damage as would lead a reasonable person who has an interest in the damaged property at the time when those facts become known to him to consider it sufficiently serious to justify his instituting proceedings for damages against a defendant who did not dispute liability and was able to satisfy a judgment.

(6) For the purposes of this section a person's knowledge includes knowledge which he might reasonably have been expected to acquire—

(a) from facts observable or ascertainable by him; or

(b) from facts ascertainable by him with the help of appropriate expert advice which it is reasonable for him to seek;

but a person shall not be taken by virtue of this subsection to have knowledge of a fact ascertainable by him only with the help of expert advice so long as he has taken all reasonable steps to obtain (and, where appropriate, to act on) that advice.

(7) This section shall bind the Crown, but as regards the Crown's liability

in tort shall not bind the Crown further than the Crown is made liable in tort by the Crown Proceedings Act 1947.

Supplementary

4 Transitional provisions

(1) Nothing in section 1 or 2 of this Act shall—

(*a*) enable any action to be brought which was barred by the 1980 Act or (as the case may be) by the Limitation Act 1939 before this Act comes into force; or

(*b*) affect any action commenced before this Act comes into force.

(2) Subject to subsection (1) above, sections 1 and 2 of this Act shall have effect in relation to causes of action accruing before, as well as in relation to causes of action accruing after, this Act comes into force.

(3) Section 3 of this Act shall only apply in cases where an interest in damaged property is acquired after this Act comes into force but shall so apply, subject to subsection (4) below, irrespective of whether the original cause of action accrued before or after this Act comes into force.

(4) Where—

(*a*) a person acquires an interest in damaged property in circumstances to which section 3 would apart from this subsection apply; but

(*b*) the original cause of action accrued more than six years before this Act comes into force;

a cause of action shall not accrue to that person by virtue of subsection (1) of that section unless section 32(1)(*b*) of the 1980 Act (postponement of limitation period in case of deliberate concealment of relevant facts) would apply to any action founded on the original cause of action.

5 Citation, interpretation, commencement and extent

(1) This Act may be cited as the Latent Damage Act 1986.

(2) In this Act—

'the 1980 Act' has the meaning given by section 1; and
'action' includes any proceeding in a court of law, an arbitration and any new claim within the meaning of section 35 of the 1980 Act (new claims in pending actions).

(3) This Act shall come into force at the end of the period of two months beginning with the date on which it is passed.

(4) This Act extends to England and Wales only.

Law Reform Committee Interim Report on Limitation of Actions

SUMMARY OF CONCLUSIONS

148. Our conclusions may be summarised thus:—

(1) three years should be retained as the normal period of limitation in personal injury actions (paras. 39 and 69(1));

(2) the principle underlying the Limitation Act 1963, whereby the injured person is entitled to sue outside the normal three-year limitation period provided he starts proceedings within three years of his 'date of knowledge', should be retained (paras. 29 to 38 and 69(2)(*a*));

(3) an injured person's date of knowledge should be the date on which he first knew (or could reasonably have ascertained) the nature of his injury and its attributability to an act or omission on the part of the defendant (paras. 53 to 55 and 69(3));

(4) it is arguable whether an injured person should, or should not, be fixed with constructive knowledge of a fact which he could have ascertained only with the help of expert advice if he has taken reasonable steps to obtain such advice but has not ascertained that fact (paras. 60 to 68 and 69(3)(*c*));

(5) ignorance of matters of law should not postpone the running of time and the 'worthwhile cause of action test' should not, therefore, be accepted (para. 53);

(6) the court should have a discretion to override a defence of limitation notwithstanding that the plaintiff has not sued within three years of his date of knowledge (paras. 56 to 58 and 69(2)(*b*) and (5));

(7) a plaintiff should not be required to obtain the leave of the court as a condition of suing outside the normal limitation period (para. 86);

(8) no effect should be given to supervening disability, save to the extent that it should be a factor relevant to the exercise of the court's discretion where the plaintiff sues more than three years after his date of knowledge (para. 95);

(9) the rule whereby time runs against a person under a disability who is in the custody of a parent should be abolished (para. 110);

(10) save that our principal recommendations as to the 'date of knowledge',

the court's discretion and the abolition of 'leave', should be applied to claims under the Fatal Accidents Acts and the Law Reform (Miscellaneous Provisions) Act 1934, the effect of the present legislation on claims brought after the injured person's death should be preserved (paras. 121 to 125);

(11) if the 'custody of a parent rule' is abolished for claims made by injured persons, it should also be abolished for claims on behalf of dependants (para. 136);

(12) any legislation implementing our recommendations should apply to causes of action accruing before, and to proceedings pending at, its commencement (para. 147).

ALAN S. ORR, *Chairman.*
HUGH GRIFFITHS.
RAYMOND WALTON.
W. GRANVILLE WINGATE.
T. H. BINGHAM.
A. G. GUEST.
C. A. HINKS.
DAVID HIRST.
LLOYD OF HAMPSTEAD.
ANDREW MARTIN.
E. G. NUGEE.

J. W. Bourne, *Secretary.*
M. C. Blair, *Assistant Secretary.*
March 1974.

Law Reform Committee
Twenty-First Report
Final Report on Limitation of Actions

To the Right Honourable the Lord Elwyn-Jones, C.H.,

Lord High Chancellor of Great Britain

Part I
INTRODUCTION AND GENERAL PRINCIPLES

Introduction

1.1 We were invited by your Lordship's predecessor on the 26th April 1971 to consider 'what changes in the law relating to the limitation of actions are, in the opinion of the Committee, desirable'. We have already submitted a report on the limitation of actions in cases of personal injury[1], a subject to which we gave priority at the request of Lord Hailsham. In this, our final report, we consider, and make recommendations on, the law of limitation outside the field of personal injury.

1.2 For the purpose of conducting our inquiry into limitation, we circulated a detailed questionnaire to those bodies and individuals whom we thought might be particularly interested in the subject and we invited comments from members of the public. A list of those who responded to our request for comments appears in Part A of Annex 1 to this report. We have found the memoranda we have received most helpful and we would like to take this opportunity of thanking all those who have assisted us for the trouble they have taken in responding to our request. We are, in addition, grateful to the representatives of the British Insurance Association and of Lloyd's who gave oral evidence to us on some particular aspects of our inquiry where insurance considerations appeared to us to be important. We have also received valuable assistance in other ways, and would like to express our indebtedness to those who responded to questions which we asked, or whose views were made known to us through the good offices of the Law Commission. A list of those concerned appears at Part B of Annex 1.

1.3 We would also like to express our warm thanks to Mr. J. W. Bourne for his unstinting service as Secretary of this Committee for the last nine years. He has played an important part in the consideration leading to, and the

---

[1] *Interim Report on Limitation of Actions in Personal Injury Claims;* (1974) Cmnd. 5630. This report was substantially implemented by the Limitation Act 1975.

preparation of, five reports, including this one, and we would like to acknowledge our appreciation of his judgment and experience and to wish him well in his new appointment as your Lordship's Permanent Secretary.

1.4 Although the history of limitation goes back a long way, we have not thought it necessary to consider the earlier statutory provisions in force before the enactment of the Limitation Act 1939. That Act followed a comprehensive review of the whole of the field of limitation by the Law Revision Committee, whose report[2], presented in December 1936, is the foundation of the 1939 Act. We shall refer in this report to some of the detailed recommendations of the Law Revision Committee where they are relevant to particular recommendations made by us; at this stage, it is sufficient to note that the Committee based its general recommendations on the principles that—

(a) a multiplicity of different periods applicable to different causes of action was undesirable and that it would be advantageous to have a single period covering most forms of action;

(b) although there were conflicting arguments (to which we refer in greater detail below), the common law rule whereby the limitation period started to run from the accrual of the cause of action should be preserved;

(c) in general, a system based on limitation (barring the remedy) rather than on prescription (extinguishing the right) by lapse of time was preferable[3].

1.5 The Committee's recommendations were substantially (though with some modifications) implemented by the Limitation Act 1939, which remains the basis of the law of limitation in England and Wales today. It has, however, been subject to major changes in the field of personal injury, to which we referred in detail in our earlier report[4] and to which we do not, therefore, need to refer again. Another, and less radical, modification to the 1939 Act was effected by the Law Reform (Limitation of Actions etc.) Act 1954 which (in addition to reducing the six-year period in cases or personal injury) did away with the special protection previously accorded to public authorities. This change has simplified our task since it is not now necessary to consider what has in the past proved to be a controversial field.

1.6 There are two further developments outside England and Wales which have proved relevant to our task. First, the Scottish Law Commission submitted in 1970 a report dealing comprehensively with the reform of the law relating to prescription and limitations of actions in Scotland[5], a report which has been substantially implemented by the Prescription and Limitation of Actions (Scotland) Act 1973. This Act has proved important from our point of view because it has introduced in Scotland a short five-year negative prescription covering a very wide field of actions corresponding, in English law, to claims in contract and in tort. It has also introduced a new solution to the vexed problem

---

[2] *Fifth Interim Report;* (1936) Cmd. 5334.
[3] *ibid.*, paras. 5, 7 and 24.
[4] Cmnd. 5630, paras. 3–16.
[5] Scot. Law Com. No. 15; *Reform of the Law Relating to Prescription and Limitation of Actions.*

of 'latent damage' to which we refer in greater detail in Part II, paragraphs 2.5 to 2.38 of this report.

Secondly, there have been moves to achieve a measure of uniformity for limitation or, in certain cases, special provision for certain types of proceedings, both in the United Nations and on the Continent of Europe. These are referred to in more detail in Annex 2, Part A.

General principles

1.7 In our interim report, we expressed our agreement with the views of the Edmund Davies Committee who stated the true purpose of limitation as being:—

(a) first, to protect defendants from stale claims;

(b) secondly, to encourage plaintiffs to institute proceedings without unreasonable delay and thus enable actions to be tried at a time when the recollection of witnesses was still clear, and

(c) thirdly, to enable a person to feel confident, after the lapse of a given period of time, that an incident which might have led to a claim against him is finally closed.[6].

We have, as we did in our examination of the law relating to personal injury, sought in our recommendations to give full weight to those three basic purposes, recognising that their relative importance will vary from case to case and that, inevitably, the object of protecting defendants cannot always be achieved without causing prejudice to plaintiffs.

1.8 It appeared to us at an early stage of our examination of limitation that the first and fundamental question (assuming always that the law must impose *some* time limit on the bringing of legal proceedings) is what should start time running or, to use the traditional Latin phrase, what should be the *terminus a quo*? This is fundamental, because if, for example, the rule were that time did not start to run until the plaintiff first knew that he had a cause of action, then the length of the limitation period could be appreciably shorter than it is at present and there would be a weaker case for giving the court any discretion to extend the time. Further, there would be less need to give any special consideration to a plaintiff who was the victim of fraud or who had suffered damage which became apparent only after many years.

1.9 The next fundamental question is the determination of the length of the limitation period. As we have said above, this depends greatly on the choice of the *terminus a quo*, but, apart from that, there is a conflict between the general convenience of having one single period (at present six years) covering the great majority of causes of action and the practical advantage to particular classes of litigant of having 'tailor-made' periods suitable to particular causes of action.

1.10 The ideal of a single uniform period applicable to every cause of action is plainly unattainable. Not only is the United Kingdom a party to a number of international conventions providing for different limitation periods applicable to particular claims, but the longest period reasonable for ordinary claims in

---

[6] *Report of the Committee on Limitation of Actions in Cases of Personal Injury;* (1962) Cmnd. 1829, para. 17.

tort and contract would be far too short for some claims affecting title to land, in particular claims to recover possession from a squatter. There could also be good reasons for distinguishing between classes of contract where a comparatively short (for example, two or three years) limitation period would cause no injustice and others where such a period would be manifestly too short: fairly obvious examples of the former are claims based on cheques and other negotiable instruments; of the latter, actions for breach of building contracts and for the repayment of loans of money between members of the same family. That different periods may also be suitable for different claims in tort is evident from the history of limitation in personal injury and fatal accident claims, since experience has proved that, for the ordinary 'running-down' or industrial accident case where there is no question of latent injury, the six-year period originally prescribed by the Limitation Act 1939 is too long. A further possible example is defamation, in respect of which we note that the Faulks Committee has recommended a normal period of three years in the place of the present six-year period[7].

1.11 We discuss these matters in greater detail in Parts II and III below; at this stage we need say no more than that we agree with the approach of the Law Revision Committee in 1936 and we do not, as a general rule favour the creation of a multiplicity of different limitation periods. One very relevant factor is that the same incident may give rise to a number of causes of action and it merely causes confusion if they are subject to different limitation periods. This can already happen under the current law, but we do not wish to make its occurrence more frequent.

1.12 Disability raises another general question. As the law now stands (and as it has stood since before 1939), a person who, because of minority or mental illness, is unable to prosecute a claim, is afforded special protection in that time does not normally start to run against him until his disability ceases. This rule can obviously impose considerable hardship on a potential defendant who may be exposed to an action arising out of events occurring in the distant past, if at the time the claimant happens to have been a very young child or a mental patient. Nevertheless, although there are certain features of the law relating to disability which have attracted some criticisms (to some of which we have referred in our *Interim Report on Personal Injury Claims*[8]), we have not received any evidence to suggest that it is wrong in principle to give effect to disability in the way the law now does. We deal with various facets of disability in more detail in Part II, paragraphs 2.39 to 2.48 below; at this stage we need say no more than that, having considered the principle, we see no need to make any fundamental change.

1.13 Another question which affects limitation in every field of the law is: what should stop time running? While all those who have commented on this subject agree that, as a practical matter, it must be some definite and readily identifiable step taken by the plaintiff, there is an issue of principle involved, namely whether it is sufficient that it should be some formal act (such as the issue of a writ) which may not come to the defendant's knowledge for an appreciable time. We have given considerable thought to this question, which

---

[7] *Report of the Committee on Defamation;* (1975) Cmnd. 5909, para. 543.
[8] Cmnd. 5630, Part VI.

is not altogether easy to resolve, and we discuss it in more detail in Part II, paragraphs 2.72 to 2.83, below.

1.14 A third fundamental question is the effect of the running of the limitation period: should it extinguish the plaintiff's right or merely bar his remedy? Although the distinction may not often be of practical importance, it can have substantial repercussions in the field of private international law. We discuss these matters in Part II, paragraphs 2.84 to 2.96, below.

Part II

RULES OF GENERAL APPLICATION

A. THE START OF THE LIMITATION PERIOD (THE *'terminus a quo'*)

General considerations

2.1 The ideal *terminus a quo* would be an event which satisfied three conditions:—

   (*a*) it would be sufficiently near in time to the incidents giving rise to the claim to ensure that proceedings were instituted before the relevant evidence became either unobtainable or too stale to be reliable;

   (*b*) it would be unmistakable and readily ascertainable;

   (*c*) its occurrence would necessarily become known forthwith to the plaintiff.

2.2 It is obvious that in practice no *terminus* can satisfy all these conditions in every case. The traditional *terminus* in English law is the accrual of the plaintiff's cause of action; in some—indeed in many—cases accrual will satisfy all three conditions mentioned above, the normal 'running-down' action affording an everyday example. But, as was shown by the circumstances which led to the setting up of the Edmund Davies Committee[9] and the enactment of the Limitation Act 1963, accrual as the *terminus a quo*, even if it does (as it normally will) satisfy conditions (*a*) and (*b*) above, will often fail to satisfy condition (*c*).

2.3 An alternative approach, which we discuss in some detail below, is to make time run from the date on which the plaintiff discovered or could have discovered the relevant facts—the 'date of knowledge' principle now adopted for personal injury claims[10]. This *terminus* satisfies condition (*c*), but will obviously fail to satisfy condition (*a*) in some, and condition (*b*) in many, cases.

2.4 In our opinion—and the tenor of the evidence we have received supports this view—there are strong arguments in favour of retaining accrual of the cause of action as the *terminus a quo*. It provides a degree of certainty and in most, though not all, cases the plaintiff knows that his cause of action has accrued immediately on, or shortly after, the occurrence of some overt and unmistakable event. On the other hand, the date of knowledge principle involves much uncertainty, as has been shown in the context of personal injury claims by the difficulties to which, in practice, the 1963 Act gave rise and which we discussed in detail in our *Interim Report*. Moreover, it is clear that the date of knowledge could never form an appropriate *terminus a quo* for claims involving title to property, or, possibly, for some other cases where certainty is of paramount importance. If, therefore, the solution to the problem posed by latent damage were to lie in the adoption of the date of knowledge principle, the causes of action to which that principle is appropriate would have to be identified and distinguished from those to which it is not. Although it might not prove to

---

[9] See Cmnd. 5630

[10] As a result of a recent decision in the House of Lords, it seems possible that a 'date of knowledge' principle has been incorporated into the substantive tort of negligence in some cases at least: we deal with the effect of this on the law of limitation later in this Part.

be as difficult as at first sight appears to draw such a distinction, on general principles we are not in favour of introducing further complications into the law of limitation.

The problem of latent damage

2.5 Were it not for the problem of latent damage, we would have no hesitation in recommending that English law should (apart from personal injury claims) retain the rule that time runs against the plaintiff from the accrual of the cause of action, subject to special provisions affecting persons under a disability and the victims of fraud and mistake.

2.6 The problem of latent damage is, however, serious and has caused us much difficulty. Indeed, this report was nearly ready to submit to your Lordship when the problem of latent damage was highlighted by the decision of the Court of Appeal in *Sparham-Souter v. Town and Country Developments (Essex) Ltd.*[11] and the subsequent appeal to the House of Lords in *Anns v. London Borough of Merton*[12]. In view of the importance of the issues raised in these cases, we decided to await the outcome of the appeal to the House of Lords before completing our report. We were, in the event, able to consider representations which we received about these cases at a very late stage in our deliberations.

2.7 Apart from personal injury, with which we are not now concerned, it is probably not very often that a plaintiff is unable to discover within the normal limitation period that he has suffered damage. Nevertheless, this can happen and if it does it can cause considerable financial hardship. Such hardship is particularly likely to arise out of building or civil engineering contracts, where a breach of contract may give rise to physical damage which remains latent for very many years and then causes heavy financial loss. Apart from building and engineering contracts, hardship can also be caused in the context of professional negligence where defective advice may cause the adviser's client to take steps which prove to be financially unsound, but only after the lapse of a period much longer than the limitation period; an obvious example is the purchase of a house from a vendor with a defective title, where the defect comes to light only when the purchaser tries to re-sell. We have not been able to obtain any reliable information about the number of cases in which difficulties of this nature occur. But the evidence we have received, and the experience of some of our own members, leaves us in no doubt about the reality of the problem even if, in truth, the hard cases are not numerous.

The current law

2.8 The problem of latent damage is not new and, before considering how it can best be resolved, it is necessary to examine the current law relating to an extension of time, in any class of case, under the so-called doctrine of 'concealed fraud' as well as the recent cases concerning the problem of latent defects arising in relation to the tort of negligence.

---

[11] [1976] 1 Q.B. 858.
[12] [1977] 2 W.L.R. 1024 (12th May 1977).

(i) *Concealed fraud*

2.9 The law relating to 'concealed fraud' is contained in section 26 of the Limitation Act 1939, the legal purport of which has been considered in a number of decided cases. The section is in the following terms:—

'Where, in the case of any action for which a period of limitation is prescribed by this Act, either—

(*a*) the action is based upon the fraud of the defendant or his agent or of any person through whom he claims or his agent, or

(*b*) the right of action is concealed by the fraud of any such person as aforesaid, or

(*c*) the action is for relief from the consequences of a mistake the period of limitation shall not begin to run until the plaintiff has discovered the fraud or the mistake, as the case may be, or could with reasonable diligence have discovered it:

Provided that nothing in this section shall enable any action to be brought to recover, or enforce any charge against, or set aside any transaction affecting, any property which—

(i) in the case of fraud, has been purchased for valuable consideration by a person who was not a party to the fraud and did not at the time of the purchase know or have reason to believe that any fraud had been committed, or

(ii) in the case of mistake, has been purchased for valuable consideration, subsequently to the transaction in which the mistake was made, by a person who did not know or have reason to believe that the mistake had been made.'

2.10 The occasion for the enactment of this section was the recommendation of the Law Revision Committee who had reported[13] that the law was in a state of obscurity and uncertainty by reason of conflicting decisions in relation to the equitable doctrine of concealed fraud (which had been developed from 1714 onwards and had received limited statutory recognition in section 26 of the Real Property Limitation Act 1833); the effect of the section was to codify the existing law and to remove doubt as to its application to all causes of action. It is unnecessary for present purposes to refer in any detail to the equitable doctrine as it existed prior to 1939, save to point out that—

(*a*) its basis was that the defendant must have acted in an 'unconscionable' manner, either by concealing the plaintiff's cause of action from him or by failing to make the plaintiff aware of the facts from which a cause of action would arise, and

(*b*) there could be no 'fraud' unless the defendant had been aware of the facts alleged to have been concealed.

2.11 Following the enactment of section 26 of the 1939 Act, the doctrine of concealed fraud was developed in further decided cases, the effect of which

---

[13] Cmd. 5334, para. 22.

is summarised in the following passage from the judgment of Lord Denning, M.R., in *King* v. *Victor Parsons & Co.*[14]—

'The word "fraud" here is not used in the common law sense. It is used in the equitable sense to denote conduct by the defendant or his agent such that it would be "against conscience" for him to avail himself of the lapse of time. The cases show that, if a man *knowingly* commits a wrong (such as digging underground another man's coal); or a breach of contract (such as putting in a bad foundation to a house), in such circumstances that it is unlikely to be found out for many a long day, he cannot rely on the Statute of Limitations as a bar to the claim: see *Bulli Coal Mining Company* v. *Osborne*[15] and *Applegate* v. *Moss*[16]. In order to show that he "concealed" the right of action "by fraud", it is not necessary to show that he took active steps to conceal his wrongdoing or breach of contract. It is sufficient that he *knowingly* committed it and did not tell the owner about it. He did the wrong or committed the breach secretly. By saying nothing he keeps it secret. He conceals the right of action. He conceals it by "fraud" as those words have been interpreted in the cases. To this word *"knowingly"* there must be added "recklessly": see *Beaman* v. *ARTS Ltd.*[17]. Like the man who turns a blind eye, he is aware that what he is doing may well be a wrong, or a breach of contract, but he takes the risk of it being so. He refrains from further enquiry lest it would prove to be correct; and says nothing about it. The Court will not allow him to get away with conduct of that kind. It may be that he has no dishonest motive; but that does not mater. He has kept the plaintiff out of the knowledge of his right of action: and that is enough: see *Kitchen* v. *Royal Air Force Association*[18]. If the defendant was, however, unaware that he was committing a wrong or a breach of contract, it would be different. So if by an honest blunder he unwittingly commits a wrong (by digging another man's coal), or a breach of contract (by putting in an insufficient foundation) then he could avail himself of the Statute of Limitations.'

(ii)   *Latent defects in negligence*

2.12 In *Sparham-Souter* v. *Town and Country Developments (Essex) Ltd.*, the Court of Appeal held on a preliminary issue (which one Lord Justice thought should never have been tried) that a cause of action in negligence in the assumed circumstances of that case (which concerned alleged negligence on the part of a local authority relating to inspection of foundations of dwelling houses) was not complete until physical damage to the structure became reasonably detectable. The decision was reached as a result of consideration of the substantive law relating to the tort of negligence, but has implications for the law of limitation. The effect of the decision, for those purposes, was to create a new *terminus a quo* in, at any rate, some cases of negligence, by the extension to such cases of a date of knowledge principle comparable to that which is applied to cases

---

[14] [1973] 1 W.L.R. 29 at p. 33.
[15] [1889] A.C. 351.
[16] [1971] 1 Q.B. 406.
[17] [1949] 1 K.B. 550, 565–566.
[18] [1958] 1 W.L.R. 563.

of personal injury, fraud (including concealed fraud) and mistake, by virtue of sections 2A and 26 of the Limitation Act 1939.

2.13 It is not altogether clear from the judgments in *Sparham-Souter* whether the Court of Appeal was enunciating a new principle applicable to all cases of negligence other than personal injury claims, to the effect that the cause of action in negligence is not complete until the damage caused by the negligent act or omission becomes reasonably ascertainable; or, alternatively, whether the Court was declaring that on facts analogous to those in the *Sparham-Souter* case no damage resulting from the negligent act or omission is suffered until some outward and visible sign reveals the fact that the property affected is not in truth in as sound a condition as it had appeared to be.

2.14 The difference between these two differing constructions of the judgments in *Sparham-Souter* is, of course, of great importance for our review of the law of limitation. The wider construction would have the effect of making section 26 of the Limitation Act 1939 largely irrelevant to negligence cases, and the law as laid down by the Court of Appeal, without much consideration of section 26, would be substantially more favourable to a plaintiff than that section, because he would not have to show that the defendant had concealed the cause of action. On the other hand, the effect would be more limited if the Court of Appeal were saying that, in practice, where the negligent act causes physical damage to property and the loss to the plaintiff is only the fall in the market value of that piece of property caused by the physical damage, then, as a question of fact, the plaintiff suffers no damage until the defect is readily discoverable and produces an effect on the market value.

2.15 The local authority in *Sparham-Souter* did not appeal to the House of Lords, but the local authority in a substantially similar case (which was determined by the Court of Appeal on the basis of *Sparham-Souter*[19]) did so. The judgment of the House of Lords in this case, (sub nom. *Anns* v. *London Borough of Merton*), was given on 12th May 1977 with speeches from Lord Wilberforce (with whom three other Lords of Appeal[20] agreed) and Lord Salmon. The House unanimously dismissed an appeal by the London Borough of Merton against the decision of the Court of Appeal which reversed a decision of an Official Referee on a preliminary issue relating to limitation. The allegations in question concerned negligence in failure to examine, or careless examination of, defective foundations for a block of flats which was completed in 1962. The various plaintiffs had acquired their leases in 1962, 1967 and 1968. In 1970, structural movement began to occur and cracks etc. appeared. The local authority pleaded the Limitation Act as their defence to the actions begun in 1972.

2.16 Both speeches concentrated to a large extent on the question whether the local authority owed a duty of care and the discussion of the limitation point was comparatively brief. Lord Wilberforce devoted two short paragraphs at the end of his speech to this question, while Lord Salmon dealt with it in some greater detail.

2.17 Lord Wilberforce considered that a cause of action arose in the case in question when the state of the building was such that there was a present

---

[19] *Anns* v. *Walcroft Property Co. Ltd* [1976] 1 Q.B. 882.
[20] Lord Diplock, Lord Simon of Glaisdale and Lord Russell of Killowen.

or imminent danger to the health or safety of persons occupying it; in the following paragraph he implied that the cause of action arose when the defects first appeared. He had earlier described the *Sparham-Souter* case as a decision 'that the cause of action did not accrue before a person capable of suing discovered, or ought to have discovered, the damage' but his speech does not necessarily imply outright approval of *Sparham-Souter*.

2.18 Lord Salmon referred to two earlier *obiter dicta*[21] which suggested that, in a case concerning defects in a structure, the damage was done when the foundations (or drains) were improperly constructed, and he firmly disapproved of that view. He suggested that there might be a difference between foundations and drains, if a defect in drains caused immediate damage running from occupation. Although, therefore, Lord Salmon has departed from the act of negligence in question as the *terminus a quo*, the date when the damage occurs is not, in his view, necessarily the date when it was discoverable. His discussion of *Cartledge* v. *E. Jopling and Sons Ltd.*[22] shows that he regards the present law, outside the personal injury field, as not containing a test of reasonable discoverability.

2.19 We have found some difficulty in ascertaining precisely what the *ratio decidendi* of *Anns* is, and, indeed, we are not all agreed on the way in which the decision may be applied in future cases. In particular we are not certain whether the *Sparham-Souter* decision has been approved or disapproved and, if approved, whether on the wider or narrower basis mentioned at paragraph 2.13 above. We consider that the House of Lords were not attempting to lay down any broad statements of principle about the tort of negligence, but were principally concerned with the particular (assumed) facts of the case in question. The test of present or imminent danger to the health or safety of occupiers is plainly applicable only to defects in immoveable property, and probably to a proportion of such defects only: it is not suitable for general application.

2.20 It is not, of course, for us to say how the courts will interpret the decision in *Anns* in any given case, but we consider that it is likely to be viewed as a decision concerning questions of fact and, in particular, as to the date when damage occurred on the facts of that case. If so, then it will probably not be seen as deciding that discoverability of a hidden defect is necessarily a precondition to the occurrence of damage in the tort of negligence as a whole. In some cases, that is where damage is suffered only when loss in value is ascertainable, it may be that damage is not suffered until the fact that a defect exists can be found out. In due course, this line of authority may have to be considered against the decision of the House of Lords in *Darley Main Colliery* v. *Mitchell*[23]. We expect, also, that the courts are likely to confine the decision in *Anns* within fairly narrow limits and not to apply it outside the particular

---

[21] Of Diplock, L.J. in *Bagot* v. *Stevens Scanlan & Co. Ltd.* [1966] 1 Q.B. 197, 203, and Lord Denning, M.R. in *Dutton* v. *Bognor Regis Urban District Council* [1972] 1 Q.B. 373, 396.
[22] [1963] A.C. 758.
[23] [1886] 11 App. Cas. 127.

sphere of activity concerned[24]. In particular we are of the view that the courts are unlikely to find that *Anns* has disturbed the established view that a cause of action in contract accrues when the breach occurs: the decision may make the distinction between actions in negligence and actions in contract more noticeable in certain circumstances and in certain classes of case, but we do not think that it should be taken as having undermined the law of contract, which we believe to be right (although we should observe that changes in the substantive law of contract are not within our terms of reference). The fact that a plaintiff who has no cause of action in contract may now sue in negligence more than six years after the occurrence of the act which gives rise to the damage may, however, lead to renewed attempts to establish that a plaintiff who *does* have a cause of action in contract may similarly sue in negligence after that cause of action is barred (unless the terms of the contract have excluded his right to do so)[25] If, therfore, it were to turn out that our view about *Anns* is wrong, the remedial steps which we recommend at paragraph 2.38 below might have to be considered further.

Possible approaches

2.21 Against this background we have had to consider what ought to be the policy of the law for dealing with cases of latent damage. Any temptation to ignore cases of latent damage would involve the reversal of a policy which has had the support of the judiciary for over two and a half centuries and would fly in the face of the recent difficulties in the tort of negligence concerning hidden defects in property. On the assumption, therefore, that the law must make some special provision for cases of latent damage, we have reached the conclusion that there were three possible approaches which could be adopted, namely—

(i) adherence to the 'concealed fraud' principle, involving the retention of section 26, reformulated so as to express its true legal purport as decided by the courts;

(ii) acceptance of some form of 'date of knowledge' principle;

(iii) conferring on the court a discretion to override a defence of limitation in a hard case.

This last approach could be combined with either of the two earlier approaches or could be adopted independently of either.

(i)   *The 'concealed fraud' approach*

2.22 The essential feature of the concealed fraud approach (as distinct from the date of knowledge approach) is that it operates on some degree of blameworthiness on the part of the defendant beyond his mere failure to comply with his legal obligations; the traditional expression is 'unconscionable conduct'. If this is thought to be the best approach, it will not, in our view, be difficult

---

[24] It will, for instance, be plain that the decision is inapplicable in cases covered by s. 1 of the Defective Premises Act 1972 (at any rate where an alternative claim is not available in negligence) since s. 1(5) of that Act provides that the cause of action for breach of duty generally arises when the dwelling is completed.

[25] The law at present appears to be that he cannot do so: *Bagot* v. *Stevens Scanlan & Co. Ltd* [1966] 1 Q.B. 197; *Clark* v. *Kirby-Smith* [1964] Ch. 506.

to reformulate section 26 in a way which, while incorporating the feature of unconscionability, reproduces in a more readily intelligible form the construction placed on that section by the courts.

2.23 It is evident from the judgment of Lord Denning, M.R. quoted above, that both the title and the wording of section 26 are misleading in that it:—

(i) is not limited to fraud in the common law sense;

(ii) embraces recklessness; and

(iii) is not limited to cases of active concealment.

2.24 In the suggested reformulation which follows we have attempted to cure these defects and, accordingly, we suggest that section 26 might be redrafted thus (the precise wording would, of course, be a matter for Parliamentary Counsel to settle):—

'26.(1) Subject to subsection (2) below, where, in the case of any action for which a period of limitation is prescribed by this Act—

(a) the action is based on the fraud of the defendant or his agent or any person through whom he claims or his agent; or

(b) the action is for relief from the consequences of a mistake; or

(c) the action is based on a deliberate or reckless breach of duty (whether or not arising under a contract); or

(d) the right of action is concealed by the dishonest conduct of any such person as is mentioned in paragraph (a);

the period of limitation shall not begin to run until the plaintiff has discovered the fraud or mistake or breach of duty or the right of action, as the case may be, or could with reasonable diligence have discovered it.

(2) Nothing in subsection (1) above shall enable any action to be brought to recover or enforce any charge against or set aside any transaction affecting any property, or recover damages in respect of any property[26], which has been subsequently purchased for valuable consideration by a person who—

(i) in the case of paragraph (a), was not a party to the fraud and did not at the time of the purchase know or have reason to believe that any fraud had been committed, or

(ii) in the case of paragraph (b), (c) or (d), did not at the time of the purchase know or have reason to believe that the mistake or breach of duty or dishonest conduct had occurred.'

2.25 Our re-draft does not, deliberately, include any reference to the likelihood (viewed at the time of its occurrence) of the defendant's wrongful act remaining undiscoverable for a substantial period, or at all. We considered in some detail the desirability of including such a reference. If it were to be included, it would then be necessary for the legislation to specify whether the test of foreseeability was to be entirely objective or whether the foresight of the particular defendant, or the capacity of the particular plaintiff to discover the breach of duty, should

---

[26] See para. 3.18 below for the reason for including these words.

be relevant. It might also be necessary to consider whether anything should turn on the length of period for which the breach was likely to remain undiscovered. We came to the conclusion that it would be possible (though at the cost of greatly complicating the subsection) to draft a paragraph dealing with all these matters; but in the end we concluded that to attempt to make the operation of the provision depend on the probable undiscoverability of the defendant's breach of duty would be somewhat unrealistic. The provision would anyhow be relevant only if the breach had in fact remained undiscoverable and (although it is not difficult to construct hypothetical cases) the court would in practice not find it easy to hold that a cause of action which it was satisfied had in fact remained undiscoverable for (for example) six years was not, at the time of its accrual, likely so to remain. In our view, there is much merit in legislative simplicity and we have therefore reached the conclusion that the section ought not to cater for these complexities.

(ii)   *The 'date of knowledge' approach*

2.26 The date of knowledge approach is essentially different from the concealed fraud approach, because it ignores the 'unconscionability' of the defendant's conduct and operates solely on the position of the plaintiff. In their evidence to us, the Law Society have advocated this approach and Scots law has, since the Prescription and Limitation (Scotland) Act 1973 came into force in July 1976, adopted it. Both the Law Society's recommendation and the Scottish Act restrict the date of knowledge approach so as to exclude claims involving title to property.

2.27 The Scottish Act deals with issues very relevant to the problem with which we are immediately concerned. It is a comprehensive restatement of Scots law incorporating amendments suggested by the Scottish Law Commission[27]. The provisions immediately relevant for our purposes are sections 6, 7 and 11. In very general terms (and subject to a number of exceptions and qualifications which we need not here specify) the effect of section 6 is to provide for a five year negative prescription covering most claims in contract or delict (tort), apart from personal injury claims. There are excluded from the computation of the five years any period during which either—

(a) the 'creditor' was induced by the 'debtor's' fraud or by error due to the debtor's conduct, not to prosecute his claim; or

(b) the creditor was under a disability.

Section 6 is, by virtue of section 7, subject to an overall 'longstop' of 20 years.

2.28 Section 11(3) caters specifically for cases of latent damage, again outside the field of personal injury. It implements a recommendation of the Scottish Law Commission[28] by providing that, in the case of an obligation (whether contractual, delictual or statutory) to make 'reparation' for loss, injury or damage where the creditor 'was not aware and could not with reasonable diligence have been aware' that the loss, injury or damage had occurred, the five-year period is to start running, not on the date the cause of action accrued, but on the

---

[27] Scot. Law Com. No. 15.
[28] *ibid.*, para. 97.

date when the creditor first became, or could with reasonable diligence have become, so aware.

2.29 Translated into English terms, this means that the prescriptive period starts to run against a plaintiff who has a claim for damages for breach of contract, or for tort, or for breach of statutory duty, only when he first knew, or could reasonably have discovered, that he had sustained the loss or damage in question. The Commission's report makes it clear that they did not propose to make anything turn on the plaintiff's knowledge either of the attributability of his loss or damage to the defendant's wrongful act, or of his right in law to be compensated; the Commission's intention was simply that time should start to run when the plaintiff first knew, or could reasonably have discovered, that he had in fact suffered the loss or damage in question. Whether this is the effect of the statutory language is, we are advised by those familiar with Scots law, a question about which doubt is felt. However, for the purpose of our consideration of the Scottish solution to our problem, we have assumed that the Act will be held to have implemented the Commission's recommendation.

(iii)   The 'discretionary' approach

2.30 The third possible approach (which, as we have said, could be adopted either independently of, or in conjunction with, concealed fraud or the date of knowledge) is to give the court a discretion to override an otherwise effective defence of limitation. There are precedents for this, of which the most important is now to be found in section 2D of the Limitation Act 1963[29] embodying our own recommendation for conferring such a discretion on the court in cases of personal injury. Another precedent is to be found in section 8 of the Maritime Conventions Act 1911, which imposes a normal two year limitation period for claims arising out of collisions at sea with a wide discretion for the court to extend the time.

Arguments for and against each approach

2.31 Each of these approaches has advantages and to each there are objections. The advantage of adhering to concealed fraud is that it affords to a defendant who is not in any 'moral' sense blameworthy the protection of a limitation period which, so long as the current six year period is retained, errs if at all on the side of generosity to the plaintiff. It thus avoids causing hardship to a defendant who, while admittedly in breach of his legal obligation, has not in any way contributed to the plaintiff's failure to appreciate in time the occurrence of the damage. Against this, there is the objection to the concealed fraud approach that, considered from the plaintiff's point of view, the loss is just as severe whether the defendant's conduct was deliberate or merely inadvertent (or, indeed, free from all blame) and it may be difficult for the plaintiff to prove on which side of the line that conduct fell. Thus, while affording a considerable measure of protection to defendants, the concealed fraud approach will not prevent a plaintiff who is in no way to blame from suffering severe hardship.

2.32 The obvious advantage of the date of knowledge approach is that, in most cases, it will prevent the diligent plaintiff from suffering hardship. The objections to it are that, first, it can cause hardship to a defendant who has

---

[29] Inserted in that Act by the Limitation Act 1975.

no reason to suppose that he may have incurred a liability and who has therefore destroyed his records after the expiry of the normal limitation period; secondly, it is bound to lead to a degree of uncertainty, not least because it is difficult to define by statute the precise matters knowledge of which is to be necessary before time can start running; thirdly, because the date of knowledge cannot be a universal *terminus a quo*, it involves drawing a distinction between those causes of action for which accrual is to remain the *terminus a quo* and those for which it is not.

2.33 The obvious advantage of conferring a wide discretion on the court is that it enables hard cases to be dealt with on their particular facts and without putting the court into the difficult position of having either to 'bend' the statutory provision or to fail to do justice. On the other hand, it involves a greater measure of uncertainty than does the date of knowledge principle, even if 'guidelines' are specified in the statute (and in this connection we think that it would be more difficult to formulate guidelines appropriate to the exercise of discretion 'across the board' than in personal injury claims alone).

The Committee's conclusion

2.34 These three possible approaches were considered by the Law Revision Committee in 1936[30]. Their conclusion was that the objections to the date of knowledge principle and to discretion outweighed the advantages of either. Since the implementation of their report by the Limitation Act 1939, we have had more experience of the operation of the date of knowledge principle in the limited field of personal injury claims; we have not yet had any substantial experience of the operation of a discretionary power in this limited field, but we were ourselves persuaded that some such power was necessary and our recommendation to that effect has been accepted by Parliament. Against this background, we have re-considered the whole question of latent damage and its relation to the *terminus a quo*. On this crucial issue we have not been able to reach a unanimous decision.

(i)   *The majority view*

2.35 The view of the majority is that, though admittedly far from perfect, the best solution is to reformulate section 26 of the Limitation Act 1939 in the way suggested above and to accept the corollary that there will be some hard cases where a plaintiff, through no fault of his own, is unable to ascertain before the expiry of the limitation period that he has suffered damage. The majority take the view that certainty is the prime consideration; that hard cases are likely to be few; and that justice to the defendant whose conduct has not in any way been 'unconscionable' demands that he be protected once the limitation period has run. A further factor to which the majority attach importance is the difficulty (and expense) of insuring against claims to which such professional persons as architects, engineers, surveyors, accountants and solicitors are particularly likely to become vulnerable if either the date of knowledge becomes the general *terminus a quo* or the court is given a wide discretion. The cost of insuring against professional negligence claims is already high and the evidence of the underwriters' representatives was to the effect that any substantial increase

---

[30] Cmd. 5334, paras. 6 and 7.

in the number of potential claims could make it very difficult to obtain cover. This, in turn, would reflect back on the prospects of recovery by all plaintiffs and the majority consider that it would not be sensible to put all plaintiffs in a potentially worse position for the sake of avoiding hardship to relatively few of their number. In the absence of any clear evidence that the current law causes serious hardship in a significant number of cases, the majority therefore take the view that the best course will be to preserve that law, reformulated in more readily intelligible language.

(ii) *The minority view*

2.36 The minority share the general view of the Committee that accrual of the cause of action should be retained as the standard *terminus a quo*, while also agreeing that the running of time should automatically be retarded in cases falling within section 26 of the Limitation Act, as reformulated. The combined effect of these rules is, however, to deny any remedy to a party who could not reasonably have learned of his cause of action within the standard limitation period and who after that lapse of time is unable to prove that the conduct of which he complains was fraudulent, or deliberate, or reckless. Absolute denial of remedy in such circumstances is in the view of the minority apt to lead to injustice. Theoretically, it is unsatisfactory that a plaintiff's right to relief should depend on the quality of the defendant's conduct alone, when this is outside both the knowledge and the control of the plaintiff. Practically, the plaintiff will encounter severe difficulty in establishing the nature of the defendant's breach years after the event, and hard cases are bound to arise and tempt courts towards a strained interpretation of any absolute statutory rule. The minority accordingly favour granting to the court a residual discretion to override a defence of limitation in the limited class of case in which problems of latent damage in practice arise (namely, professional advice and building and engineering contracts)[31], this discretion being exercisable in a plaintiff's favour if, but only if, after considering the nature of the claim and the circumstances of the parties, the court thinks it just to allow the action to proceed. The number of cases to which this provision would apply woud be relatively small when compared with the total body of claims, and the minority do not agree with the view of the majority as to its likely effect on the cost or availability of insurance. In the view of the minority, problems are encountered sufficiently often in practice to justify special treatment of a situation in which hardship on a significant scale would otherwise occur. They believe their solution to be consistent with that recommended by the Committee in respect of personal injuries, which has been adopted by Parliament and accordingly favour treating this smaller, but analogous, problem in a similar way[32].

(iii) *Anns v. London Borough of Merton*

2.37 On any view, it is necessary to consider the decision in the *Anns* case. It may be that by the time when any decision to implement our report is taken, the effect of *Anns* will have become clearer and, if so, the recommendations

---

[31] It is of interest that similar classes of action, together with personal injuries, were singled out by the Alberta and Ontario Law Reform Commissioners, reporting in 1968 and 1969, as requiring special treatment.

[32] This paragraph expresses the view of Mr. Bingham, Mr. Hinks, and Mr. Martin.

which follow may have to be adjusted. We have felt able to put forward both the majority view in paragraph 2.35 and the minority view in paragraph 2.36 despite the fact that, on one interpretation at least, the decision in *Sparham-Souter* (if it survives) would render much of the analysis that leads to these recommendations inapplicable in cases of negligence. We have put forward our recommendations on the footing (which we hope will be found to be the case in any further litigation of this kind) that *Anns* has not substantially changed the law, or, if it has changed the law, has done so only to the extent that it shows that damage of a certain kind in a certain type of case (that is, pecuniary loss caused by a defect inherent in a building or chattel) does not 'occur' until the loss in market value (which itself is dependent upon discoverability of the defect) is sustained or foreseeable.

2.38 We do, however, readily recognise that our view of the *Anns* case may not be the right one and we are agreed that the step which would be necessary to ensure that the law of limitation continued to work satisfactorily to all parties if we were wrong would be as follows. In general, it would then be necessary to ensure that the test as apparently laid down in *Sparham-Souter* were abrogated, since it could have unfortunate effects for the law of limitation, particularly on the 'reasonable discoverability' point. First, it would be necessary to make it plain that the decision in *Anns* has no effect in cases where liability lies in contract only: here, as we have stated at paragraph 2.20 above, time runs from the breach, and this is a principle which we would not wish to disturb. Secondly, we consider that the legislature should endorse the view expressed by Lord Salmon in *Anns*, namely that in cases where the *dictum* of Diplock L.J. in the *Bagot* case is not, for one reason or another, applicable, it is the law that the occurrence of damage is a question of fact to be determined by the evidence, without any interposition of a rule of law to the effect that damage does not occur until it is reasonably discoverable[33].

Disabilities

2.39 In paragraph 1.12 above we alluded briefly to the general principle whereby time does not run against a plaintiff who is under a disability at the time of the accrual of his cause of action. Although, as we have stated above, the comments we have received do not suggest that there is any demand for making a fundamental change in this well-established principle, certain aspects of that principle have been criticised by those who have submitted evidence to us.

2.40 The major criticism of the current law has been directed against the 'custody of a parent' rule, under which time ran against a minor who was in

---

[33] The Royal Institute of British Architects, one of the bodies which submitted evidence to us about the decision in *Anns*, suggested, in the course of a memorandum proposing a number of changes in substantive law (which are outside our terms of reference, but which no doubt would deserve consideration in any review of the law relating to defective premises), that the normal limitation period for actions in connection with defects in a building, howsoever arising, should be six years from completion of the building or ten years from the occurrence of the alleged breach of duty whichever first occurred. The Institute take the view that a limitation period running from the accrual of a cause of action is unsatisfactory for the purpose of determining fixed periods of reasonable duration for civil liability; but, for the reasons already given in this report, we have been unable to accept this suggestion.

the custody of a parent at the time his cause of action accrued. The rule applied only to personal injury claims and, following the recommendation contained in our interim report[34], it has been abolished by the Limitation Act 1975. There is, therefore, no need for us to consider this particular criticism further.

2.41 The second point that has been made is that the scope of 'disability' is not wide enough. Since the enactment of the Limitation Act 1939, the only forms of disability are minority and mental illness. The criticism that has been made is that there are other forms of illness which effectively prevent a potential plaintiff from exercising his legal rights and that a person suffering from one or other of these forms of illness ought to be treated as being under a disability. We appreciate the force of this argument; however, it would in our view be difficult to draw an effective and precise line between those forms of physical illness which could properly be treated as creating disabilities and those which could not. Moreover, such hardship as may be caused to potential plaintiffs is seldom likely to arise in practice outside the field of personal injury claims where an accident may produce in the plaintiff a state of incapacity, not amounting to mental illness, which makes it difficult for him to take legal advice and exercise his rights. The implementation by the Limitation Act 1975 of our recommendation that in personal injury claims the court should have a discretion to extend the time in order to meet hard cases will, in our view, meet this particular criticism. In other fields of litigation, particularly those relating to title to property, we think it could cause considerable hardship to the defendant if the plaintiff's physical illness were a ground for the suspension of the running of time against him and the conclusion of most of us (we were not unanimous on the point) is that any extension of the scope of disability to include physical illness would, on balance, be a mistake.

2.42 There is, however, evidently a case for defining more precisely mental illness giving rise to disability. The point was considered by the Law Revision Committee in 1936 who criticised the interpretation given to the old Latin phrase (used in the Limitation Act 1623) 'non compos mentis'; but that Committee made no recommendation about the interpretation given to this phrase on the ground that the question was 'so intimately associated with the Lunacy Laws that it ought only to be dealt with if such laws are under revision'[35].

2.43 Since the Law Revision Committee's report, the 'Lunacy Laws' have been revised and are now contained in the Mental Health Act 1959, Part VIII of which deals with the management of the property and affairs of mental patients. Section 101 of that Act defines a mental patient for the purposes of Part VIII as being a person in respect of whom the Court of Protection is satisfied that he is incapable by reason of mental disorder of managing and administering his property and affairs. 'Mental disorder' is defined in section 4(1) of the Act as meaning 'mental illness', arrested or incomplete development of mind, psychopathic disorder, and any other disorder or disability of mind. If there is to be a statutory definition of 'disability', we think it must be consistent with these provisions.

2.44 On the authorities, incapacity to manage one's own affairs is the essential feature of 'unsoundness of mind' where that phrase is used in the context of

---

[34] Cmd. 5630, para. 136.
[35] Cmd. 5334, para. 17(b)

disability. The language of section 101 is already reflected in the Rules of the Supreme Court governing persons under a disability[36] and was in effect adopted by the Court of Appeal in *Kirby* v. *Leather*[37]. It follows that a statutory definition based on section 101 would not make any substantive change in the law. Indeed, we were at first inclined simply to adopt the definition of 'patient' in that provision; this would not, however, be entirely satisfactory, because the definition of 'patient' operates on the Court of Protection's being satisfied about the mental condition of the person concerned at the time the matter comes before the Court, whereas a court considering limitation has to determine what *was* the plaintiff's mental condition at some time in the past. Nevertheless, we see no difficulty in defining disability in terms of a person who, 'by reason of mental disorder as defined in section 4(1) of the Mental Health Act 1959, is incapable of managing and administering his property and affairs'. Admittedly, the terms used in section 4(1) are necessarily themselves somewhat imprecise, but we do not think it would be practicable to improve upon them and it is clear from the decision in *Kirby* v. *Leather* and from the Rules of the Supreme Court that in practice the courts already determine questions of unsoundness of mind by reference to these terms.

2.45 Our conclusion is, therefore, that any statutory definition of disability should follow the Mental Health Act and that there would be some marginal advantage in having such a definition, since it would make it clear beyond argument that unsoundness of mind for the purposes of the law of limitation means exactly the same as it does in other contexts where disability is relevant. If such a definition were incorporated in any legislation following our report, we think it should retain those provisions in section 31(3) of the Limitation Act 1939 under which a patient who is (or in some circumstances has been) liable to be detained or subject to guardianship under the Mental Health Act is presumed to be of unsound mind. These provisions have an obvious practical advantage.

2.46 The third criticism that was made of the existing law related to 'supervening disability'. As the law stands, disability (necessarily in this context mental illness) occurring after the accrual of the plaintiff's cause of action does not suspend the running of time against him. This rule was considered by the Law Revision Committee in 1936[38], who thought that suspension of the running of time in the case of a claimant becoming subject to a disability during the statutory period would impose grave hardship on defendants. Accordingly they concluded that, although the rule could cause hardship to plaintiffs in some cases, it should be left unchanged.

2.47 We ourselves considered the matter further in the context of personal injuries and have dealt with it at some length in our interim report[39]. Our conclusion was that, insofar as any hardship might be caused by the current rule in the context of personal injury claims, this could best be mitigated by the adoption of our suggestion that the court should have a discretion to extend the time in order to avoid such hardship, a suggestion which, as we have stated above, has been adopted in the Limitation Act 1975.

---

[36] See R.S.C., O. 80, r. 1.
[37] [1965] 2 Q.B. 367 (see Lord Denning, M.R., at pp. 383G to 384A).
[38] Cmd. 5334, para. 16.
[39] Cmnd. 5630, paras. 91 to 96.

2.48 Our examination of the question showed that, even in the context of personal injury claims, the suspension of time in the case of supervening disability would raise serious problems and, although we did not at that stage form any view on the desirability of amending the rule 'across the board', it seemed obvious to us that those difficulties would be very much greater if effect were to be given to supervening disability in relation to other claims, particularly those affecting the title to property; further consideration of the subject has confirmed these views. Although, therefore, it must be accepted that, in the absence of any general discretion to extend the time in particular circumstances, supervening disability could cause hardship to claimants outside the field of personal injuries, in our view the balance of advantage lies with leaving the rule undisturbed and we so recommend.

B.   THE RUNNING OF THE LIMITATION PERIOD

The length of the period

2.49 The general limitation period is six years, running from the accrual of the plaintiff's cause of action. This six-year period applies to most causes of action, the major exceptions being claims for personal injuries (for which the relevant period is now three years running, in effect, from the plaintiff's 'date of knowledge') and claims for the recovery of land (for which the period is 12 years). There are also some less important exceptions, to some of which we advert in Part III of this report.

2.50 There is, inevitably, an arbitrary element in the selection of any limitation period and there is no magic about a six-year period which makes it inherently preferable to any other period. The question we have had to consider is whether—on the assumption that, as we recommend, time should normally start running from the accrual of the plaintiff's cause of action—some other, equally arbitrary, period should be substituted for the six years prescribed by the Limitation Act 1939.

2.51 There was virtually no support from those whom we consulted for a general limitation period longer than six years. Indeed, most of those who expressed views on the subject were of the opinion that for most transactions (particularly in the field of commerce) six years constitute an unnecessarily long period. It was accordingly suggested by some that a period of four or five years should be adopted, on the ground that in practice such a period gives ample time for a potential plaintiff to obtain legal advice and institute proceedings. Moreover, a five-year period for contract and tort has now, in effect, been accepted by Scots law and a shorter period has a measure of international support[40].

2.52 We agree that for most claims the six year period is usually unnecessarily long and we do not think that the substitution of a five-year period would cause any hardship. (Adoption of a substantially shorter period might, however, cause difficulty unless English law were to abandon, as the normal *terminus quo*, accrual of the plaintiff's cause of action). On the other hand, we have received no evidence to suggest that the six-year period causes any difficulty and we do not think that it would be right to change a rule which has become

---

[40] See, *e.g.*, the UNCITRAL convention on Limitation in the International Sale of Goods, 1974 (prescribing a four-year period).

familiar to the general public as well as to the legal profession unless it can be shown that there would be a substantial advantage in doing so.

2.53 The only advantage we can see in adopting a shorter period would be the achievement of a greater measure of uniformity with other legal systems, in particular with Scots law. In practice, this result could be achieved only if a five-year period were chosen and the choice before us lies between adhering to the six-year period and substituting a five-year period. On balance, we think that the objection to changing a familiar rule which causes no difficulty in practice outweighs the advantages to be derived from such additional measure of uniformity which a five-year period might afford. We do not, therefore, consider the change worth making and we recommend that the normal limitation period should continue to be six years.

Abridgment and extension of time and the effect of negotiations

2.54 In our consultative document we invited comments on the desirability of parties to a dispute being free, by mutual agreement, to abridge or extend the limitation period in a particular case. We also invited comment on an allied question, namely whether the running of time should be suspended during the course of negotiations aimed at effecting a compromise between the parties.

2.55 As the law stands, it is open to parties to a contract to stipulate by their contract that a claim for any breach must be brought within a specified period of its occurrence, a period which may be (and very often is) much shorter than the normal six years, and, by recourse to a deed under seal which creates a 'specialty', they can attract the longer 12-year period prescribed by section 2(3) of the Limitation Act 1939. After a dispute has arisen, irrespective of the nature of the cause of action, the parties are also free to extend the time by agreement, which may be express or implied from conduct. Negotiations, however, do not by themselves have any effect on the running of time. Unless there is a contract between the parties to extend the time, or not to rely on a defence of limitation or unless the conduct of the defendant has been such that he is estopped from raising that defence, the fact that negotiations aimed at a compromise were still in progress when the limitation period expired will not enable the plaintiff to defeat a defence based on the expiry of that period.

2.56 Most of those who commented on these matters considered it right, in principle, that parties to a contract should be free to abridge the time for making a claim under that contract. The point was, however, made that this question is involved with the general problem of 'exemption clauses', since, by stipulating for a short period within which a claim must be made, a party can greatly reduce his liability for breach of contract and in an extreme case could virtually exclude it. Parliament has, however, already stepped in to regulate by legislation this freedom in the field of 'consumer' contracts, a recent and striking example being afforded by the Supply of Goods (Implied Terms) Act 1973[41]. Moreover, we note that the two Law Commissions have made further recommendations for controlling exemption clauses in a much wider field, which are now the subject of a Bill before Parliament[42].

---

[41] The effect of this and comparable enactments is summarised in Part B of Annex 2.
[42] *Second Report on Exemption Clauses*, (1975) Law Com. No. 69; Scot. Law Com. No. 39, (1974–75) H.C. 605; Unfair Contract Terms Bill.

2.57 In our view 'consumer protection' and comparable matters do not fall within the true purpose of the law of limitation and the control of exemption clauses raises questions of social policy not covered by our terms of reference. If, in a particular field, it is socially undesirable for one party to a contract to be free to insist on any claim against him arising out of the contract being brought within an especially short period, his freedom to do so should be regulated, if at all, by legislation directed at that particular field; not by a rule of general application which restricts freedom of contract where no such restriction is necessary and where, indeed, it may be undesirable. Accordingly, on the basis that we may expect *ad hoc* legislation to control exemption clauses where control is needed, we see no need to restrict the freedom of parties to abridge the limitation period by contract.

2.58 The extension of time by contract may raise rather different considerations since there is an argument based on public policy for excluding from the courts trials of very stale claims and some of those who have submitted evidence to us favour an overall 'longstop' which would operate irrespective of the wishes of the parties. However, we see considerable difficulty about this. So long as the law retains the principle that a defendant intending to rely on a defence of limitation must raise that defence expressly, no such overall longstop is practicable. More importantly, we think it unlikely that any defendant would agree, without good reason, to an indefinite extension of time, since such an extension cannot do him anything but harm and, if he will not agree, time will not be extended. Moreover, we have received no evidence to suggest that freedom to extend time by contract is in practice abused. For all these reasons, we do not recommend restricting by legislation freedom to extend the time. We recognise that on this matter we are taking a view opposed to that taken by the Scottish Law Commission, who recommended[43] that there should be a statutory prohibition on contracting out, a recommendation now embodied in section 13 of the Prescription and Limitation (Scotland) Act 1973. However, the Scottish Law Commission's recommendation was made in the context of the 'traditional approach to prescription in Scots law', which is fundamentally different from the approach to limitation in English law. In view of this difference we see no good reason why English law should follow Scots law in this respect.

2.59 Although usually considered as a separate subject, 'specialties' are relevant to the extension of time by agreement, since (as we have stated above) the adoption of this particular form of obligation automatically attracts a 12-year limitation period. The nature and origin of specialties were authoritatively explained by Viscount Maugham when delivering the advice of the Judicial Committee of the Privy Council in *R* v. *Williams*. For practical purposes, a specialty may be treated as an obligation entered into by deed under seal, a form often used for, among other transactions, major building contracts. For some transactions, there is a good sense in making the form of the relevant instrument import a specially long limitation period; for example, since actions for the recovery of land are subject to a 12-year period and since many dispositions of an interest in land have to be made by deed under seal, it is not unreasonable that the deed itself should import a 12-year period. However, where the transaction is

---

[43] Scot. Law Com. No. 15, para. 141.
[44] [1942] A.C. 541, at pp. 554–556.
[45] This point was made by the Law Revision Committee: see Cmd. 5534, para. 5.

not by its nature subject to any special limitation period, it is not entirely logical to make the limitation period applicable depend on the form of the instrument by which it is effected. Although most of those who have submitted evidence to us favour the repeal of section 2(3) of the Limitation Act 1939 for the sake of uniformity, our view is that so long as parties remain (as we recommend) free to stipulate for an abnormally long limitation period, the use of a specialty may be a convenient way of going about it. We have no evidence to suggest that the current rule does in practice cause any difficulty and we do not think there is a sufficient case for abrogating it.

2.60 We received very little support for the suggestion that the running of time should be suspended during the currency of negotiations. One firm of solicitors who submitted evidence to us suggested that an exception to the general rule should be made for a party acting in person and the Hire Purchase Trade Association favoured suspension generally, in the interest of promoting settlements. However, the majority of those who commented on our consultative document were opposed to any change in the current law, on the grounds that such a change would lead to uncertainty. Furthermore, the current rule is a strong incentive to those representing plaintiffs to act with expedition. The point was also made that, if the parties really want to extend the time, they can do so by express agreement.

2.61 We find these arguments convincing. Moreover, it would not be practicable to define 'negotiations' in terms which made it clear at what precise moments the suspensory period started and stopped. It is true that a party acting in person may not appreciate that time is running against him, but solicitors are fully alive to the need to issue a writ if no firm agreement to extend the time has been made and the possibility of a party acting in person failing to appreciate this and being thereby met by a defence of limitation is one which, we think, must be accepted. As far as personal injury claims are concerned, the discretionary power which we recommended and which has now been conferred on the courts by the Limitation Act 1975 should be sufficiently flexible to deal with any really hard cases.

Acknowledgments and part-payments

2.62 The Law Revision Committee[46] made a number of detailed recommendations dealing with various aspects of the effect on limitation of acknowledgment or part-payment of a debt. The Committee's proposals were in substance implemented by sections 23–25 of the Limitation Act 1939.

2.63 We invited comments on these provisions and the tenor of the evidence we have received does not suggest that there is any serious dissatisfaction with the current law. In particular, there is no dissatisfaction with the general rule that an acknowledgment or part-payment made during the currency of the limitation period starts time running again and we do not, therefore, propose to canvass the principle underlying this well-established rule; nor do we find it necessary to discuss in detail each of the relevant statutory provisions. There are, however, three points arising out of those provisions on which it has been suggested that the law is unsatisfactory and which, therefore, we think it appropriate to examine more fully.

---

[46] Cmd. 5334, paras. 19–22.

2.64 First, some of those who have submitted evidence criticise the law for its lack of clarity. On the authorities, it is by no means always easy to say whether a particular statement will amount to an acknowledgment of a debt, and there have been some fairly fine distinctions drawn. For example, it is not always easy to reconcile the various decisions dealing with the question whether an admission contained in a solicitor's letter is an authorised acknowledgment sufficient to bind his principal[47]. However, although we recognise that this question, and other similar questions, may in particular circumstances be difficult to answer, we do not think that the difficulties could be avoided by any elaborate statutory definition of 'acknowledgment' and we do not, therefore, recommend any legislation directed to this point.

2.65 Secondly, the rule now set out in section 24 of the 1939 Act that, to be effective, an acknowledgment must be in writing and signed by the debtor or his agent, has given rise to criticism. The rule is not new and was in force before 1939; the Law Revision Committee did not criticise it, but it can be argued on principle that the extension or preservation of a remedy (or of a title to property) should not depend on the form of an acknowledgment, but on the fact that it has been made and that if an oral acknowledgment can be proved it should be as effective as a written one.

2.66 This argument is advanced by the Law Society and is one with which we have some sympathy. In recent years the law has in some respects (though by no means in all) moved in the direction of insisting less on writing than used to be the case, an obvious example being the repeal of the provision in the Sale of Goods Act 1893 requiring written evidence of a contract of sale for over £10[48]. Moreover, where a debt has been incurred between friends, an oral acknowledgment may be freely given and accepted in circumstances in which the creditor would never think of asking for anything in writing.

2.67 Against this, it remains true that oral evidence is usually less reliable than written evidence and, if effect is to be given to an oral acknowledgment, not only will the creditor be tempted (particularly if the debtor is dead) to embroider a remark not intended to amount to an acknowledgment, but also the courts will be faced with difficult conflicts of evidence. Our conclusion is that there are good practical reasons for continuing to insist on a written and signed acknowledgment; we reach this conclusion the more readily because in Part III below we make an allied recommendation which we think will go a long way towards avoiding unjust results in a particular field (namely loans of money between friends and relations) where the current law on acknowledgment is likely to cause hardship.

2.68 The other question, which has given rise to some difference of opinion, is whether an acknowledgment or a part-payment made *after* the expiration of the limitation period should start time running again. Before 1939, although there had been some conflict of authority in the 19th century, it had become the rule that if expiration of the limitation period had extinguished a title to property no subsequent part-payment or acknowledgment could revive that title[49].

---

[47] See the judgment of Harman, J. in *Wright* v. *Pepin* [1954] 1 W.L.R. 635.
[48] Law Reform (Enforcement of Contracts) Act 1954, s. 2.
[49] *Sanders* v. *Sanders* [1881] 19 Ch. D. 373.

But if only the remedy was barred, the obligation was revived by an acknowledgment or part-payment made at any time.

2.69 The Law Revision Committee[50] treated this rule as well settled by 1936 and, although they gave careful consideration to the matter, did not recommend any fundamental change, though they did propose that an acknowledgment or a part-payment made out of time should bind only the person making it and his personal representatives. The Committee's recommendation on this point was implemented by section 25 of the 1939 Act, which left the pre-existing general rule unchanged.

2.70 In our consultative document we sought views on the desirability of changing that rule. There was general support for the principle that, once lapse of time had extinguished a title, no subsequent acknowledgment should be capable of reviving it. But there was a marked difference of opinion on the question whether a similar principle should apply to the barring of a remedy where the right still persisted. It was argued, in favour of making the change, that the contrary rule gives rise to much uncertainty and is also something of a trap in that, for example, a company's accounts required by law to be published may have to include a balance sheet showing statute-barred debts and these may then be revived as having been 'acknowledged', although no such revival was intended to be the result of the publication of the accounts.

2.71 On the other hand, we recognise that the current rule, by which legal effect is given to an 'out-of-time' acknowledgment, is logically consistent with the principle that limitation only bars the remedy and leaves the right unaffected. Nevertheless, we think the rule is somewhat unreal and serves no very useful purpose. If the debtor and creditor both wish to preserve the former's liability, they can do so easily in some other manner and it seems to us better, and to make for a greater measure of certainty, that once a debt has become statute-barred it should remain irrecoverable by action. Therefore, although the issue is not one of prime importance, we think the law should be changed so that no acknowledgment or part-payment made after expiration of the relevant limitation period should be capable of reviving a time-barred remedy.

The 'terminus ad quem'

2.72 In paragraph 1.13 above, we referred briefly to the question of what step taken by the plaintiff should stop time running against him; again, we use to describe this step the convenient and traditional Latin phrase 'terminus ad quem'.

2.73 If the matter is put very broadly, it is plain that, provided the plaintiff 'institutes proceedings' within the relevant limitation period, he is not to be time-barred. But this is an over-simplification because it leaves open the question of what precisely is meant by 'instituting proceedings'.

2.74 Ideally, the institution of proceedings for this purpose would be a step taken by the plaintiff which fulfilled three conditions—

(a) it should be unmistakable, so that there could be no argument about whether or when it had been taken;

---

[50] Cmd. 5334, para. 19(e).

(b) it should be simple, so that a plaintiff against whom time had nearly run could act immediately and effectively to preserve his rights;

(c) on being taken, it should come at once to the notice of the defendant.

Not all of these conditions can be fully satisfied by any single step and the question we have had to consider is what step comes nearest to satisfy them.

2.75 Under the current law, issue of process is the *terminus ad quem*. Issue entirely satisfies conditions (a) and (b) above, because both in the High Court and in a county court issue consists merely in the presentation to the appropriate court office of a document (a writ or a summons) which, on the proper fee being tendered, thereupon receives the official court seal recording the date of issue. It is a unilateral process in the sense that only the plaintiff and the court staff are involved, so that time can thereby be stopped running forthwith so long as the plaintiff knows what his cause of action is and whom he wishes to sue.

2.76 On the other hand, issue of process does not satisfy condition (c) because it is inherent in the procedure that some time may elapse between a writ or summons being issued and the defendant's becoming aware of it. In practice, the defendant becomes aware that process against him has been issued when it is served on him and not before. For this reason, some of those who have submitted evidence to us on the point have suggested that the *terminus ad quem* ought to be service, rather than issue, of process and we have accordingly examined this suggestion in some detail.

2.77 The suggestion is, at first sight, attractive because one of the objects of the law of limitation is to enable a potential defendant to be confident, after the lapse of the relevant period, that he can no longer be sued and can therefore safely destroy his records and arrange his affairs on the basis that there can be no question of his being made liable. This object is not achieved if the *terminus ad quem* is a process which may not come to his notice until a considerable time after it has taken place.

2.78 Before any conclusion can be reached as to the desirability of substituting service of process for issue as the *terminus ad quem*, it is essential to bear in mind just what is involved in service. Very briefly, the general rule in the High Court is that personal service of a writ on the defendant is essential, though the court has power in particular circumstances to order service by some other method or to dispense with service altogether; service in the High Court is the responsibility of the plaintiff, not of the court staff. In the county court, on the other hand, considerable use is made of service by posts and the normal practice, where personal service is to be effected, is for this to be done by the bailiff, though the party is entitled if he so wishes to effect service himself. As in the High Court, the county court has power to direct that service be effected in some way other than the normal manner.

2.79 A further point of considerable practical importance is the time within which process must be served. In the High Court, a writ can be served at any time within 12 months of issue and the court has power, on application, to renew the writ for a further period. Similar provisions apply in the county court in respect of a default summons; an ordinary summons has necessarily to be served within a comparatively short time of issue, because the return date is fixed at the time of issue and service must be effected before the return date. If this is not done, a successive summons can be issued.

2.80 The choice of service as the effective *terminus ad quem* evidently raises a number of practical problems. In the first place, whether process has been effectively served is a question that cannot always be answered as precisely as the question whether it has been issued; this is particularly true where service is effected by post. Secondly, some special provision would be required to cater for substituted service (which may take the form of a series of notices in newspapers spread over a period of time) and for orders dispensing with service altogether. Thirdly, it would not be altogether satisfactory in the county court that the answer to the question whether the plaintiff had effectively instituted proceedings in time should depend on the zeal and competence of the bailiff entrusted with the duty of serving the summons. Fourthly, it is unfortunately true that an unscrupulous and determined defendant can without great difficulty evade service for a considerable period of time by moving and leaving no address; he may also delay service by going abroad, since process cannot be served out of the jurisdiction without leave of the court. These last considerations might put considerable difficulties in the path of the plaintiff if, for example, negotiations with the defendant broke down shortly before the expiration of the limitation period, leaving the plaintiff insufficient time to make an application to the court for leave to serve out of the jurisdiction or to effect substituted service or to dispense with service altogether.

2.81 No doubt all these difficulties could be overcome by appropriate rules designed to meet particular circumstances. But such rules would involve a measure of complexity which we think ought to be avoided: there is, in our view, and in the view of the majority of those whom we have consulted and who have commented on the matter, an advantage in having, as the *terminus ad quem*, the taking of a simple step, applicable in every kind of proceeding whatever the circumstances. In spite, therefore, of the legitimate criticism of the current law, we have (though some of us have felt reservations on the point) come to the conclusion that the balance of advantage lies in retaining the issue of process as the step which effectively stops time running against the plaintiff, even if the taking of that step may not immediately come to the notice of the defendant.

2.82 Nevertheless, it remains true that as far as the defendant is concerned the effective limitation period appears to be seven, rather than six, years, because a writ or summons issued at the very last moment may not be served on him for another 12 months. Although the matter does not lie within our terms of reference, we think the Supreme Court and County Court Rule Committees might care to consider whether this 12-month period could with advantage be shortened or whether the rules of court should require the plaintiff to give to the defendant notice of the issue of process within a comparatively short time of its having taken place.

2.83 There is one further point in connection with the *terminus ad quem* which requires mention. A number of those who submitted evidence to us commented on the difficulties that can be caused when a limitation period, or a period prescribed by statute within which a particular step (such as the giving of a formal notice) must be taken, expires on a day when the relevant court office is not open. Difficulty had been caused in this connection by a number of judicial decisions which were not easy to reconcile. However, since we started our examination of the problem, the Court of Appeal has overruled a number of earlier decisions and the law is, in our view, now both clear and satisfactory. In effect, if a statute prescribes a period (whether or not a true limitation period) for doing an act which involves taking a step in the court office and the period expires on a day when the court office is not open, the period is treated as being extended to the first day thereafter on which the office is open[51]. In view of this decision, we have not considered it necessary to examine the question further.

C. THE EFFECT OF THE RUNNING OF TIME

Prescription or limitation

2.84 Except for the provisions governing extinction of title in relation to land and advowsons (section 16 of the Limitation Act 1939) and to chattels (section 3 of that Act), the effect of the English law of limitation is to bar the remedy and not to extinguish the right itself. The rule is a procedural one rather than one of substance, and has to be pleaded by way of defence. In practice this distinction is usually of little importance, although barring the remedy means that payment of most, though not all, statute-barred debts cannot thereafter be attacked as improper, and that a lien, charge or other security (though not, because of section 28 of the Limitation Act 1939, a right of set-off) may be enforced even though the debt itself is statute-barred[52].

2.85 In our consultative document we asked, as our first question, for views on the desirability of retaining this principle or of abandoning it in favour of a system of negative (that is extinctive) prescription. We also asked whether there should be any extension to other subject matters of the rule in section 75 of the Land Registration Act 1925, which confers a positive title to registered land after a certain period.

2.86 The question was carefully considered by the Law Revision Committee in 1936[53] and has also been examined in three recent reports relating to New South Wales[54], Ontario[55] and Scotland[56]. The Law Revision Committee considered the practical differences between prescription and limitation and came to the conclusion that no general case could be made in favour of changing the present law. Six of their nine cases of difference were, they thought, of little importance: the other three concerned collateral rights against property, conversion and private international law. The first of these constituted a reason for leaving the law unchanged: the right of a creditor to enforce a *security* which he has in his possession ought not, they thought, to be brought to an end by a prescriptive period applying to the debt itself, since creditors holding sufficient security do not sue and should not be compelled to enforce the security or else lose the

---

[51] *Pritam* v. *S. Russell & Sons Ltd.* [1973] Q.B. 336.
[52] An account of the case law was given by the Law Revision Committee in their *Fifth Interim Report*; Cmd. 5334, para. 24.
[53] Cmd. 5334.
[54] Report of the Law Reform Commission of New South Wales on the Limitation of Actions of October 1967.
[55] Report of the Ontario Law Reform Commission on Limitation of Actions 1969.
[56] Report of the Scottish Law Commission on Reform of the Law Relating to Prescription and Limitation of Actions: (1970) Scot. Law Com. No. 15.

right altogether. The difficulty caused by the old rule in *conversion* cases was not, in their view, sufficient to justify a change to a rule of prescription, although that particular change was, in the event, made by the Limitation Act 1939. They drew attention to the effect of the distinction in *private international law* and suggested that the problem, which they described as being of importance but of considerable difficulty, should be considered separately.

2.87 The views of the Law Revision Committee were considered in detail by the Law Reform Commission of New South Wales, where the law was until 1969 virtually the same as the English law of limitation at the accession of Queen Victoria. The Commission concluded that extinction of the claim or title should be made the general rule, instead of a rule applicable only to land. Their reason was that, if the claim or title were left in existence without the support of a remedy by action, the result would be that expectations would be open for ever afterwards to disturbance by accident or by contrivance. The Commission described the change as rarely important in practice, but of basic importance to the principles of the law of limitation. This recommendation was adopted by the legislature of New South Wales in the Limitation Act 1969[57].

2.88 The Ontario Law Reform Commission also recommended in 1969 extinction of the right in relation to any cause of action, once the time for instituting proceedings had expired. They did not accept that there was any need for special provision for possessory liens and suggested that limitation should in future be classified in the Ontario courts as a substantive matter. As far as we know, this report has not yet been implemented.

2.89 When recommending proposals for the reform of the law of Scotland relating to prescription and limitation of actions, the Scottish Law Commission considered[58] whether their new general period of five years should be a period of limitation or of prescription; they recommended the latter, except for certain rights involving retention of possession of goods (an exception which was not in the event made when the Commission's recommendations were implemented by section 6 of the Prescription and Limitation (Scotland) Act 1973). In making the choice, the Commission attached importance to the 'general philosophy of Scots law' and to the greater simplicity in Scots law of making prescriptive a five-year period within an overall prescriptive period of twenty years.

2.90 Despite the detailed previous consideration of this subject, as evidenced by these reports, and of its theoretical importance, we received very little evidence in favour of abolition of the present basis of the law of limitation. It was pointed out that in practice the exceptions in English law for real property and for chattels produced prescription in the areas where the case for prescription is strongest, that is where title to property is involved. (In passing, we have noted with interest the view of the Ontario Commissioners that the most important effect of a change from limitation to prescription in Ontario would be in relation to title to tangible personal property.) Much of our evidence was in favour of leaving the rule as it is on the ground that there is little practical difference

---

[57] S. 63–69. S. 68 preserves ('so far as is necessary to support and give effect to the lien') a debt protected by possessory lien until an action in conversion or detinue in respect of the goods themselves is barred, and thus makes a special, though limited, exception for securities of the kind which the Law Revision Committee themselves had considered.
[58] Scot. Law Com. No. 15, paras. 84–88.

between the two systems and that the change would therefore not be worth making. It was also suggested that it would be possible to treat the choice between prescription and limitation as an issue separate from the admittedly similar question whether limitation should be a substantive or a procedural matter for the purposes of private international law.

2.91 We find ourselves attracted to the view which commended itself to the Law Revision Committee, as opposed to that more recently advocated in relation to other legal systems. The cases where an approach based on limitation can cause problems principally concern goods and land and in such cases Parliament has already made provision, with which in general we are in agreement, for extinction of rights. A change in the law would therefore have very little practical effect, at any rate in relation to cases without any international element, and we do not consider that there is any need, or indeed any significant demand, for such a fundamental change in approach. The possible hardship that can be caused by an acknowledgment out of time (for example, in a company's annual statement of accounts of a statute-barred debt) should, as we have recommended above, be met by a substantive provision. We think that there are advantages in retaining the rule that limitation is a matter that has to be pleaded and that this rule fits more conveniently with a procedural system of limitation than with a substantive rule. The same can also be said of the general freedom which we have proposed for abridgement or extension of the statutory period by agreement[59]: our recommendation in favour of such a freedom would be hard to reconcile with any proposal for a wider degree of extinction of rights by operation of law.

Classification

2.92 As we have explained, English law treats limitation as part of the law of procedure. An English court will, therefore, always apply English law (*lex fori*) to an issue of limitation, notwithstanding that the substantive rights in question are governed by foreign law[60]. In determining the existence of those substantive rights a distinction has to be drawn between a foreign rule of limitation and a foreign rule of prescription: if the 'proper law' of the transaction (*lex causae*) extinguishes the right through lapse of time, the English court will give effect to that extinction; if, on the other hand, under the relevant *lex causae* lapse of time merely bars the remedy (as it does in most cases in English law), the English courts will ignore the foreign limitation period and apply English law alone.

2.93 Classification of limitation is not itself part of the law of limitation but of private international law and therefore not within our terms of reference. For that reason, we make no positive recommendation about it. Nevertheless, we received from Dr. F. A. Mann a memorandum arguing persuasively in favour of making a change in the English rule (which has been heavily criticised by

---

[59] Paras. 2.54 to 2.58, above.
[60] *Harris* v. *Quine* [1869] L.R.4 Q.B. 653, recently approved by the House of Lords in *Black-Clawson International Ltd* v. *Papierwerke Waldhof-Aschaffenburg A.G.* [1975] 1 All E.R. 870.

academic writers[61]) and we think it right to mention the matter so that it may be considered as a possible subject for reform.

2.94 Although classified as procedural, limitation has an effect which is normally substantive rather than adjectival; the barring of a remedy by lapse of time makes the right to which it relates as worthless as if it had been extinguished by prescription, except in the unusual, and rare, cases mentioned in paragraph 2.84 above. If the English courts are prepared to give effect to Ruritanian law in order to ascertain whether a particular right has been created and, if so, what is its extent, it does not seem unreasonable that the Ruritanian law should also govern its effective termination. On general principles, therefore, we see much force in Dr. Mann's contention that questions of limitation should be decided by the *lex causae*, a contention which is reinforced by consideration of the somewhat anomalous results which English law can bring about in a case such as *Black-Clawson*, cited above. Moreover, as the Scottish Law Commission has pointed out[62], classification of limitation as a matter of procedure can expose the debtor to the risk of proceedings abroad without there being any effective time limit, since the foreign court will ignore English procedural rules and will not apply its own substantive rules to an obligation governed by English law. This was one of the considerations which led the Scottish Law Commission to recommend that the new five-year prescriptive period in Scotland should extinguish the right and not merely bar the remedy.

2.95 We have not examined in detail the possible consequences of accepting Dr. Mann's suggestion. It did, however, appear to us that outside the field of contract (where the concept of *lex causae* is well recognised) there could be considerable difficulties in ascertaining what was the relevant foreign law. For example, English law does not yet fully recognise the concept of *lex causae* in the field of tort[63]. Moreover, it could be the case that on grounds of policy an English court ought not to be bound by the rules of limitation applicable under a foreign *lex causae*, because, for example, the time limit was either unreasonably short or unreasonably long. We appreciate that the difficult task of ascertaining what law governs substantive rights may have to be undertaken in any event and that, if so, it might ,be no great additional burden on the court to ascertain what was the limitation period under that law. However, the possibility that some foreign law of limitation might apply in a case where there was no clear *lex causae* governing all substantive issues, could, we think, raise problems for the courts.

2.96 These questions have occurred to us as raising possible difficulties; there may be others which a thorough examination of Dr. Mann's proposal would bring out. Nevertheless, we are impressed by the fundamental argument that the law under which a right is created should be the law under which it is extinguished, and that the difficulties of the present rule are real. We do, therefore, think that there is a case for the re-examination of the English rule which classifies limitation as procedural, though we are not ourselves able to make any positive recommendation.

---

[61] *E.G.*, J.D. Falconbridge, *Essays on the Conflict of Laws*, 2nd ed., ch. 12; Cheshire, *Private International Law* 9th Ed. (ed. North) pp. 687–90.
[62] Scot. Law Com. No. 15, para. 87(3).
[63] See *Boys* v. *Chaplin* [1971] A.C. 356.

Part III

LIMITATION IN PARTICULAR CASES

A. CONTRACT AND TORT

Conversion and detinue

3.1 Section 3 of the Limitation Act 1939 provides one of the relatively few instances in English law of limitation extinguishing a right instead of merely barring a remedy. Once the six-year limitation period has run from the accrual of a cause of action for the conversion or detinue of a 'chattel' (an expression which includes most forms of tangible property other than land), section 3 operates to extinguish the owner's title and, if there have been successive conversions, the six years run from the first of those conversions.

3.2 Section 3 was enacted to meet the criticism directed against the common law rule under which, if O's chattel was converted first by A and subsequently by B, O could successfully sue B for the subsequent conversion notwithstanding that his remedy against A was already statute-barred. The effect of that rule was to put an entirely blameless B (who might have no idea that the goods had originally been converted by A) in a worse position than the relatively culpable A.

3.3 None of those who has submitted evidence to us has criticised the principle underlying section 3, which is, in our view, right. Our examination of the section has, however, led us to the conclusion that it can produce an unacceptable result where a valuable object has been stolen and the owner is unable to trace it until more than six years after the date of the theft. The fact that the identity of the thief is unknown and undiscoverable is not enough to bring the case within section 26 (and therefore to postpone the running of time in the thief's favour)[64]. Thus, the owner of the stolen property may have no effective opportunity to sue the thief in time and may yet lose his title to what might be an object of great value, such as an Old Master or an irreplaceable piece of jewellery. It also appears that, by virtue of section 3, a transferee from the thief, whether a dishonest receiver or a *bona fide* purchaser for value, will acquire a good title to the stolen property unless the owner starts proceedings against him within six years *from the date of the theft*. (It is possible that this consequence may not follow if the theft falls within section 26: see footnote to paragraph 3.6 below).

3.4 It does not seem to us right that a thief or receiver should, whether or not he has been prosecuted, be able to establish by limitation a valid title to the stolen goods. The criminal law does not provide a complete answer to the problem even if the offender is prosecuted to conviction, since the convicting court can order restitution of the property under section 28 of the Theft Act 1968 only to a person 'entitled to recover' the property and, *ex hypothesi*, an owner whose title has been extinguished is not such a person. Equally, the Police Property Act 1897 may not help, because it goes no further than to empower a magistrates' court to order property coming into police hands in connection with a criminal charge to be delivered to a person 'appearing to be the owner

---

[64] *R.B. Policies at Lloyd's* v. *Butler* [1950] 1 K.B. 76.

thereof'. Once the owner's title has been extinguished by limitation, it appears that all a convicting court can do is to order compensation to be paid to him under section 35 of the Powers of Criminal Courts Act 1973. Furthermore, since criminal courts can exercise their powers only if there is a prosecution (and in some cases a conviction) and since it is not difficult to envisage circumstances—such as the death of the thief before apprehension—in which no criminal process can be instituted, it seems to us that the problem with which we are faced can be resolved only by an amendment to the civil law.

3.5 Although the situation which troubles us may not often arise in practice, we think it is wrong for the law to extend the protection of limitation to the thief or receiver at the expense of the true owner and we note that in Scots law time will never run in favour of a thief or a person 'privy to the stealing', an expression which, we are advised, includes a receiver[65]. This appears to us to be a precedent which English law could well follow and we have accordingly examined the possible consequence of making theft and allied offences 'imprescriptible'.

3.6 If time is not to run in favour of a thief, it will still be necessary to give some protection to the bona fide purchaser of stolen property. As the law now stands, such a purchaser will acquire a good title 6 years from the theft[66]. To preserve this rule would not be consistent with making theft imprescriptible and a more logical rule would be to provide for time to start to run in favour of the bona fide purchaser of stolen property only from the date of his purchase. In our view, this is the right principle.

3.7 We considered, as an alternative to adopting the Scottish principle, the reversal by legislation of the decision in R.B. Policies at Lloyd's[67] and the extension of section 26 to a case in which the identity of the converter was unknown and undiscoverable. This would not, however, be an altogether satisfactory solution where, though identified within the 6-year period, the thief had hidden the stolen property. In such a case the owner could protect his title only if he was prepared to start civil proceedings against a man who, at the time, would probably appear to be 'not worth powder and shot' and it seemed to us unrealistic to expect a victim of theft to go to that expense. In our view, the Scottish provision is more satisfactory in that it affords better protection to the owner, who need institute civil proceedings only when he sees a reasonable chance of recovering his property or obtaining damages for its conversion.

3.8 Accordingly, we propose that the right of an owner of goods to recover his property (or to claim damages for its conversion) should never be barred by lapse of time as against a thief or receiver, but that, as against either a bona fide purchaser of the stolen property or a person claiming through such

---

[65] Prescription and Limitation (Scotland) Act 1973, sch. 3, para. 9(g).
[66] This follows from the effect of s. 3 of the Limitation Act 1939 on successive conversions. It is not altogether clear whether the same result would follow if the theft were clandestine so as to fall within the doctrine of 'concealed fraud'. There is authority (see Eddis v. Chichester Constable [1969] 2 Ch. 345, per Lord Denning, M.R., at p. 356) for the proposition that s. 26 of the Act postpones the extinction of title under s. 3; but the proviso to s. 26 (which prevents that section from prejudicing a defence of limitation which could otherwise be set up by a bona fide purchaser) may perhaps exclude such postponement as against a purchaser. There is no clear authority on the point.
[67] [1950] 1 K.B. 76.

a purchaser, the owner's title should be extinguished, and his right to claim damages barred, after six years from the date of purchase. As far as the burden of proof is concerned, it appears to us right on principle that the onus should be on the owner to prove that the property was stolen from him and that, once he has done this, the onus should be on the defendant to prove that the property was subsequently the subject of a *bona fide* purchase.

3.9 We considered whether our proposal ought to operate on dishonest acquisition generally or on the commission of a specific criminal offence. There are many forms of acquisition which can properly be described as dishonest, of which only some constitute criminal offences. In the interests of certainty we think it better to make our proposed 'imprescriptibility' operate on the commission of one of a number of specific offences under the Theft Act 1968: namely, theft (section 1); obtaining by deception (section 15); blackmail (section 21); and dishonest handling (section 22). To these we would add the doing of an act abroad which, if done in England or Wales, would constitute one of these offences. Normally, conviction by a criminal court will be sufficient evidence that the offence was committed, but we do not think it would be either logical or sensible to restrict our proposed new rule to cases in which the thief or receiver has in fact been convicted.

3.10 Not every transferee of property from a dishonest acquirer is himself either dishonest or a *bona fide* purchaser for value: such a transferee may be an honest 'volunteer' to whom the property has been given or bequeathed. We have, therefore, had to consider what should be the position of, for example, an honest donee of stolen property if the thief himself is never to have the protection of the limitation period. On the one hand, on grounds of public policy it may be thought desirable that long and honest possession should not be disturbed by the revival of an old title and it is not difficult to envisage circumstances in which an entirely honest man has for many years been in possession of property which was in fact stolen before he acquired it without having any reason to suppose that it had ever been stolen. If such a man's long possession is to be protected, it may be argued that he should not be liable to a claim at the suit of the true owner notwithstanding that the true owner was the victim of the theft. Moreover, even if it be the fact that the property was the subject of a *bona fide* sale after the theft, the honest possessor may have difficulty in proving this after many years have elapsed since the sale. There is, therefore, an argument for treating the honest volunteer on a par with the *bona fide* purchaser and giving him a good title if six years have passed since he acquired the goods without a claim having been made by the true owner.

3.11 On the other hand, donees of valuable stolen property are often not entirely honest even if their knowledge of its having been stolen may be impossible to prove and, if the property is sufficiently valuable for the owner to be able to prove after many years that it was stolen from him, any subsequent dealing with it which was in truth a *bona fide* sale is likely (though this will not always be the case) to be well-documented and therefore capable of proof by an honest person relying on that sale. As between the volunteer, even if in fact honest, and the true owner whose property has been stolen, we think the law should favour the owner. Accordingly, we recommend that, as against the owner, time should not run in favour of a gratuitous transferee of stolen property; though some of us are concerned at the possibility of a genuinely honest volunteer, who has sold the property in good faith, being subsequently faced by a claim in conversion in which the damages will be measured by the value of the property at the time of the claim, not of the sale.

3.12 Our proposals would remedy a defect in the law to which attention has been drawn by, among others, Professor Heuston[68]. As the law stands, the honest purchaser of stolen property is in a better position than the honest purchaser of lost property: for the former, time runs from the theft (because the theft is necessarily a conversion); for the latter, it runs from the date on which the property was first converted (a date which may be as late as the sale to him), since taking possession of lost property is not by itself, and without any denial of the owner's title, a conversion. Consideration of this point led us to examine the related question whether a finder of lost property should be able to acquire title by lapse of time and, if so, from what *terminus* time should run.

3.13 Under the current law time runs in favour of a finder and against the owner only from the moment when the finder converts the object found. It may be difficult to ascertain the precise point of time at which a conversion occurs, because the finder himself may be the only person who can give evidence as to the moment when he first treated the object as his own and it follows that, where a question of limitation arises, it is always in the finder's interest to say that he committed the tort of conversion at an early date. There is something rather artificial about this situation and we therefore considered whether there was a sufficient case for changing the current law.

3.14 One possibility would be to make time run in favour of a finder from the date of the finding. Such a rule would be consistent with the policy of not disturbing long possession and, if made subject to our proposal that the most common forms of dishonest acquisition should be imprescriptible, would not benefit dishonest finders whose criminal conduct could be proved; (it appears, though there is no clear authority on the point, that the Theft Act 1968 has enlarged the circumstances in which a dishonest finder may be guilty of stealing). This would however, involve a departure from the basic principle that limitation periods start to run only after something has occurred which gives rise to a cause of action and since, as we have said, taking possession of lost property does not, without more ado, constitute a legal wrong actionable at the suit of the owner, it cannot start a limitation period running. It follows that, if the finder of lost property is to be given a prescriptive title running from the date of finding, a change in the substantive law will be required.

3.15 Another (and opposite) course would be to provide that time *never* ran in favour of a finder, whether or not he had converted the property found. This would, in effect, mean, if our main recommendation is accepted, equating the finder with the thief. In favour of this proposal it can be argued that in practice the question of limitation arises only in relation to property which is both durable and valuable (a claim for the return of an umbrella lost more than six years previously is not a reality) and that the finder of such property who is not prepared to return it when the true owner has been identified is unlikely to be an honest man. On this basis, there is no reason (it may be said) why the law should give the finder an 'uncovenanted benefit' at the expense of the true owner. There is certainly force in this argument, but we think that

---

[68] *Salmond on Torts*, 16th Ed., ch. 5, para. 36, p. 112.

it would be difficult to distinguish between finders and other gratuitous acquirers; moreover, hardship could be caused where the goods had been honestly disposed of (whether or not for value) by the finder, who might become liable to a claim for substantial damages many years later. Furthermore, it would hardly be reasonable to preserve the owner's title if, notwithstanding his knowledge of the finding of his property, he had not, over a period of years, taken any action to assert that title.

3.16 In the end, our conclusion was that the adoption of either of the courses canvassed above would raise more problems than it would solve. In these circumstances, and bearing in mind that we have received no evidence to suggest that the current law leads to any practical difficulties, we recommend no change as far as finders are concerned.

3.17 There is one minor point on which clarification is desirable. This point was referred to by Lord Denning, M.R., in *Eddis* v. *Chichester Constable*, when he criticised the proviso to section 26 of the Limitation Act on the ground that it purported to protect the *bona fide* purchaser only if the claim against him was for the recovery of the property he had purchased, as distinct from a claim for damages for the conversion of that property[69].

3.18 We think that Lord Denning's criticism is well founded and that any reformulation of section 26 (such as we have suggested above[70]) should make it clear that the proviso does extend to a claim for damages for the conversion of property which has been the subject of a *bona fide* purchase.

Loans of money

3.19 Our consideration of the rules relating to acknowledgments has brought out a point which, though not strictly a matter of limitation, does, we think, reveal a defect in the law which may cause considerable injustice, in that a defence of limitation can be successfully raised in answer to a claim for the repayment of a loan when, if effect were given to the true intention of the parties, the claim would be well within the limitation period.

3.20 This particular defect is caused by the rule that where no time is specified in a contract of loan, or where the loan is expressed simply to be repayable 'on demand', time starts to run in favour of the borrower from the date of the loan. Although the precise scope of this rule may be open to some doubt, it has been applied in a number of cases and was treated as well settled as respects promissory notes and other straight-forward loans by the end of the 19th Century[71]. The principle underlying this rule appears to be that the cause of action accrues from the first moment the lender could have taken steps to claim the money.

3.21 Although the courts have declined to apply a similar rule to a guarantee[72] and have shown themselves in more recent cases disposed to treat the question whether a demand is a prerequisite to the accrual of the cause of action as

---

[69] [1969] 2 Ch. 345 at p. 357.
[70] At paragraph 2.24.
[71] See, e.g., *Re Brown's Estate* [1893] 2 Ch. 300 and *Reeves* v. *Butcher* [1891] 2 Q.B. 509.
[72] *Bradford Old Bank* v. *Sutcliffe* [1918] 2 K.B. 833.

being a genuine question of construction[73], nevertheless it seems that a loan made without any express provision as to repayment, or expressed to be repayable simply 'on demand' without any further qualification, is still likely to be treated as giving rise to a cause of action forthwith, with the result that the Limitation Act can be successfully pleaded to a claim made more than six years from the date of the loan.

3.22 It has been represented to us that, although this rule probably causes little injustice in the case of commercial loans, it can cause real hardship where the loan is made between friends or members of the same family. It is by no means uncommon for money to be lent in these circumstances without any written contract and without any legal advice having been obtained, on the tacit understanding that the borrower will not be expected to repay the money until it is asked for. However, as the law appears to stand, once the loan has been outstanding for more than six years (which not infrequently happens), the borrower has a complete defence to the claim, notwithstanding that it is perfectly well known 'in the family' that the money was lent and not given and was never expected to be repaid before demand.

3.23 A rule which does not, in many cases, give effect to the true intention of the parties and which enables an unscrupulous borrower to 'get away with it' is open to criticism; moreover, if, as we recommend, the law on acknowledgments is to be changed so that an acknowledgment of a debt made out of time is to have no effect, the number of hard cases in this field can only be increased. We have, therefore, thought it right to consider some modification to the general rule referred to above, notwithstanding that (as we have said) strictly speaking it is not a rule of limitation but a rule which forms part of the substantive law of contract.

3.24 That we are not alone in feeling concern about this aspect of the law of contract and its repercussions on limitation is shown by recent changes in the law of Scotland. Following a recommendation in the Report of the Scottish Law Commission[74] (to which we have referred above), Parliament has enacted in the Prescription and Limitation (Scotland) Act 1973 a provision which does make a substantial change in the law of contract for the specific purpose of meeting this particular defect. Paragraph 2 of Schedule 2 to the Act provides, in effect, that in the case of a loan of money time begins to run in favour of the borrower—

    (a) if a date for repayment is specified, from that date; and

    (b) if no date is specified, from the date when a written demand for repayment is first made.

In our view, this provision does make the law more consistent with what the parties to a contract of loan really intend. We felt some doubt about the need to insist on a demand in writing before time begins to run, but on balance we think the arguments in favour of insisting on writing outweigh those against, for very much the same reasons that led us to conclude that an acknowledgment of a debt should not be effective unless made in writing.

---

[73] *Joachimson* v. *Swiss Bank Corporation* [1921] 3 K.B. 10.
[74] Scot. Law Com. No. 15, para. 79.

3.25 Before concluding that English law ought to follow Scots law in this respect, there were three matters which we thought it necessary to consider. *First*, we were concerned that a provision on the lines of the Scottish Act might interfere with the settled practice of banking. It is well settled that, in the case of a credit balance on a current account, the limitation period *does not* begin to run in favour of the bank until the customer has made a demand for payment of the money due to him; it is equally well settled that in the converse case of an overdraft time *does* begin to run in favour of the customer from the latest dealing on the account. Although at first sight this rule may appear to put the bank at a disadvantage, in practice bankers are unlikely to be taken by surprise since they are entirely familiar with this rule of law and no prudent banker will leave an overdraft outstanding for six years without taking steps, by obtaining an acknowledgment or in some other way, to prevent the limitation period running against him. In practice, therefore, our proposal would make no real difference to the relationship of banker and customer.

Secondly, we considered whether adoption of the Scottish rule would prejudice the right of a creditor to garnish a banking account; we are, however, satisfied that it could not do this, since it is well settled that the service of a garnishee summons by the creditor is tantamount to a demand for payment of the amount standing to the credit of the debtor's account[75].

Thirdly, we wanted to satisfy ourselves that the change we proposed would not affect the existing law relating to promissory notes, cheques and bills of exchange. As the law stands, the right of action against the parties primarily liable on such an instrument normally accrues on the date on which the instrument falls due. If a bill or note is payable 'on demand', no demand is ordinarily necessary to enforce payment and the limitation period therefore starts to run from the date of the instrument (or of its delivery if later,) and not from the date of the demand. It is not our intention to affect these well-known rules of commercial law or to suggest that a demand in writing should be necessary to start time running in, for example, the case of a cheque or promissory note given in return for a loan of money repayable on demand. If, in the 'family loan' case, the borrower discharges his liability by giving the lender a cheque (whether or not postdated) or promissory note which is not acted on until the limitation period has expired, then the consequence must be accepted that the lender will have lost his remedy. However, in practice, a loan made in the circumstances we envisage is unlikely to lead to the execution of a promissory note: an ordinary letter thanking the lender for the money and promising to repay it would not, in our view, be likely to be construed as a promissory note, but rather as a mere acknowledgment of receipt accompanied by an expression of the writer's intention to repay. Moreover, if a cheque is given by the borrower, it is likely to be a post-dated cheque and in any event to be given as security for the loan rather than in payment of the amount due.

3.26 We have considered whether, in order to achieve our object of preserving the existing law in the field of bills and notes, it would be necessary to make any specific reference in the legislation to instruments of this nature, so as to exclude them from our proposal. Our conclusion is that no such express reference is necessary and we are confirmed in this view by the fact that the corresponding

---

[75] *Joachimson* v. *Swiss Bank Corporation* [1921] 3. K.B. 10.

Scottish legislation contains none. Since the instrument constitutes a distinct and separate contract from the contract of loan, it will not be affected by our proposal, which relates solely to loans. Accordingly, we recommend that where money is lent and no date specified for its repayment, then, for the purpose of limitation, time should not begin to run in favour of the borrower until the date on which a written demand for repayment is first made.

Defamation

3.27 In Chapter 18 of their Report the Committee on Defamation[76] under the chairmanship of Mr. Justice Faulks made a number of recommendations about the law of limitation in actions for defamation. They suggested that the period should be capable of extension from the normal *terminus a quo* of publication (which the Committee suggested should be retained) in cases where the plaintiff was in exceptional circumstances unable to ascertain that he had been defamed until after the expiry of the three-year period. In such a case, the plaintiff should have to seek leave to sue in proceedings *inter partes*, and should be debarred if he did not start proceedings for leave within 12 months of his 'date of knowledge'.

3.28 The Committee received evidence from many witnesses to the effect that the six-year period is too long in actions for defamation, and that plaintiffs should have no difficulty in starting such proceedings well within a shortened period of three years. They put forward their suggestion for a date of knowledge extension in order to remove any doubt about the plaintiff's ability, under the present law, to sue outside the six-year period in cases of secret or clandestine defamation. They thought it doubtful whether section 26 of the Limitation Act 1939 would cover all the cases which they had in mind.

3.29 The Faulks Committee thus propose that a rule not unlike that now prevailing in personal injury cases should be introduced for defamation actions. In a sense, injury to reputation is not unlike personal injury[77] and this similarity may be thought sufficient to justify treating defamation in the same way, despite the general view which we have formed that there are advantages in adhering to a single uniform period[78] (and a uniform set of rules for extension in cases for concealment[79]) for as many different sorts of case as possible.

3.30 Since, however, we have not ourselves received any evidence either in favour of or against the change advocated by the Faulks Committee, we do not feel qualified to dissent from the recommendations made by a body which was very well suited to consider the special problems of defamation and which received a substantial body of evidence in favour of the changes proposed. We therefore make no recomendation on the point.

---

[76] Cmnd. 5909.

[77] Indeed, as the law stands, a man's reputation can no longer be injured in law after his death: Law Reform (Miscellaneous Provisions) Act 1934, s. 6. The Committee propose that this should be changed.

[78] para. 1.11 above.

[79] paras. 2.24 and 2.25 above.

Contribution and indemnity

3.31 Section 4(2) of the Limitation Act 1963 prescribes a two year period for the bringing of a claim for contribution by one tortfeasor against another. The period runs from judgment against the first tortfeasor or, if the claim against him has been compromised, from the date on which he admitted liability. The purpose of this provision was to reduce the period of six years which was previously applicable to such claims[80]. Some of the evidence we received suggested to us that there should be a three-year instead of a two-year period, or that the period should be either one year from judgment, or three years from service of process, in the original proceedings against the first tortfeasor, whichever is the longer.

3.32 In their Working Paper on Contribution[81] the Law Commission drew attention to the possibility that, in an extreme case, the present law could lead to the second tortfeasor first learning of the possibility of a claim against him more than nine years after the original cause of action accrued. They invited views on the need to make any change in the law and on the merits of two alternative proposals. Of these one (described in paragraph 34) would involve a change in the substantive law to the effect that, once the limitation period for an action by the plaintiff against the second tortfeasor had expired without any such action being commenced, the plaintiff would be limited in his claim against the first tortfeasor to the damages which, had both tortfeasors been sued in time, the first tortfeasor would have had to pay himself, that is excluding those which he could have passed on to the second tortfeasor in proceedings against him. Since this solution, which is to be found in the Republic of Ireland, relates to the substantive law, we have not considered it, or the difficulties which it presents, in any detail.

3.33 The second suggested solution would be to bar a claim for contribution if, at the time when the contribution proceedings were started, the defendant in those proceedings could have relied on a defence of limitation against the original plaintiff, unless, exceptionally, the contribution proceedings were started within a relatively short period from the service on the first tortfeasor of the original plaintiff's writ.

3.34 The Law Commission have now reported on the topic of contribution in general in their report No. 79[82]. They made no recommendations concerning limitation, because of the existence of our inquiry. They kindly informed us of the tenor of evidence which they have received in response to their request for views and those who assisted in this way we included in Part B of Annex 1 to this report. With one or two exceptions it confirms the view which we ourselves have formed that, despite the theoretical possibility of a long period from the original cause of action, section 4 of the 1963 Act causes few problems in practice and that there is no compelling case for abandoning it in favour of the more complex solutions adumbrated by the Law Commission. It is rarely necessary to invoke section 4(2) of the 1963 Act, because well-advised plaintiffs

---

[80] The claim arises by statute, under s. 6 of the Law Reform (Married Women and Tortfeasors) Act 1935, with the result that there was, until 1963, a six year period running from the accrual of the cause of action: s. 2(1)(d) of the Limitation Act 1939.

[81] Working Paper No. 59 of March, 1975, paras. 31–35.

[82] *Report on Contribution*, (1977) Law Com. No. 79; H.C. 181 (1976–77).

in practice sue all likely defendants, and if one only is sued, he is quick to suggest that others are really to blame.

3.35 In their *Report on Contribution* the Law Commission suggest that the right to claim contribution should be extended from claims arising in tort so as to cover claims arising by way of breach of contract, of trust or of other duty. They deal with a number of problems associated with limitation (including the protection now given to a defendant who has defeated the plaintiff on a limitation point, and is then exposed to proceedings by another defendant for contribution), and we do not propose to cover this ground again.

3.36 We have considered the question whether the two year period in the 1963 Act should be made applicable to third party claims generally. This issue can most conveniently be considered in the context of procedure, and we revert to it (at paragraphs 5.4–5.6) below.

Products liability

3.37 We have also considered briefly the suggestions that are now being made for special provisions for products liability both in the Council of Europe and in the European Communities. The subject is discussed in a recent Report of the Law Commissions[83]. We have noted in particular that at paragraphs 141–149 the two Commissions are not able to arrive at an agreed view concerning the provisions in the proposed EEC directive. Since, however, both Commissions are agreed (at paragraph 137) that the proposal to extend the scheme for strict liability to property damage is unsound as a matter of policy, we do not propose to go into these matters in more detail. The subject of products liability is still under examination by the Royal Commission on Civil Liability and Compensation for Personal Injury, and we therefore content ourselves with the suggestion that those concerned should bear in mind the general basis upon which we have proceeded.

B. CLAIMS RELATING TO LAND

The length of the limitation period

3.38 Under section 4(3) of the Limitation Act 1939, the normal limitation period for an action to recover land is 12 years and if there has been adverse possession for that period the original owner's title to the land is extinguished and the squatter's title becomes indefeasible. The majority of those who submitted evidence to us were satisfied that any period appropriate to claims to recover land must be appreciably longer than the normal six-year period applicable to claims in contract or tort. We agree with this view and, although a minor reduction of the period to 10 years (which was suggested to us by the Institute) would in our view be acceptable, any substantial reduction would be bound to have serious repercussions on titles to property. This would, in our view, be undesirable. Our conclusion is that a minor reduction to 10 years is, in the absence of any particular reason for preferring that period to the existing 12-year period, not worth making and, therefore, that the general rule should be preserved. Whatever

---

[83] *Liability for Defective Products*, (1977) Law Com. No. 82; Scot. Law Com. No. 45; (1976–77) Cmnd. 6831, following Law Commission Working Paper No. 64 (Scottish Law Commission, Memorandum No. 20) of June 1975.

the period may be, we agree that its expiration should serve to extinguish the claimant's title.

3.39 We have not thought it necessary to examine again the relationship between the 12-year period applicable to a claim to recover land and the periods of prescription relative to the acquisition of easements and profits. This subject was discussed in detail in our 14th Report[84], where we expressed the view that, should a new and simplified statutory system of prescription be adopted, the appropriate period would be 12 years so as to make this form of prescription consistent with section 4 of the Limitation Act. No legislation has followed our 14th Report; for our present purposes it is sufficient to say that we adhere to the views expressed in that report about the length of the period of prescription.

3.40 We have received some evidence criticising the abnormally long limitation periods prescribed by section 4(1) and (2) of the Limitation Act. These periods apply to claims to recover land instituted by the Crown or by a spiritual or eleemosynary corporation. The relevant periods are 30 years or, in the case of a claim by the Crown to recover foreshore, 60 years. Most of those who commented on these provisions were of the opinion that such claims should be subject to the normal rule, that is to say, they should be barred after 12 years or whatever is to be the period applicable to claims to recover land generally.

3.41 Those who favoured the retention of abnormally long periods did so on the ground that both the Crown and the Established Church were distinguished from ordinary landowners. On behalf of the Crown it was argued that in practice the Treasury Solicitor often has to enforce claims against squatters who have been in possession of Crown Land for more than 12 years. Some Government Departments (notably the Ministry of Defence) own considerable tracts of remote and uncultivated land, encroachment on which may well not come to the notice of officials of the Department until many years after it has been started. Similar considerations apply to the foreshore, the extent of which also changes gradually through the operation of natural forces. Secondly, land may devolve on the Crown as the *ultima haeres* (because there is nobody who can inherit on an intestacy) without the Crown's becoming aware of this having occurred until somebody reports it. The Crown is, therefore, said to be peculiarly likely to own or acquire land the existence or extent of which is unknown to it and in respect of which it is, therefore, not readily in a position to assert its title.

3.42 The case for special treatment of the Established Church runs on different lines: it would be virtually impossible for the Church to attempt to keep track of the ownership of all the parcels of land, often in remote areas where such problems are more likely to arise, during the incumbency of each of its ministers. It would be quite unreal to suggest that the Church would have any adequate remedy against one of its ministers, so that, even if the law relating to future interests were to be altered so as to permit 12 years' adverse possession against trustees to bar all the equitable interests in the land (see paragraph 3.64 below), we would not consider that the same rule should apply to the Church. We are confirmed in this view by the fact that we have no evidence at all to suggest that the existing law causes any practical difficulty. In the circumstances we do not feel justified in recommending any change in respect of either Crown or Church lands.

---

[84] *Acquisition of Easements and Profits by Prescription*; (1966) Cmnd. 3100.

3.43 We have also considered the abnormally long periods applicable, under section 14 of the Limitation Act, to claims to enforce advowsons. We have not, however, thought it necessary to examine this complex provision in any details because such claims are of no practical importance in modern conditions. Moreover, it seems likely that, within the fairly near future, the General Synod will promote legislation to abolish (or greatly to modify) existing rights of private patronage and, if such legislation is enacted, section 14, already obsolescent, seems likely to become entirely obsolete. In these circumstances, we do not see that any useful purpose would be served in attempting to re-cast it in a different form.

The St. Marylebone case

3.44 We also invited comments on the decision of the House of Lords in *St. Marylebone Property Co. Ltd.* v. *Fairweather*[85], where it was held that a lessee whose own title had been extinguished by adverse possession could nevertheless, by surrendering the lease, enable his lessor to evict the squatter. The evidence we received revealed a considerable difference of opinion among those who commented on this decision. Those who disapproved of it argued that, as a matter of logic, the lessee could, once his title was extinguished, have nothing left to surrender and that, therefore, no action on his part should be allowed to prejudice the squatter. They accordingly suggested that the squatter ought to be entitled to remain in possession for the remainder of the term. Those who supported the decision thought that the law should not assist squatters and that the rule declared by the House of Lords could not cause any injustice, because the squatter would not, at the time of taking adverse possession, have any knowledge of the duration or conditions of the lease and would, therefore, have no expectation of remaining in possession for any particular time.

3.45 The current law is, in our view, certainly open to criticism on grounds of logic and we were informed by Mr. Ruoff, then Chief Land Registrar, that in his experience it gave rise to special difficulties over the registration of title to leasehold property where the boundaries on the conveyancing plans did not correspond with those on the ground, and that in strictness it precluded the Land Registry from registering a lessee in such a case even with a possessory title. On the other hand, where a lease contains a covenant against assignment, reversal of the *St. Marylebone* decision might prejudice the lessor, who could find himself saddled with a 'tenant' whom he had never wanted and to whom he would never have allowed the real tenant to assign the lease (though under a carefully drawn covenant such prejudice would be unlikely to arise). No general rule is likely to produce absolute justice in every case, but it can be argued that, since the lessor can, by careful drafting of the lease, take steps to protect himself and since the problem appears to arise mainly in connection with the boundaries of properties forming part of the same leasehold development and usually held for the same terms of years, the general law should protect the squatter during the term originally granted rather than the lessor. The contrary argument is that if there is going to be a possibility of hardship or injustice to either the squatter or the lessor, the law ought to lean in favour of the lessor, since it ought not to encourage trespassers.

---

[85] [1963] A.C. 510.

3.46 We have not been able to reach a decided view on this difficult issue and we are about equally divided on it. Some of us feel that an amendment of the law under which the lessor obtained no greater rights by virtue of a surrender of the lease than he would by virtue of an assignment would produce a more logical situation[86]; and although it seems that the problem does not often arise in practice as between squatter and lessor, a statutory reversal of the *St. Marylebone* decision would provide a solution to some of the difficulties to which Mr. Ruoff drew our attention. The contrary view is that, although the law is not entirely satisfactory and does give rise to the difficulties referred to by Mr. Ruoff, no alternative is likely to be more satisfactory. Further, since the situation arises but rarely and since a carefully drawn covenant would anyhow circumvent a statutory reversal of the *St. Marylebone* decision, there is not sufficient justification for a change in the law. In view of the disagreement, we make no recommendation on the point.

Adverse possession

3.47 In our consultative document, we invited those who had submitted evidence to us to say whether, in practice, they found it difficult to establish that, in particular circumstances, possession was 'adverse' in the sense given to that expression by the courts. A number of those who have dealt with this matter have informed us that this is a real difficulty and the Institute suggested that it would be better if there were a presumption that possession was adverse. We were also informed that the difficulty was particularly felt when it came to establishing a claim for the payment out of court, under the procedure prescribed by R.S.C. Order 95, rule 5, of sums that have been paid in because an acquiring authority has been unable readily to ascertain the identity of a landowner entitled to compensation.

3.48 We have, throughout our examination, appreciated the force of the criticisms that have been voiced; but until recently we would have said simply that the difficulties arise from the great variety of circumstances which may occur, that the inevitable emergence of borderline cases would not be altered by changing the law and that on the whole we did not consider that any change was justified. However, as the result of a series of recent decisions[87], we consider that it is no longer possible to take such a complacent view. The law now appears in one very important respect uncertain, and possibly to have taken a direction which we do not consider justifiable, so that some reform is required.

3.49 The nature of the difficulty may be simply stated. When considering the initial step towards acquiring a title by 12 years adverse possession, namely

---

[86] The Supreme Court of Ireland has declined to follow the *St. Marylebone* decision: *Perry v. Woodfarm Homes Ltd.* [1975] I.R. 104. See also J.C.S. Wylie, 'Adverse Possession: An Ailing Concept?', [1965] N.I.L.Q. 467; Herbert Wallace, 'Adverse Possession of Leaseholds—The Case for Reform', [1975] The Irish Jurist 74.

[87] *Wallis's Cayton Bay Holiday Camp Ltd.* v. *Shell Mex and B.P. Ltd.* [1975] 1 Q.B. 94; *Gray v. Wykeham-Martin , Goode* [1977] Bar Liberty Transcript No. 10A (C.A. affirming the decision of Goulding, J., who had followed *Wallis* by implying a licence without any factual basis); *Powell v. McFarlane* [1977] Unreported—Slade J. held he was bound by these cases if necessary to find an implied or hypothetical licence, but actually found that possession had not been taken. The contrary approach, along traditional lines, was demonstrated in *Treloar* v. *Nute* [1977] 1 All E.R. 230.

the taking of possession, the courts—in our view rightly—have never been astute to find that possession has in fact been taken. This approach has been particularly marked in relation to small pieces of land which cannot immediately be economically exploited—for example, a narrow strip of land ultimately intended as an access road—and for which the true owner had no immediate use. None of us would wish to detract from the necessity of jealous scrutiny of acts alleged to have resulted in possession being taken of such a parcel of land. Thus what have happily been called 'trivial' acts of trespass, even if repeated over many years, have never been equated with the acquisition of possession.

3.50 However, as the result of the cases we have referred to, there has now apparently been established a quite general doctrine of an implied licence from the true owner to the would-be adverse possessor permitting him to commit the acts of possession upon which he seeks to rely, without any specific factual basis for such an implication. The effect of implying such a licence is to prevent time running in favour of the adverse possessor, since time does not run in favour of a licensee. If this doctrine extends as far as it appears to have been extended by the most recent decision of the Court of Appeal[88], it amounts in, effect, to a judicial repeal of the statute. The philosophy behind this approach has been expressed by the Master of the Rolls, Lord Denning, as follows:—

> 'The reason behind the decisions is because it does not lie in that other person's mouth to assert that he used the land of his own wrong as a trespasser. Rather his user is to be ascribed to the licence or permission of the true owner'.

We, however, prefer the more traditional approach recently restated by Sir John Pennycuick, delivering the judgment of the Court of Appeal in *Treloar* v. *Nute*[89], in which he said:—

> '... if a squatter takes possession of land belonging to another and remains in possession for 12 years to the exclusion of the owner, that represents adverse possession and accordingly at the end of the 12 years the title of the owner is extinguished. That is the plain meaning of the statutory provisions ...'

3.51 It is clear that these two approaches cannot be reconciled, except on the basis that the 'implied licence' theory is an attempted rationalisation of the 'trivial acts of trespass' approach. This might have been possible with the decision in the earlier of the two cases already cited (*Wallis*): it is not possible with the decision of the latter case (*Gray* v. *Wykeham-Martin*). It is also impossible to reconcile the approaches of the Court of Appeal in those cases and in *Treloar* v. *Nute*.

3.52 We consider that the law should be restored to the law as stated in *Treloar* v. *Nute*. There can, in our view, be no justification for implying a licence, or other similar position, in any case in which there is no factual basis for such an implication. The precise formula for such a restoration is not easy, since the present law is that if the land is in the possession of some person in whose favour the period of limitation can run, then such possession is 'adverse' (Limitation Act 1939 section 10(1)) and this appears to be quite plain. We do not consider that the suggestion of the Institute—that there should be a

---

[88] *Gray* v. *Wykeham-Martin & Goode, supra.*
[89] at pp. 234–5.

presumption that possession is adverse—would really add anything to this existing provision. Accordingly, we think that it may be necessary for amending legislation expressly to provide that for the purposes of the Limitation Act 'possession' is to bear its ordinary meaning in law, so that it is not to be artificially stripped of its character of being adverse by the application of any implication or presumption not grounded upon the actual circusmtances of the case. Such a formula, whilst leaving full scope for the application of the 'trivial acts of trespass' approach, would effectively reverse the recent unsatisfactory line of cases.

Landlord and tenant

3.53 There were two aspects of limitation in the field of landlord and tenant law which appeared to us likely to require consideration and on which we therefore asked specifically for comments, namely, the *terminus a quo* relating to a claim to recover land from a tenant at will and the effect of failure to pay rent over the normal six-year period.

3.54 As the law stands, the 12 years for an action to recover land start to run in favour of a tenant at will after one year from the creation of the tenancy so that, if the landlord takes no action for 13 years from the start of the tenancy, his interest is extinguished. This result flows from section 9(1) of the Limitation Act 1939, by virtue of which a tenancy at will is deemed to have been terminated after one year from its creation, with the result that thereafter the tenant's possession is 'adverse'.

3.55 Most of those who commented on this point criticised the rule as being artificial and unduly prejudicial to lessors and it was suggested to us that a better principle would be to make the 12 years run from an actual, not a fictitious, termination of the tenancy. We agree with those who have made this suggestion. Moreover, in the light of recent authorities, the distinction between a tenancy at will and a gratuitous licence is, at the best, tenuous and the rule to which we have referred does not apply to a licensee, in whose favour time does not run as long as the licence endures[90]. We think there would be a distinct advantage in prescribing a common limitation period for these frequently indistinguishable interests and we accordingly recommend that, whether the land be occupied under a tenancy at will or under a gratuitous licence, time should not begin to run in favour of the occupier until the tenancy or licence has actually been determined.

3.56 If this recommendation is accepted, we think that as a corollary the same rule should be applied to periodical tenancies where there is no written lease. As the law stands, section 9(2) of the Limitation Act applies to these tenancies the same rule as subsection (1) applies to tenancies at will, subject to the qualification that payment of rent after the first 12 months starts time running again. If the law is changed for tenancies at will, we think a corresponding change should be made for periodical tenancies where there is no written lease and we so recomend.

3.57 We also recommend that the opportunity should be taken to bring section 9(3) of the Limitation Act up to date. Subsection (3) provides for the extinction of a lessor's title if the rent reserved by a lease in writing is paid to the 'wrong'

---

[90] *Hughes* v. *Griffin* [1969] 1 W.L.R. 23.

landlord for 12 years. This general rule, however, applies only if the rent is £1 or more. The reason for excluding very small rents is to protect the lessor where the amount is so small as not to be worth collecting, so that he is unlikely to know that it is being paid to the wrong person. The figure of £1 is by now out of date and we think a figure of £10 would be more realistic.

3.58 This change should apply, in our view, to any lease in writing which is entered into after the change in the law has taken place. If it were to apply to existing leases an injustice could be done to a lessee where the rent was between £1 and £10.

Future interests

3.59 Section 6 of the Limitation Act 1939 deals comprehensively with the accrual of a cause of action (and therefore with limitation) in respect of a future interest in land. The basic principle underlying section 6 is that time begins to run against the owner of the future interest when that interest falls into possession. This principle is subject to qualifications where the owner of the preceding interest was not in possession of the land at the time of its determination and there are special provisions in section 6 affecting Crown and Church property and entailed estates; however, for our present purposes, it is not necessary to consider these complications.

3.60 In adopting this principle, section 6 preserves the effect of the law of property as it stood before 1925. Future interests were then, in general, legal estates which could not be affected by anything which happened in relation to a preceding interest. The 1925 property legislation converted all future interests into equitable interests and vested the legal estate in the land in one or more trustees who were given exclusive powers to dispose of the land, leaving any equitable interests to subsist in the proceeds of any dispossession, and since they hold this right in trust for any beneficiaries entitled to equitable interests, it can be argued that it would have been more consistent with the 1925 policy if 12 years' adverse possession against trustees had been made effective to bar not only the trustees' legal estate but also all equitable interests in the land; any beneficiary damnified by the extinction of the legal estate would be entitled to claim damages against the trustees for their failure to protect his interests. The effect would have been to assimilate the law relating to land with that relating to investments.

3.61 This subject was mentioned very briefly by the Law Revision Committee in 1936[91]. That Committee referred to the statute law then in force[92] and recommended no change. The relevant provisions of the pre-existing law have, in substance, been reproduced by section 6 of the Limitation Act 1939. It therefore appears that there was a deliberate decision to treat the 1925 legislation as having, in this respect, changed only the form and not the substance of the law relating to future interests so that the owner of such an interest is still treated as having an interest separate and distinct from any preceding interest in the land. However, there is nothing in the report of the Law Revision Committee to show whether the point was considered.

---

[91] Cmd. 5334, para. 8.
[92] Real Property Limitation Act 1833, ss. 2 and 24.

3.62 The evidence we have received shows that there is a difference of opinion among those who have experience of the operation of section 6. On the one hand, it is argued that the present law leads to undesirably long limitation periods and to the possibility that long established possession may be upset by the falling in, after many years, of a future interest and the accrual of a cause of action to the person entitled to that interest. Those who advance this argument think it would be better if adverse possession did bar a future interest so that the beneficiary concerned would be able, not to claim the land, but to proceed against the trustees of the estate. The contrary arguments advanced by a number of those who have commented on the matter, are that, first, any departure from the current law would unduly prejudice the owners of future interest whose remedies against the trustees might be ineffective and, secondly, that trustees do not, in practice, always exercise effective supervision over the trust land and may therefore remain unaware of an encroachment.

3.63 A number of suggestions have been made to us which, while not going so far as to make time run against the beneficiary from the moment the trustee is dispossessed, would go some way towards meeting the criticism of the current law that it fails to protect long possession. One such suggestion was that time should begin to run against the beneficiary either when his interest falls into possession or when he first knows of the adverse possession having been taken, whichever is earlier. Another suggestion was that the running of time should not be suspended during the minority of the beneficiary since there is always a legal estate vested in an adult; or, alternatively, that the minor's interest, though still in remainder, should be barred six years after he attains his majority.

3.64 We have not found it easy to reach a conclusion on this controversial subject. There are persuasive arguments on either side; if the problem were confined to the encroacher who extends his boundary by a few yards only, we think there would be a definite advantage in leaving the remainderman to his remedy against the trustees and thus not upsetting possession which has been enjoyed for very many years simply because a future interest falls in long after the limitation period has run against the trustees. But the difficulty is that encroachment can extend to misappropriation far more serious than mere adjustment of a boundary; the amount of money involved could be large and the remedy against the trustees could be valueless. In the end we concluded (though with some reservations) that, in the absence of evidence that the current law causes much difficulty in practice, it would be better not to make any change. But the question is admittedly an open one on which different views may well be held.

Mortgages

3.65 Under section 18 of the Limitation Act 1939 there is a 12-year limitation period for an action to recover the principal sum secured by a mortgage and a six-year limitation period applicable to an action to recover arrears of interest. In our consultative document we asked for views on the appropriateness of these two limitation periods; we also enquired whether any of the provisions of the Limitation Act relevant to mortgages caused particular difficulty.

3.66 The response we received to our enquiries showed that there was general approval of the 12-and six-year periods. The action to recover the principal was considered by those who expressed views on the point to be analogous to a claim for the recovery of land (though section 16 applies also to mortgages of personal property), while an action to recover interest was considered to be indistinguishable from a claim to recover any other debt. We agree with these views and therefore recommend that, as long as the limitation periods applicable to actions for the recovery of land and actions for the recovery of debts remain 12 and six years respectively, the same periods should apply to actions to recover the principal and interest due under a mortgage.

3.67 The Chief Chancery Master drew our attention to one circumstance in which arrears of interest may be recoverable notwithstanding that they have not been claimed within the normal six-year period. These are the circumstances that arose in *Holmes* v. *Cowcher*[93] where Stamp, J., (as he then was) followed the earlier decision of Kindersley, V.-C. in *Edmunds* v. *Waugh*[94] where it was held that a mortgagor must, as a condition of redeeming the mortgage, pay all arrears of interest, however old. This rule enables the mortgagee to recover in redemption proceedings interest which, if claimed in a separate action, could not be recovered because of the expiration of the limitation period. As applied to redemption proceedings, we think that the rule is sound, because, in seeking to redeem the mortgage, the mortgagor, having lost his legal right, is seeking the intervention of equity to help him recover his property. It seems to us only reasonable that, as a condition of being allowed to do so, he should pay all the interest which he ought to have paid and we do not advise any statutory reversal of the rule.

3.68 In *Holmes* v. *Cowcher*, Stamp, J., was concerned with the converse rule, namely that a mortgagee who realises his security is entitled to retain out of the purchase price both the principal sum and all arrears of interest. The Chief Chancery Master has suggested to us that this rule goes a long way to rendering ineffective the six year period applicable to a claim for arrears of interest, because in practice mortgagees very rarely sue for the arrears and prefer to take possession of the property and sell. He accordingly suggested that a mortgagee who is realising his security ought not to be able to retain arrears of interest more than six years overdue. We see the force of this argument; nevertheless, we think the current rule is consistent with the general principle that a secured creditor should be able to rely on his security to recover all the money due to him, irrespective of the running of the limitation period[95].

3.69 As mentioned above, section 18 of the Limitation Act 1939 applies to mortgages of personal property. On the other hand section 12, which deals with redemption actions, is restricted to mortgages of land. We did not receive any representations about this difference, but have considered whether it is right and have borne in mind the possibility that any legislation to carry further the implementation of the Crowther Report on Consumer Credit[96] might make the use of chattel mortgages more prevalent. It seems to us, however, that the restriction of section 12 to land is justified by the different nature of real and personal property. When a mortgagee of land has been in possession of the mortgaged land for 12 years, then it seems consistent with general policy that the mortgagor should no longer be able to redeem the mortgage. Where, however,

---

[93] [1970] 1 All E.R. 1224; [1970] 1 W.L.R. 834.
[94] (1866) L.R. 1 Eq. 418.
[95] See the Report of the Law Revision Committee, Cmd. 5334, para. 24, especially at (e) (lien and equitable charge on shares).
[96] Cmnd. 4596.

there is a mortgage of securities, the mortgagee will typically be in possession of the documents of title, and may also, particularly if the mortgagee is a bank, be in receipt of the dividends pursuant to an arrangement between the parties. It seems to us that the extension of section 12 to mortgages of securities could therefore cause considerable difficulty and the Law Revision Committee's suggestion[97] that there should be no change in the law seems to us still sound.

3.70   Accordingly, we do not recommend that the law of limitation as it applies to mortgages should be in any way altered.

Land registration

3.71   The Law Commission drew our attention[98] to three points on the law of limitation in relation to registered land. Of these the first relates to rectification and the remaining two to indemnity.

(i)   *Rectification*

3.72   There is no express period of limitation for claims for rectification of the land register and we consider that no such period is required. If there is an error in the land register and the 'owner' of the land has been dispossessed of it for 12 years, then in practice the 'owner' will not be successful in attempting to have the register rectified, since his substantive right to the land itself will by then have disappeared[99] If, however, the owner of the land is still in possession, there seems to us to be no reason for denying rectification of an error relating to his title at any time: any period of limitation would either be unnecessary or else would prevent correction of a faulty register, even though the substantive right itself was still enforceable, though incorrectly registered. We also think that in cases falling between these two extremes the court has sufficient powers to prevent any injustice arising through the absence of limitation period for claims for rectification; it can refuse rectification either through the application of its statutory discretions, or through the equitable principles such as laches or acquiescence which, it seems, apply to an issue of rectification even when the question is whether effect should be given to an over-riding interest.

(ii)   *Indemnity*

3.73   The Law Commission's second and third points concern the rights conferred by the Land Registration Act 1925 to indemnity out of public funds for injury suffered through the operation of the land registration system. We have, therefore, had to consider first what sort of limitation period or periods ought to be prescribed for such claims; and, secondly, how long any such period or periods should be.

3.74   At present a claim to indemnity can arise where the register is rectified[100];

---

[97] Cmnd. 5334, para. 10.
[98] Working Paper No. 45 of July 1972, paragraph 110.
[99] By the operation of s. 75(1) of the Land Registration Act 1925.
[100] The claim arises under s. 83(1) or (4) of the Land Registration Act 1925.

or where there is an error or omission in the register which is not rectified[101]; or where there has been an administrative error which occasions loss[102].

3.75 For the first and third of these categories the present limitation period is six years from the date when the claimant knows, or but for his own default might have known, of the existence of his claim[103]. This we think is broadly right, although we think that it would be both simpler and more consistent with principle that the six-year period for the first category should run from the date of rectification rather than from the date of the claimant's knowledge.

3.76 The second category (where the register is not rectified and the claimant thus loses his title to the land in dispute) is much more difficult. The present law is contained in the very complex proviso to section 83(11) of the Land Registration Act 1925 and we are much indebted to the present Chief Land Registrar and to his predecessor for the help which they have given to us over the history and purpose of this provision. In short, leaving aside special cases (such as claims by an infant or a remainderman under a trust) the claim to indemnity is statute-barred after six years from the date of the erroneous registration, whether or not the claimant knew of the error at the time it was committed. The Law Commission thought that a period of 12 years, rather than six, running from the erroneous registration, might be appropriate, since a claim for indemnity when the register is not rectified is in some respects analogous to a claim for damages in a real property action. We think that this would represent some improvement, but that the present law contained in section 83(11) is open to the much more fundamental objection that it would deny a claim to indemnity after a period running from registration when the substantive right itself would not (but for the erroneous registration and the subsequent refusal to rectify[104]) have been lost. It seems to us that a person who loses his title because someone else's title has been wrongly entered on the register and the register is not rectified, ought not to be put in a worse position than he would have been if the land had been unregistered and that accordingly he should be fully compensated for any loss he suffers even if the error was committed more than six (or 12) years before the claim for rectification was made. A change in the law to this effect may, it is true, make it more difficult in some cases to determine whether an indemnity should be paid, since in place of the relatively simple rule providing for a fixed period from the commission of the mistake, there would be a test which depended solely on whether the error in respect of which rectification was refused was the cause of loss to the claimant; and this in turn might involve inquiring whether his title would, apart from the error, have been extinguished by adverse possession[105], a problem which has given rise to considerable difficulties in the past in the case of unregistered land (see paragraphs 3.47–3.51 above). To some extent, however, this problem is

---

[101] *ibid.* s. 83(2).

[102] Such as loss of deeds, a mistake in a search, or in an office copy, or failure to serve notice: see ss. 30, 83(3) and 113 of the Land Registration Act 1925.

[103] Land Registration Act 1925, s. 83(11) read without the proviso which is not relevant either to cases where the register is rectified (*Epps* v. *Esso Petroleum Co. Ltd* [1973] 1 W.L.R. 1071 *per* Templeman, J., at p. 1082) or to cases of administrative error.

[104] Which might have been based on the fact that the erroneously registered proprietor was in possession (s. 83(3) of the 1925 Act) even though he had not been in possession for more than a few days.

[105] See *Re Chowood's Registered Land* [1933] Ch. 574.

already to be encountered in rectification cases because the Land Registration Act 1925 relies on the concepts of 'actual occupation'[106] and a 'proprietor who is in possession[107]; and the question whether the title of a proprietor of registered land would have been extinguished by adverse possession had the land not been registered is one which may arise for decision by the registrar under the existing provisions of the Act[108]. In any event, we do not think that any argument about complication should be allowed to stand in the way of the removal of a provision which is capable of working considerable injustice[109] and which, when fully analysed, stands out as one of the very few places where it can be said that the present English system of land registration is inferior to the unregistered system which it is in course of replacing.

3.77 We therefore recommend that the proviso to section 83(11) should be repealed and replaced by a provision which would ensure that a claim for indemnity is not to be defeated by a defence of limitation except in a case where (had the land not been registered) a claim to the right itself would have been lost. In recommending the repeal of the proviso we have not lost sight of the fact that it contains special provisions[110] for claims relating to restrictive covenants: such claims should, we think in future be governed by the general principle which we favour for other refusals to rectify, as should claims in respect of other third party rights (such as easements, estate contracts or options).

3.78 Section 83(6) imposes an upper limit on the amount of indemnity payable which, in a case where the register is not rectified, is not to exceed the value of the estate, interest or charge of the claimant at the time when the error or omission which caused the loss was made. Since we consider that the date of the error or omission should be treated as irrelevant to the claimant's right to indemnity, it follows that, if any upper limit is required, it should be expressed by reference to the value (if rectification had been ordered) of the estate, interest or charge immediately before rectification is refused: and we so recommend.

3.79 This subject is complex and we think that it would help the readers of our report if we were to set out succinctly what we propose by way of a replacement for section 83(11), though we do not wish to suggest that this formulation should necessarily find its way verbatim into any Bill that may be put forward to implement our report. We suggest that section 83(11) could with advantage be reframed on the following lines:—

'83(11). A liability to pay indemnity under this Act shall be treated as a simple contract debt, and for the purpose of the law relating to limitation:—

(a) the cause of action in any case of loss suffered by reason of rectification shall be deemed to arise on the date of rectification;

(b) the cause of action in relation to a claim arising under subsection (2) of this section shall be deemed to arise on the date when the court or the registrar determines that the register is not to be rectified:

---

[106] S. 70(1)(g) (definition of overriding interest)
[107] S. 82(3) (prohibition on rectification against a proprietor in possession).
[108] See s. 75 (acquisition of title by possession).
[109] cf. Epps v. Esso Petroleum Co. Ltd., (1973) 1 W.L.R. 1071 at pp. 1081F–1082D.
[110] See exception (c) to the proviso, which prescribes a period, for claims for indemnity in respect of restrictive covenants or agreements, of six years from 'the breach'.

provided that the question whether the claimant has suffered loss by reason of the error or omission in the register in respect of which rectification is refused shall be determined on the same principles which would have been applicable if the land had been unregistered and as at the date on which he brought an action for rectification or applied to the registrar for rectification whichever is the earlier[111];

(c) the cause of action in relation to any other claim to indemnity arising under this Act shall be deemed to arise when the claimant knows, or but for his own default might have known, of the existence of his claim'.

Rentcharges

3.80 The Law Commission also invited[112] us to consider a point on rentcharges which was made in an article in *The Law Times* of 1953[113] to the effect that section 10(3) of the Limitation Act 1939 is defective. That subsection provides that for the purposes of the rule of adverse possession (that is, that no cause of action accrues unless the land is in the possession of some person in whose favour the period of limitation can run), possession of land subject to a rentcharge by a person who does not pay the rent due to the person entitled is deemed to be adverse possession of the rentcharge. It was suggested in the article that where the land is unoccupied there may be no period of limitation in respect of the rentcharge. We think however, that there is no substance in this point, since, if the land is unoccupied, it must in law be in the possession of its owner. It follows, in our view, that if the owner of the 'unoccupied' land does not pay the rentcharge there is sufficient adverse possession of the rentcharge to enable the relevant period of limitation to run against the owner of the rentcharge.

C. EQUITY

Claims by beneficiaries against trustees

3.81 The effect of section 19(1) of the Limitation Act 1939 is that limitation affords no defence to a claim brought by a beneficiary under a trust against his trustee, if the claim is made either—

(a) in respect of fraud, or a fraudulent breach of trust, on the part of the trustee; or

(b) to recover trust property (or its proceeds) in the hands of the trustee.

Subject to these exceptions, the normal six-year period applies to claims in respect of a breach of trust or to recover trust property from third parties[114].

3.82 In our consultative document, we sought views on the question whether there should be any limitation period applicable to the claims mentioned in

---

[111] The need to specify alternative dates arises from the fact that an application for rectification may be made to the Court or to the registrar (s. 82(1)); and time ought to stop running against the claimant when the application is made in either case, whether or not he applies for indemnity in the alternative.

[112] In their Working Paper No. 49 of April 1973, para. 113.

[113] H.E. Easton in (1953) 215 L.T. 106.

[114] Limitation Act 1939, s. 19(2).

paragraph 3.81(*a*) and (*b*) above and, if so, what the length of such period should be. All of those who submitted evidence on this matter were opposed to the imposition of any statutory limitation period on claims based on the trustee's fraud, a view with which we agree. There was, however, some difference of opinion about claims to recover trust property (or its proceeds) in the hands of an honest trustee. It was proposed by some that such a trustee should have the benefit of the normal six-year period and thus be treated in the same way as an honest third party into whose hands the property had come. However, the majority (including the Bar Council and The Law Society) were opposed to any change in the law, largely on the ground that the equitable doctrines of laches and acquiescence already afford sufficient protection to a trustee whose beneficiary has had, but has not availed himself of, an adequate opportunity to recover the trust property or its proceeds.

3.83 On this issue we agree with the majority and we do not, therefore, recommend any change in the general rules embodied in section 19(1) and (2) of the Limitation Act. There is, however, a particular case in which those provisions can, in our opinion, operate unfairly against a trustee and which calls for an amendment to the law. This is the case of the trustee who, in good faith, distributes the trust property among all those whom he reasonably believes to constitute the class of beneficiaries entitled to it, including himself. As the law stands, a 'late-comer' who appears after six years from the distribution can recover his share out of what the trustee took, but nothing from any of the other beneficiaries, who are protected by the Limitation Act. The trustee's liability is not limited to the contribution he would have had to make had the late-comer's claim been instituted in time to bring in the other beneficiaries: the trustee is liable to the whole of the extent of the new-comer's share (up to the amount of what he paid to himself) and he will not be able to recover anything from the other beneficiaries, because they can raise against him a defence of limitation.

3.84 We do not consider that this is a satisfactory result. It is true that the doctrines of laches and acquiescence apply to a claim by a late-comer in these circumstances, but they are not likely to provide an effective defence against a beneficiary who was genuinely unaware that he had any rights under the trust. In our view, a trustee/beneficiary who has acted prudently and honestly in distributing the trust property should be in no worse position as the result of a claim by a late-comer than he would have been if the late-comer had been included in the original distribution. Accordingly, we propose that section 19 of the Limitation Act should be amended[115] so as to enable a trustee/beneficiary, in the circumstances described above, to rely on a defence of limitation, save in respect of the share of trust property which he would have had to pay to the late-comer had all the beneficiaries, including himself, been sued in time. For example, if the trustee has distributed one-third of the trust property to himself and one-third to each of two other beneficiaries in ignorance of the existence of a fourth, he should be liable to pay to the newcomer only the difference between the one-third share he has taken and the one-quarter share which was truly his; the trustee would thus be liable for only one-twelfth of trust property, not (as he now is) for one-quarter.

---

[115] A consequential amendment to s. 27(2)(*a*) of the Trustee Act 1925 may be necessary.

Personal representatives

3.85 In our consultative document we sought views on the rule under which the running of time is suspended in relation to a debtor who becomes the administrator of his creditor, but not in relation to the debtor who becomes executor of his creditor or the creditor who becomes either executor or administrator of his debtor.

3.86 The rule governing a debtor/administrator, known as the rule in *Seagram* v. *Knight*[116], provides one of the very few examples of an exception to the fundamental principle that once time begins to run it continues to run whatever may happen[117]. The explanation of the rule, and the difference between the treatment afforded by the law to the debtor/administrator and the debtor/ executor, is historical. At common law, the right of action for debt was suspended when the debtor became the executor of the creditor's estate (he could not sue himself) and since the rule was that the suspension of a personal action as a result of the voluntary act of the creditor prevented the revival of the action, the effect was that the creditor, by appointing the debtor to be his executor, extinguished the debt when that appointment became effective on the creditor's death[118]. But the appointment of an administrator of the creditor's estate was not the voluntary act of the creditor and therefore fell outside the rule barring revival of the action. The debt was therefore not extinguished, but was suspended for the duration of the administration.

3.87 In the case of the debtor/executor, the extinction of the debt prevented any question of limitation arising and in the event equity intervened by treating him as if he had paid the debt to himself, so that he became accountable for the amount of the debt as being an asset of the estate[119]. Thus, equity effectively overrode the common law rule that the right to claim the debt was suspended. However, equity did not intervene in the case of the debtor/administrator, whose liability was merely suspended during the period of administration; the solution adopted was to suspend the limitation period so long as the action itself was suspended.

3.88 From this it will be seen that suspension of the limitation period in the case of the debtor/administrator is derived from the substantive rule of law that, since he (like the debtor/executor) cannot sue himself, the action for the recovery of the debt is suspended. Consequently, the apparent anomaly in the law of limitation is really a matter of substance and cannot be cured without an amendment to the substantive law.

3.89 Those who commented on the rule in *Seagram* v. *Knight* were virtually unanimously in favour of abolishing the distinction between the debtor/ administrator and the debtor/executor. We agree that the distinction is anomalous and, although for the reasons we have given this anomaly cannot be cured without

---

[116] (1867) L.R. 2 Ch. 628.
[117] *Re Bencom* [1914] 2 Ch. 68, at p. 76, *Halsbury's Laws of England* (3rd ed. vol. 24, paras. 352 and 353) mentions a number of other situations in which the running of time may be suspended, the only one of any practical importance being the rule that, in bankruptcy, time ceases to run in respect of provable debts during the currency of the bankruptcy proceedings.
[118] *Nedham's case*: (1610) 8 Co. Rep. 135a.
[119] *Re Greg* [1921] 2 Ch., 243.

an amendment to the substantive law (which, strictly speaking, falls outside our terms of reference), the question is so closely connected with the law of limitation that we have felt it right to make a positive recommendation on the point.

3.90 There are, in our view, two possible ways in which the anomaly could be cured. First, the substantive law could be changed so that, on appointment as administrator to his creditor's estate, the debtor became accountable to the estate for the amount of the debt in the same way as does an executor under the equitable rule to which we have referred. If the law were changed in this way, then, as a corollary, there would be no occasion to suspend the running of time in relation to the debtor. Alternatively, the law could provide that the running of time was suspended whenever a personal representative (whether executor or administrator) was either the creditor or the debtor of the estate. This would in effect, extend the rule in *Seagram* v. *Knight* to any case where a debtor or creditor becomes personal representative.

3.91 The first solution to the problem has the advantage that it makes for simplicity in the law by removing one of the very few exceptions to the general rule that the running of time is not suspended by subsequent events. The advantage of the second solution is that it would remove any possibility of prejudice to a creditor who, for one reason or another, ceased to be personal representative before having completed the administration of the estate but after the period of limitation had run against him, with the result that his claim against the estate became statute-barred before he could pay himself. On the other hand, this proposal would mean introducing yet further exceptions to the general rule referred to above.

3.92 On balance, we think that the better course would be to make the debtor/administrator accountable to the estate for the amount of his debt and to reverse the rule in *Seagram* v. *Knight*. We realise that this solution would not assist the creditor in the circumstances mentioned in the last paragraph, but we think that this particular difficulty is, unlikely to arise often in practice, and the possibility of its doing so does not, in our view, justify a further complication to the law.

3.93 Accordingly, we recommend that the running of time should not be suspended in favour of a debtor who becomes administrator to his creditor's estate but that he should, in the same way as an executor, be required to account to that estate for the amount of the debt.

Equitable remedies

3.94 In our consultative document we sought views on two questions relating to equitable relief:—

(a) whether the power of the court to refuse relief on the ground of 'acquiescence' or 'laches' should be retained and, if so, extended to other forms of relief; and

(b) whether there should be a short, statutory, limitation period applicable to certain forms of equitable relief, such as specific performance and injunction.

3.95 Section 29 of the Limitation Act provides expressly that the Act is not to affect any 'equitable jurisdiction to refuse relief on the ground of acquiescence or otherwise'. This provision has generally been held to preserve the power of the court to refuse relief on the ground of delay on the part of the plaintiff, usually termed 'laches'.

3.96 On the authorities, a party can lose his remedy if he either stands by and does nothing while his rights are, to his knowledge, being violated, or if, on learning of a violation of his rights which has already taken place, he so conducts himself that it would be inequitable thereafter to permit him to enforce those rights. 'Acquiescence' may connote either of these forms of conduct and delay ('laches') in asserting his rights may be an element in the plaintiff's acquiescence, particularly in the second sense of that term. Laches may also serve to bar a plaintiff from enforcing a right arising only in equity where there is no statutory limitation period, or from obtaining an equitable remedy to enforce a legal right.

3.97 'Acquiescence' in either of the senses referred to above is a defence distinct from, and independent of, limitation and its operation is not confined to equitable relief. This point was made by Lord Cranworth, L.C., in *Ramsden* v. *Dyson*[120], where he made it clear that acquiescence could prevent an owner of land establishing his legal title after having stood by while a stranger was building on that land. There is, therefore, no need for us to consider whether the doctrine of acquiescence should be extended to forms of relief other than equitable remedies, since it can already be invoked notwithstanding that the relief sought takes the form of a remedy available at common law; nor have we received any evidence to suggest that there would be any advantage in discarding the doctrine of acquiescence, or in restricting its scope.

3.98 Laches, in the sense of delay, though not amounting to acquiescence, may be a ground for refusing relief in either of two cases; first, where a cause of action arises only in equity and there is no limitation period, relief may be refused if the party seeking to enforce his remedy has delayed unreasonably in doing so. Within this class of case there may fall a claim in respect of breach of trust; proceedings to set aside a sale of property on the grounds of undue influence; a claim to redeem a mortgage of personality; a claim to rescind or rectify a contract; and other similar proceedings. The doctrine of laches is also relevant where the cause of action arises at common law, but where equity affords a more effective remedy than does the law. Specific performance of a contract, and the grant of an injunction to restrain a party from repeating a legal injury, are obvious examples of such equitable remedies.

3.99 Our examination of the decided cases has led us to the conclusion that it would be neither practicable nor desirable to replace the doctrine of laches by one or more fixed statutory periods of limitation in either of these categories of case. One common feature is that, in deciding whether or not laches has cost the plaintiff his remedy against the defendant, the court has to look at the position of both parties, because the possible unfairness to the defendant is a very relevant factor: it plays a larger part in most of the situations where laches operates than where the remedy sought is the payment of money in the form of damages for breach of contract or for tort. The reason for this is that the equitable relief claimed often involves the transfer of title to, or some alteration to the defendant's rights in, property. Obviously, the manner in which the

---

[120] 1866 L.R. 1 H.L. 129 at p. 140.

defendant has dealt with the property in the interval is relevant if justice is to be done. The circumstances are, therefore, almost infinitely variable and to substitute one or more fixed periods must involve loss of flexibility. We do not see that any advantage would accrue from such an alteration in the law. Moreover, we have had no evidence to suggest that such a change would be beneficial. Indeed, the only major change suggested by any of those who submitted evidence to us was that, far from abolishing the flexible doctrine of laches, the law should get rid of all fixed statutory limitation periods and let that doctrine operate in every case. However, such a radical change would, in our view, serve to defeat one of the main objects of the law (to which we have referred in paragraph 1.7, above), and we do not regard it as acceptable.

3.100 For the reasons given above, we do not recommend any change in the law relating to acquiescence or laches. We have, however, considered specifically the suggestion canvassed in our consultative document that there should be a statutory limitation period (necessarily shorter than the standard six-year period) after which certain equitable remedies (notably specific performance and injunction) should not be obtainable. We are satisfied that this would be a mistake. In the first place, it is by no means uncommon for parties deliberately to contract for the sale of land with the intention of postponing (often for a period of years) the execution of a formal conveyance. It would defeat the intention of both sides if, after the lapse of a comparatively short time, the purchaser (who might well have been in possession during the interval) should be unable to obtain a good legal title to the property. Moreover, while the law already requires a party seeking specific performance to act with reasonable diligence, what will be reasonable diligence varies very much with the nature of the subject matter of the contract. For example, if it is a wasting asset (such as a short leasehold), a comparatively short period of delay before seeking specific performance may be unreasonably long, while a much longer delay may be reasonable in the case of a plaintiff who is the purchaser of a freehold estate. As far as injunctions are concerned, it would hardly be acceptable that a plaintiff should be barred from seeking a final injunction in support of a legal right at any stage before the existence of that right has been established by action: so long as his cause of action is not barred by lapse of time, there seems no reason why his most effective remedy should not remain open. On the other hand, delay in seeking an interlocutory injunction may be very relevant, because, if the party has for a long time submitted to the alleged infringement of his rights, there are grounds for supposing that the infringement is not irreparable and that he will not be seriously damnified if no injunction is granted until the substantive claim has been tried. As in the case of laches, the circumstances are variable and the court has, when deciding whether or not to exercise its discretion to grant an injunction, to weigh the circumstances of both parties. A fixed period would mean the loss of that measure of flexibility which, in our view, is essential if the court is to do justice.

3.101 There is, however, one rather unusual situation in which we think there might be some advantage if a discretionary power to refuse relief on the grounds of delay were superseded by an express statutory limitation period. This situation arises where a lessor, relying on a forfeiture clause in the lease, re-enters the demised premises peaceably (that is otherwise than in pursuance of a court order) on the grounds that the rent has not been paid and subsequently the lessee wishes to claim relief. Under section 210 of the Common Law Procedure Act 1852, there is a six-month period within which relief may be claimed if the

Part IV

MISCELLANEOUS

Admiralty

4.1 A number of those who gave evidence to us, including Mr. Justice Brandon, the Admiralty Judge, suggested that we should include Admiralty in our review of the law of limitation. Since this is a branch of the law where specialist knowledge is particularly important, and since our invitation to interested bodies and individuals and to members of the public (referred to in paragraph 1.2., above) did not include any material relating specifically to Admiralty proceedings, we decided to issue to those immediately concerned a supplementary request for views on a number of criticisms about the law of Admiralty which has been made to us. A list of those who responded to this further request for comments appears in Part C of Annex 1 to this Report and we are very grateful to those who submitted memoranda to us.

4.2 The points which, we were informed, had caused some difficulty in practice, and on which accordingly we particularly asked for assistance, were as follows:—

(a) there is doubt about the true construction of section 2(6) of the Limitation Act 1939, which excludes from the Act certain Admiralty proceedings;

(b) that subsection, on any view, leaves a wide field of Admiralty proceedings subject to no statutory period of limitation;

(c) the Maritime Conventions Act 1911 (which imposes a two year limitation period for actions for damages caused by the fault of any vessel and in respect of salvage services) entitles a plaintiff to an extension of that two year period if he could not have arrested the defendant vessel; this provision is arguably out of date as a result of the introduction in 1956 of the rights to found jurisdiction by arresting a sister ship;

(d) the 1911 Act (which also permits a discretionary extension of the two year period in any case) applies to personal injury cases where a vessel is at fault, and thus differs from the amendments made to the Limitation Act 1939 by the Limitation Act 1975 in three respects (the initial period is two years, not three; there is no right to an extension based upon a date of knowledge; the guidelines contained in section 2D of the 1939 Act do not apply to the discretionary extension);

(e) section 28 of the 1939 Act (which provides that any claim by way of set-off or counter-claim is deemed to be a separate action commenced on the same date as the main action) does not apply to Admiralty proceedings whether or not they are governed by the 1911 Act or by the Carriage of Goods by Sea Act 1924 (section 32 of the 1939 Act).

4.3 Those who responded to our request for assistance were generally agreed that there was doubt as to whether section 2(6) of the 1939 Act was apt to exclude from the Act all Admiralty proceedings which were capable of being enforced *in rem*, or only proceedings in which the plaintiff seeks to enforce his right by proceeding *in rem*. There was also general agreement that this doubt should be cleared up; since, however, there was also general agreement that section 2(6) of the 1939 Act was no longer justifiable in principle, it is not necessary for us to go further into the resolution of the doubt.

4.4 Section 2(6) of the Limitation Act 1939 provides that except for an action to recover seamen's wages, section 2 of the 1939 Act (which provides the standard limitation period for actions in contract, tort, etc.) is not to apply to any cause of action within the Admiralty jurisdiction of the High Court which is enforceable *in rem*. An analogous provision in section 18(6) provides that section 18, which deals with limitation periods in respect of mortgages and charges, is not to apply to any mortgage or charge on a ship. Section 2(6) restated the previous law on the subject[122]. Our consultation showed, however, that there is no good reason for the retention of this exception from the normal rules of limitation. Indeed, it may well be that the reason for the exception is no more than that the Statutes of Limitation were originally drafted in terms of the common law forms of action. We doubt whether abolition of the exception would create any difficulties in practice, and those whom we consulted were generally agreed that it would be desirable to apply the general law to Admiralty proceedings, whether *in personam* or *in rem*. One memorandum submitted to us suggested that there should be, for Admiralty proceedings, a short period coupled with a discretion to extend it in proper cases, but since the tenor of our evidence is that there is nothing particular about Admiralty proceedings which distinguishes them, for limitation purposes, from other proceedings, we consider that we would not be justified in recommending a discretionary approach for Admiralty proceedings when we do not favour such an approach in general[123]. The Admiralty Solicitors Group suggested that application of the normal rules of limitation could cause difficulty in the case of a mortgage of a ship, but it seems to us that the period of 12 years provided for by section 18 of the 1939 Act should suffice.

4.5 We therefore recommend that the 1939 Act should be amended so as to repeal the specific exceptions for Admiralty matters.

4.6 The point mentioned at paragraph 4.2(*c*) above concerning sister ships proved to be a contentious matter, on which the majority of those consulted considered that the better solution was to leave the Maritime Conventions Act 1911 alone in this respect. In practice, difficulties are already encountered over the identity of sister ships, and further problems could result if it were necessary to determine whether there had been a reasonable opportunity to arrest a sister-ship and whether she had sufficient value. We have, therefore, decided not to make any recommendation on the point, but we suggest that this point might deserve further consideration in any future review of the law relating to Admiralty which might be conducted by a body better qualified than ourselves.

4.7 It did, however, appear that there was substantial support for the other point concerning the Maritime Conventions Act 1911, namely that, within the limits permitted by the two Brussels Conventions which that Act enabled the United Kingdom to ratify, the limitation period applicable to actions for personal injuries under that Act should be assimilated to the sections recently inserted by Parliament into the Limitation Act 1939. As we understand it, it would not

---

[122] See the Kong Magnus [1891] P. 223, at p. 228, *per* Sir James Hannen, P., and in respect of seamen's wages, the Statute 4 and 5 Anne, c. 16, ss. 17 and 18.
[123] See paras. 2.31 to 2.36, above.

be permissible simply to enlarge the initial period from two years to three, but both Conventions permit extension of the initial period in accordance with domestic law[124]. It would, therefore be possible to build into the 1911 Act an extension of time as of right based upon a date of knowledge, and the guidelines in the 1939 Act for the exercise of the discretion to extend beyond that period. We recommend that this should be done.

4.8 Our last suggestion was that the rule relating to counter-claims in section 29 of the Limitation Act 1939 should be applied to all Admiralty proceedings, so that the limitation period for a counter-claim should start from the same date as that for the original action. It was suggested to us that this could cause difficulties to a defendant in a foreign jurisdiction, since the foreign court might take the view that it should decline to accept jurisdiction on the basis of an arrest by the person who is the defendant in the English proceedings. It was suggested that the foreign court might do this because in English law the arresting person has a counter-claim and that counter-claim is deemed to have been commenced on the same date as the original action. Further examination has, however, led us to conclude that this is not a real difficulty, since section 28 of the 1939 Act relates only to counter-claims that are in fact pleaded. We therefore recommend that section 28 of the 1939 Act should be extended to Admiralty proceedings.

Arbitration

4.9 We did not ask any specific questions about the law of limitation as it affects arbitration, and none of those who were kind enough to assist us in our examination raised any particular point of difficulty. Indeed, the provisions of section 27 of the Limitation Act 1939 (which apply the Act to arbitrations and deal with other matters such as the *terminus a quo* where there is a *Scott* v. *Avery* clause) appear to have attracted little or no case law. We have, however, noted that the learned editor of Halsbury's *Laws of England* takes the view[125] that section 27(5) of the Limitation Act 1939 has inadvertently altered the previous wording in section 16(7) of the Arbitration Act 1934 by omitting the word 'agreement' after the word 'arbitration' where it appears second in the subsection. The effect of the change 'may be that the power to adjust the time limits as between the parties which is conferred by the subsection arguably arises (under the 1939 Act) only where the High Court orders that an award be set aside, or orders that the *arbitration* shall cease to have effect. Since the normal form of order is to set aside the arbitration agreement as a whole, it may be that the subsection would now be more restrictively construed than was intended in 1934. We recommend that this anomaly be removed.

4.10 We did receive some evidence on section 27 of the Arbitration Act 1950, which enables the court to extend any time provided for by an agreement for the taking of steps to commence arbitration proceedings. This discretion which is based on 'undue hardship', was at one time restrictively construed, but a more liberal interpretation was applied to it in *Liberian Shipping Corporation*

---

[124] The 1910 Brussels Collision Convention, Art. 7 and the 1910 Brussels Salvage Convention, Art. 7.

[125] 4th Ed., vol. 2, para. 517.

v. *A. King & Sons*[126] in 1967. That authority has been followed ever since and, so far as we know, it is thought to be satisfactory by all those most closely concerned.

4.11 Accordingly, we make no recommendation concerning the law of arbitration except for the correction of what we think must have been a mistake in section 27 of the 1939 Act.

Action on a judgment

4.12 By virtue of section 2(4) of the Limitation Act 1939, the limitation period in respect of an action on a judgment is 12 years; only six years arrears of interest due on a judgment may be recovered. The subsection applies only to an action on a judgment obtained in England and Wales; the period for suing on a foreign judgment is six years, since such a claim is in the nature of a simple contract debt.

4.13 Until 1852, an action on a judgment was the simplest way in which a judgment creditor could recover his money after a year and a day had elapsed since the judgment; and a judgment was, until 1864, chargeable *per se* on, and payable out of, the proceeds of sale of real property. In view of this latter rule, it is understandable that the period for an action on a judgment has since 1833 been the same as that for an action relating to land. Actions on a judgment are, however, nowadays very rare indeed[127] and we do not think that the special provision for judgments should be preserved.

4.14 The authorities[128] show that section 2(4) has caused difficulties in practice, because it has been held apt to bar certain (though not all) forms of execution. We think that the law of limitation of actions ought not to interfere with the rules in relation to execution, which currently provide[129] for a period for issue of a writ of execution of six years, which may be extended with the leave of the court. We think that provisions of this kind are the appropriate method of dealing with execution and that they could, if necessary, be extended to cover those methods of execution which, because they are not caught by the current rule, are subject to the twelve-year period.

4.15 If these recommendations are accepted, there will in future rarely be any advantage in attempting to enforce a judgment by means of a fresh action, since the period for execution itself will be at least as long as that for the further action. It would, however, possibly be to a judgment creditor's advantage to sue on the judgment so as to give himself a fresh limitation period (running from the judgment in the new action), since he would not then be dependent on the exercise of the court's discretion to extend the time for enforcing the earlier judgment by execution. But such a situation would not often occur and,

---

[126] [1967] 2 Q.B. 86 (C.A.).
[127] The courts have held that an action on a judgment can be an abuse of the process of the court if there is another way of obtaining satisfaction: *Pritchett* v. *English and Colonial Syndicate* [1897] 2 Q.B. 428.
[128] *Lamb (W.T.) and Sons* v. *Rider* [1948] 2 K.B. 331; *Lougher* v. *Donovan* [1948] 2 All E.R. 11; *Mills* v. *Allen* [1953] 2 All E.R. 534.
[129] R.S.C., O.46, r. 2(1); in the County Court leave is required to issue execution more than two years after judgment: County Court Rules O. 25, r. 16.

in any event, the possibility of its occurrence cannot justify retention of the special 12-year period.

4.16 Accordingly, we recommend that the special 12-year period for an action on a judgment should be abolished and that the normal six-year period should apply instead.

APPENDIX 6

Part V

PROCEDURE

General

5.1 Questions of limitations are likely to arise in connection with procedure when it is sought to alter the character or scope of an action and the alteration is sought after a relevant limitation period has expired. Apart from claims between joint tortfeasors, catered for by the statutory provisions referred to in paragraphs 3.31 to 3.36 above, the evidence we have received suggests that limitation is likely to raise difficult questions in connection with:—

(*a*) the institution of third party proceedings;

(*b*) the amendment of a claim for the purpose of adding a new cause of action;

(*c*) the amendment of a writ for the purpose of altering the capacity in which a party sues or of joining a new party as plaintiff or defendant.

Third party proceedings

5.2 We use the term 'third party proceedings' to denote all those proceedings in an action which have the effect of instituting a claim by or against a person other than the original plaintiff or defendant. As the Senior Master has observed (in a memorandum from which we have derived much assistance) the number of proceedings which can be covered by the concept is large. It includes, for example (apart from the ordinary third party claims):—

(1) claim, question or issue by plaintiff against third party arising out of counterclaim by defendant against plaintiff;

(2) counterclaims by defendant against plaintiff and an added party (that is a person not originally a party brought in by the defendant in his counterclaim);

(3) counterclaim by added party against defendant;

(4) claim, question or issue by added party against plaintiff;

(5) claim (for example, contribution or indemnity), question or issue by defendant against co-defendant;

(6) claim, question or issue by defendant against third party (that is the person not originally a party brought in by the defendant in the separate proceedings);

(7) counterclaim by third party against defendant;

(8) claim, question or issue by third party against plaintiff;

(9) claim, question or issue by third party against fourth party and so on in respect of subsequent parties.

The essential features of these proceedings are that a party who is being sued is trying to 'off-load' the whole or part of his liability on to someone else against whom he himself has (or claims to have) a cause of action and that rules of court permit him to do so without requiring him to institute separate proceedings. The objects of these rules are to prevent multiplicity of actions; to enable the court to settle in one action all the disputes between the various parties; and to prevent the same issue being litigated more than once with, perhaps, different results[130]. It is, however, clear that the form of the proceedings does not affect the substantive rights of the parties.

5.3 The difficulty to which limitation gives rise in this context is simply stated: if the plaintiff (P) issues his writ against the defendant (D) at a time when D's cause of action against the third party (TP) is already, or is on the point of being, statute-barred, D may have no opportunity of obtaining from TP the relief to which he is, on the merits, entitled. As far as claims for contribution between tortfeasors are concerned, this difficulty has been dealt with by the statutory provisions referred to above[131]. We are here concerned only with those third party proceedings which do not fall within those provisions and which are instituted in circumstances where, were D to sue TP in a separate action, TP could beyond doubt rely on a defence of limitation. The problem we have had to consider is whether D should nevertheless be able to defeat such a defence because his claim against TP is one which the rules of procedure allow him to make in an existing action.

5.4 The evidence we have received suggests that, on occasion, the operation of the Limitation Act may cause hardship to D, whose defence against P's claim is weak and whose own claim against TP is met by a defence of limitation. We have, therefore, considered whether the present law should be altered in D's favour. There seemed to us to be two possible approaches:—

(a) any party wishing to start third party proceedings might be given a relatively short period in which to do so, running from the service on himself of the original proceedings; or

(b) all third party proceedings in the action might be treated as having been instituted on the date on which the writ in the original action was issued.

5.5 If the former solution were adopted, the law might provide, for example, that irrespective of when D's cause of action against TP accrued, D would always have six months from service on him of P's writ in which to start proceedings against TP, provided that his claim against TP fell within the relevant 'third-party' rules of court. This solution is at first sight attractive and would have the merit of inducing D to start proceedings against TP without delay. However, apart from the question of principle (whether in any circumstances it is right for TP to lose the protection of the Limitation Act simply because P has chosen to start an action against D and the rules allow D to claim against TP in that action) the solution proposed raises practical difficulties stemming from the fact that D's cause of action against TP may be subject to a limitation period different from that applicable to P's claim against D. Three examples may be given:—

(a) A contract for the sale of goods by TP to D contains a term (not affected by the Supply of Goods (Implied Terms) Act 1973) limiting to two years the period within which any claim in respect of the goods may be instituted by D. D resells the goods to P under a contract which contains no such term. If, four years later, P sues D in respect

---

[130] *Standard Securities Ltd.* v. *Hubbard* [1967] Ch. 1056, 1 p. 1059. *per* Pennycuick, J.
[131] Para. 3.31, above.

of defects in the goods, is D to be able to claim over against TP in spite of the terms of their contract?

(b) there is a main contract between P, the owner of land, and D, a builder, for the erection of a building on P's land. TP is a sub-contractor who supplies some of the material of which the building is made. The main contract is executed under seal (importing a 12-year limitation period) but the sub-contract is not. Ten years after the building is erected. P sues D for breach of the main contract; is D to be able to claim over against TP[132]?

(c) TP, a solicitor, acts for D on the purchase of land, the title to which is defective. Ten years later P claims the land from D under a superior title. Is D to be able to sue TP for negligence in connection with the purchase, notwithstanding that the limitation period (six years) applicable to such a claim has expired?

5.6 It is not difficult to find other examples where, because of some special feature affecting one of the relevant causes of action (particularly one arising from contract) it would be unreasonable for TP not to be able to raise the defence of limitation against a claim by D. Moreover, though we have not gone into this in detail, we think it likely that, particularly in the context of building and analogous contracts, a change in the law on the lines canvassed above could raise insurance problems.

5.7 The second solution (whereby the issue of P's writ would be the *terminus ad quem* for all third party proceedings) has been proposed to us by the Senior Master. The precedent suggested is section 28 of the Limitation Act 1939, which makes the issue of P's writ the *terminus ad quem* for D's counterclaim, a provision which is evidently just and necessary: without it, P could, by timing his writ carefully, deprive D of an effective answer to his claim. Admittedly, there is not the same justification for applying such a provision to third party proceedings because, unlike P, TP has not started the litigation and has not, therefore, brought upon himself the possibility of being sued.

5.8 There are advantages in Master Jacob's proposal, which have caused us to look at it with much sympathy. In the first place, it has the merit (assuming always that 'third party proceedings' can be suitably defined) of simplicity. Secondly, in a straightforward case involving only P, D, and TP, TP would be prejudiced only if the limitation period, as between D and himself, expired between the issue of P's writ and the issue of D's third party notice. Thirdly, if D wished to issue his third party notice *after* delivery of defence, he would require the leave of the court and the court could then use its discretion so as to avoid unfairness to TP (though most third party notices are in practice issued *before* delivery of defence, when no leave is required: R.S.C. Order 16, rule 1(2)).

5.9 We were at first much attracted by Master Jacob's proposal as providing an acceptable solution to the problem posed by late claims involving third party proceedings. However, on further examination, we found that it was capable

---

[132] The draft Bill annexed to the Law Commission's *Report on Contribution* (Law Com. No. 79), which would preclude TP from relying on a 'time-clause' as a defence to a claim by D for contribution, does not apply to a case of successive sales, or of sub-contracts.

of producing results no less capricious than those which the current law can produce. That this is so can be illustrated by an example of a 'string-contract' for the sale of goods. The following set of facts will serve:—

1st June 1970	W sells 1,000 tons of defective steel to X
1st September 1970	X sells 500 tons to Y
1st December 1970	Y sells 100 tons to Z
1st August 1976	Z sues Y
1st October 1976	Y issues Third Party notice against X
1st November 1976	X issues Fourth Party notice against W

If the *terminus ad quem* for all proceedings were 1st August 1976 (the date of the issue of Z's writ) Y's claim against X would be in time, but X's claim against W would not. So the ultimate loss would fall on X, irrespective of his knowledge of the likelihood of proceedings being brought or of his own degree of fault (W, who is mostly likely to be the one at fault, will have a good defence of limitation). Moreover, there would remain the question whether 1st August 1976 was the *terminus ad quem* only in respect of claims relating to 100 tons of defective steel (the quantity sold to Z) or to 500 tons (the quantity sold to Y). If the former, a distinction would have to be drawn between a narrower class of third party proceedings, for which the issue of the writ was the *terminus ad quem*, and a wider class, which was available where no question of limitation arose. If the latter, it is difficult to see any justification for enabling D to enforce against TP a claim which is not only *prima facie* statute-barred, but which also extends beyond the subject matter of P's claim against D. Our conclusion is that Master Jacob's proposal, though it has some advantages, would create as many problems as it would solve.

5.10 As already stated (in paragraph 5.4 above), we recognise that the current law is capable of causing hardship in the context of third party proceedings and we do not think that the criticisms that have been levelled against it are altogether met by the argument that D can issue a 'protective writ' against TP. In the first place, D will not always know in time that he is likely to be sued by P; in the second place, someone against whom there lies a potential claim does not usually consult his legal adviser, let alone start proceedings which may prove to be unnecessary, until the threat becomes a reality (though it is fair to say that in most cases the issue of a writ is preceded by negotiations and therefore does not take D wholly by surprise). We do, therefore, recognise that this argument (that in practice no hardship need be caused if D is alert) is by no means decisive. On the other hand, we are satisfied that neither of the two alternative approaches discussed above would avoid hard cases and each would cause substantive rights to depend on the procedural issue, whether D's claim against TP fell within the 'third-party' rules or required the institution of a separate action. Moreover, we are not convinced that the present law often causes hardship. That it *can* do so, as can limitation in other cases, must be admitted; we have had some evidence to show that, on occasion, it does, but we have no evidence to show that this is a frequent occurrence nor does our own experience suggest that this is so. As a result, we do not feel justified in recommending a change which would amount to no more than 'tinkering' and which might (as the examples we have given suggest) give rise to at least as many anomalies as does the current law. We therefore recommend that the law should be left as it is.

5.11 There is one minor point on section 28 of the Limitation Act 1939 to which Master Jacob has drawn our attention. The section operates on a counter-claim which is 'pleaded'; under R.S.C. Order 28, rule 7, a counterclaim can be made in an originating summons procedure without being, in the strict sense of the term, 'pleaded'. If there is any doubt whether section 28 applies to this form of procedure, we think that doubt should be resolved.

Amendment to add a new cause of action

5.12 Under R.S.C. Order 20, rule 5, an amendment to a party's pleadings may be allowed after the limitation period has expired, notwithstanding that it adds a new cause of action, if that cause—

'arises out of the same facts or substantially the same facts as a cause of action in respect of which relief has already been claimed in the action'.

The Senior Master, who has suggested to us that the discretion of the court to allow an amendment of pleadings should be stated much more widely than it now is, has helpfully drawn our attention to the terminology used in Rule 15(c) of the American Federal Rules of Procedure, under which a new cause of action may be added by amendment if—

'it arises out of the conduct, transaction or occurrence of events set forth or attempted to be set forth in the original proceedings.'

We have considered whether some such words as these might be preferable to those used in the existing R.S.C; but we doubt whether they add anything to the rule we have quoted above. The object of any such rule must, as we see it, be twofold. First, it ought to permit a plaintiff to amend his pleadings so as to make good the error of failing to tell the complete legal story at the outset. Secondly, it ought to be drawn sufficiently narrowly so as to prevent the plaintiff from instituting, under the guise of an amendment to an existing claim and after the limitation period has run, proceedings which are wholly distinct from those covered by the writ as originally framed. On the whole, we think that the existing rule achieves this object and goes as far in giving the court a discretion as the substantive law does, or should, permit. The American formula is probably consistent with our own substantive law, but we doubt whether its adoption would make any practical difference; nor do we think it is intrinsically superior to the existing words of the R.S.C.

Amendment to change capacity of a party

5.13 We are once more indebted to Master Jacob for having drawn to our attention two matters which deserve consideration. First, the Proceedings Against Estates Act 1970 has left a *lacuna* in the law insofar as it does not cover the case where a grant of probate or administration is, unknown to the plaintiff, taken out and the plaintiff subsequently sues the deceased. If the plaintiff does not discover the mistake until after the limitation period has expired, he cannot retrieve his position. We agree with Master Jacob that this is a defect in the law; we have, however, not felt it necessary to look into the matter further, because we understand that the current Administration of Justice Bill deals with it already. The converse case of proceedings issued in the name of a plaintiff who has died raises different issues which are not only issues of limitation. These, we understand, are being considered by the Lord Chancellor and we do not find it necessary to make any recommendation.

5.14 The second case arises when it is sought to alter the capacity of a party so that he can sue as administrator of a deceased person's estate. R.S.C. Order 20, rule 5 enables the court to allow a 'post-limitation' amendment to alter the capacity of a party who is also an *executor*, because the executor's title relates back to the death of the deceased. But this rule does not cover a party who is also an *administrator*, since an administrator's title dates only from the grant of representation. The result is that, for example, a widow who is not an executrix and who sues in her personal capacity as a dependant under the Fatal Accidents Act cannot, if she obtains a grant of administration after the expiry of the limitation period, amend her writ so as to claim also as administratrix on behalf of the estate.

5.15 It would not be within our terms of reference to consider whether this distinction between executors and administrators should be abolished for all purposes; indeed, we can see that there might be serious objection to such a course. We do, however, think that the particular case of the widow/administratrix illustrates a potential defect in the current law and that it should be remedied. The rules we have referred to, we are advised, go as far as the Rule Committee considered permissible under the existing substantive law. We go into this question in more detail in the context of new parties, at paragraphs 5.22 to 5.29 below, and we therefore recommend that the rule-making power should be extended to allow the capacity in which a party sues to be amended after the limitation period has expired, so as to enable him to sue as administrator, notwithstanding that, at the date the proceedings were instituted, he could not have sued as such.

Amendment to add a party

5.16 The discretion of the court to add a new party after the expiration of the limitation period is at present regulated by Order 20, rule 5(3), which is in these terms:—

> 'An amendment to correct the name of a party may be allowed under paragraph (2) notwithstanding that it is alleged that the effect of the amendment will be to substitute a new party if the Court is satisfied that the mistake sought to be corrected was a genuine mistake and was not misleading or such as to cause any reasonable doubt as to the identity of the person intending to sue or, as the case may be, intended to be sued.'

The paragraph thus relates to factual errors correction of which would not cause the other side to be taken by surprise. Obvious examples of misdescription or misnomer of this kind are afforded by wholly- or partly-owned subsidiary companies (it is easy enough to sue the wrong one), and by a company that has been wound up and superseded by another of similar name. We think that the current rule does meet most, though perhaps not all, of the 'wrong company' cases. As we see it, the court ought to have power to allow the amendment if, when the proceedings were instituted, the 'real' defendant knew, or ought to have known, that they were aimed at him. In such a situation, he is not taken by surprise and ought not to have destroyed his records, or otherwise prejudiced his chances of defending himself. The wording of Order 20, rule 5(3) seems to us apt to cover these situations.

5.17 There are, however, not wholly dissimilar cases where the existing formulation may cause injustice, that is where the plaintiff has made an error of law or procedure, the correction of which would not occasion anyone to be taken by surprise. If, for example, an equitable assignee of a debt sues the debtor without joining the assignor and the limitation period then expires, he cannot amend his pleading so as to join the assignor[133]. Secondly, if the plaintiff is one of two or more persons who have a joint right of action, a person entitled jointly with him (for example, a co-trustee) may be a necessary party to the action and cannot be joined after the limitation period has expired. We think that it would be desirable that the Rules of the Supreme Court (and the County Court Rules) should permit the addition of a new party in circumstances of this kind.

5.18 These two examples are cases where the plaintiff's mistake relates to his position as plaintiff; since the party to be joined would not have an interest adverse to that of the plaintiff, he could, with his consent, be joined as a co-plaintiff, and would be joined as a defendant only if he did not so consent. The joinder of a person with an interest which is adverse to that of the plaintiff is more difficult, since we consider that the rules of procedure should be broadly consistent with the substantive law on limitation and the joinder of a wholly new defendant after the expiry of the period of limitation would necessarily mean that he would lose his right to plead the statute. There is, however, one class of case where we think that the rules ought to permit the joinder of a new person as a defendant. Where there are persons who are jointly liable in respect of a particular claim, and where failure to join any one of those persons would result in the defeat of the action even as against those who had been joined, it seems to us that the plaintiff ought to be allowed to amend his pleadings so as to being in the additional defendant. It is true that the joinder of this defendant would mean that he would be exposed to liability despite the fact that he had not been sued before the end of the period, but we consider that in the case of joint obligations, the plaintiff who starts proceedings against some, though not all, of the persons jointly liable has in fact enabled those on the 'other side' to know that the proceedings were aimed at them. In a sense, therefore, we see the failure to join a person jointly liable as akin to the 'misnomer cases' which are covered by Order 20, rule 5(3) as it stands.

5.19 So far as we can ascertain, this amendment is not needed for the case of joint (but not several) contractual obligations, since the power of the court under Order 15, rule 4(3) to stay proceedings brought against some (but not all) persons jointly liable in contract until the other persons so liable are added as defendants does not arise where one or more of the defendants has the benefit of a limitation defence.[134]. In any event, the rule (which replaces the plea in abatement which was available to a joint contractor sued alone until 1883) has no counterpart in the county court rules[135]. Members of a partnership which is not governed by the code relating to actions by or against partnership firms set out in R.S.C., Order 81, have to be sued individually (as, for example, members

---

[133] *Hudson* v. *Fernyhough* (1889) 61 L.T. 722; affirmed (1890) 24 Sol. J. P. 288 (C.A.).
[134] *Halsbury's Law of England*, 4th ed., vol. 9, para. 617. This passage gives as an example the case where one joint debtor has acknowledged the debt, with the result that, as against him *only*, the limitation period is enlarged under s. 25(5) of the Limitation Act 1939. It appears, however, that part payment by one person jointly liable extends the period as against all (s. 25(6)).
[135] *ibid.*

of a foreign partnership); but we can find no authority to show that an action against only some of them is bound to fail if the others are not also joined in the proceedings. On the other hand, it seems to us very doubtful whether the rules at present permit a plaintiff to repair out of time his error in not suing all the trustees of a trust[136]; although we have reason to believe that in at least one unreported decision a court has given leave to add a joint trustee after expiry of the limitation period.

5.20 We have identified the following cases in which we think a new party should be capable of being added by way of amendment 'post-limitation':—

(1) where the plaintiff is beneficially entitled to equity, and the person with the legal title is a necessary party to the action (for example, the equitable assignee of a chose in action, who cannot sue without joining the legal assignor[137]; the *cestui que trust*, who cannot enforce a right of action against a stranger to the trust without joining the trustee[138]);

(2) where the plaintiff is one of two or more persons jointly entitled to a right and all of them must be joined in order that the right may be enforced (for example, an action to enforce a right vested in trustees[139]);

(3) where the plaintiff is suing to enforce a public right and the action is one which ought to have been initiated by relator proceedings in the name of the Attorney General[140];

(4) where the plaintiff is a shareholder suing to enforce a right vested in the company and the company is a necessary party to the action[141];

(5) where the plaintiff is suing to recover from persons jointly (but not also severally) liable to him *and* where his failure to join all of them, would, as the law now stands, mean that the liability could not be enforced at all[142].

5.21 We have considered whether this list should contain a further category, namely cases where the plaintiff or the defendant is under a disability, but no next friend or guardian *ad litem* is appointed to act for him before expiry of the limitation period. It was suggested to us, and here again we would like to express our thanks to the Senior Master, that in such a case the action would not be properly constituted and that the powers conferred upon the court under R.S.C. Order 20, rule 5 would not enable a next friend or guardian *ad litem* to be brought in after the period had run. We have not been able to find any authority precisely on the point, although in *John* v. *John*[143] it was held by the

---

[136] For proceedings under the Trustee Act 1925 see the Supreme Court Practice 1976 at para. 93/4/4.
[137] *Performing Right Society Ltd.* v. *London Theatre of Varieties Ltd.* [1924] A.C. 1
[138] *Harmer* v. *Armstrong* [1934] Ch. 65.
[139] *Luke* v. *South Kensington Hotel Company*, (1879) 11 Ch.D. 121.
[140] *Devonport Corporation* v. *Tozer* [1903] 1 Ch. 759.
[141] *Spokes* v. *Grosvenor Hotel Company Ltd.* [1897] 2 Q.B. 124, 128; *Cf-Wallersteiner* v. *Moir* (No. 2) [1975] Q.B. 373.
[142] See paras. 5.18–5.19 above.
[143] [1965] p. 289.

then President, Sir Jocelyn Simon, that, while failure to appoint a guardian *ad litem* under the provisions of the Matrimonial Causes Rules could not be remedied under those rules, it could be cured under Order 2, rule 1 of the Rules of the Supreme Court, on the basis that the failure was an irregularity rather than a nullity. If, therefore, that rule itself confers power to amend, it seems to us that the court could add a guardian *ad litem*, or a next friend, even after expiry of the limitation period. In our view the court does have power to amend under Order 2, rule 1, without necessarily being thrown back on to any other provision in the R.S.C.; if this is right, the restrictions imposed by Order 20, rule 5 on 'post-limitation' amendments do not apply in this case: neither a next friend nor a guardian *ad litem* is a party. In the case of a next friend, there is the further point that proceedings improperly commenced may not be proceedings at all: it seems, however, that this may be met by the wording of Order 2, rule 1(1) itself, which speaks of 'beginning or purporting to begin any proceedings'. Since we recommend (at paragraphs 5.28–29 below) that the powers of the Rule Committee should be enlarged to enable it to deal with further post-limitation amendments and since the addition of a next friend or a guardian *ad litem* would fall within the general formula which we propose, it would be possible for the Rule Committee to put the question beyond doubt if they thought this desirable.

5.22 For the cases mentioned in paragraph 5.20 there does, however, remain a serious difficulty. We understand that the Rule Committee of the Supreme Court are of the opinion that the current rules go as far as the rule-making power permits. It follows that, if the law is to be changed so as to meet the cases mentioned above (and analogous cases), primary legislation—and not merely amendments to the rules of court—will be required. We are thus faced with the question of *how* the rule-making power should be extended. There are, as we see it, three possible courses:—

(1) the rule-making authority might be given a power wide enough to enable rules to confer on the court a discretion (perhaps subject to 'guidelines') to cover such cases as the court thought appropriate; or

(2) the primary legislation could spell out in detail the *specific* cases which the rules could cover; or

(3) the rule-making authority could be given power to cover by rule only *specific* cases falling within a formula embodied in the primary legislation.

5.23 The first of these courses would accord with the views expressed to us by the Senior Master. It has the merit of flexibility and enables the court to meet unexpected and exceptional circumstances. But it is not consistent with the general principle, which we think is right, that limitation is (apart from personal injury claims to which special considerations apply) a matter of strict law and not of discretion. There is, as we see it, no good reason in the ordinary case for saying that A should be put at risk of losing his statutory defence simply because B has chosen to sue C, and any wide discretion conferred on the court *would* put A at that risk.

5.24 If we could be certain that we had identified the only cases that ought to be covered, we would advocate the course recommended in paragraph 5.22(2) above. We do, however, have to recognise that we may have failed to do this; moreover, both substantive and procedural law change and a too-precise categorisation in primary legislation would mean that further 'deserving cases' would have to await legislative opportunities. We would prefer to see the rule-making authority capable of dealing with such cases.

5.25 We have, therefore, reached the conclusion that the best course is that set out in paragraph 5.22(3) above. But, and we emphasise this, the necessary formulation will not be easy. As we see it, the essential principle is that the rule-making authority should define the categories of 'permissible added parties', but those categories should be specified in the rules and not left to the court's discretion. The difficulty lies in defining the categories.

5.26 The evidence we have received (and here we are again greatly indebted to the Senior Master) shows that, under the current law, it is by no means always easy to distinguish a correction of a misnomer from the addition of a genuinely new party. It would, inevitably, be at least equally difficult to distinguish, by reference to a generally applicable formula, between a party whose joinder was a mere 'technical' necessity and one whose joinder substantially altered the scope of the action. It would not, for example, be sufficient to confine any extension of the current rules to the joinder of a new party as plaintiff (though in practice joinder of a party as a plaintiff may well be merely a 'technical' necessity), because a 'necessary' party, who declines to be joined as a plaintiff, must be joined as a defendant, and we also consider that the case described at paragraph 5.20(5) should be included. Nor would it be practicable to base any distinction on the possibility of the new party's joinder affecting his own, or anyone else's, substantive liability: *ex hypothesi*, if the new party's addition is a *necessity*, it must affect the original defendant's liability not least in the case in paragraph 5.20(5); moreover, the addition of the new party as, for example, co-plaintiff will expose him to the risk of becoming defendant to a counter-claim or the object of an order for costs.

5.27 We have not been able to devise any entirely satisfactory formula which will cover the cases we have identified and others that may be analogous, but which will not let in the cases which, in our view, ought not to be left in (because they offend against what we consider to be the sound principle mentioned above, that A should not be deprived of his statutory defence simply because B has chosen to sue C). We think, however, that there are factors common to the cases we have identified above (and likely to be common to any analogous cases), on which Parliamentary Counsel could draft a satisfactory formula; these factors are:—

(a) the plaintiff's action is not properly *constituted* unless the new party is joined; and

(b) the *plaintiff* is not seeking any substantive relief against the new party (though, for the reasons we have given, that party's joinder may in the event involve him in substantive liability) or, if he is seeking such relief, it is sought against a person who is jointly (but not severally) liable with an existing defendant and whose joinder is necessary if the plaintiff's claim against the defendant is to proceed.

5.28 Accordingly, our conclusion is that—

(a) the rule-making power should be extended so as to permit the 'post-limitation' joinder of a new party in the circumstances we have identified and in other analogous circumstances;

(*b*) this result should not be achieved by enabling rules of court to confer on the court a wide discretion;

(*c*) (unless this presents insuperable drafting difficulties) the extension of the rule-making power should take the form of a general formula based on the factors mentioned in paragraph 5.27 above. It would then be for the rule-making authority to specify those cases, falling within the general formula, in which the court would have power (though not any obligation) to permit the 'post-limitation' joinder of a new party, and those cases might suitably include those which we have specified at paragraph 5.20 above[144].

5.29 There is one point on which we think that, in any event, the law should be clarified. As mentioned above, R.S.C. Order 20, rule 5 sets out in paragraphs (3), (4) and (5) certain circumstances in which post-limitation amendments may be allowed to correct the name of, or substitute, a party; to alter the capacity in which a party sues; to add a new cause of action. There is, however, a conflict of judicial opinion about the true construction of the rule. Widgery, L.J., (as he then was) has held that the circumstances specified in the paragraphs referred to above are exhaustive and that the court has not, in addition, a general discretion to allow a post-limitation amendment[145]. However, in other cases the view has been expressed that these circumstances are not exhaustive and that the court has, in addition, a general discretion[146]. Although it is, perhaps, not a matter for us, we think that the narrower construction placed on Order 20, rule 5 is more in accordance with the language of the rule. Moreover, in our view the rule ought to be applied in this way, because the existence of a general discretion is inconsistent with our fundamental approach to limitation.

---

[144] We doubt whether our formula would prove satisfactory for the proposal we made at para. 5.15 above which is somewhat different in kind.

[145] *Braniff* v. *Holland & Hanner and Cubitt's (Southern) Ltd.* [1969] 1 W.L.R. 1533.

[146] See, *e.g., per* Lord Denning, M.R., in *Chatsworth Investment Ltd.* v. *Cussins (Contractors) Ltd.* [1969] 1 W.L.R. 1 at p. 5. In *Marubeni Corporation* v. *Pearlstone Shipping Corporation* (*The Times*, 30th June 1977), a case concerning the one-year period for claims against carriers and ships under the Hague Rules, the Court of Appeal held that it had jurisdiction to add a party after expiry of the period. The Master of the Rolls appears to have relied upon O. 15, r. 6, and this decision perhaps underlines the need for the provision we suggest.

Part VI

CONCLUSIONS

Summary of conclusions

6.1 Our conclusions may be summarised thus:—

1. The rule that time starts to run from the accrual of the cause of action should be retained (paragraph 2.4).

2. The right to an extension conferred by section 26 of the Limitation Act 1939 should be retained, but that section should be redrafted (paragraphs 2.24, 2.35, and 3.18).

3. We are not agreed on the question whether the court should have a general discretion to set aside a defence of limitation after the time allowed at law has expired: a majority of us consider that the law should not be changed in this respect (paragraphs 2.35 and 2.36).

4. Where a cause of action depends upon proof of the occurrence of damage, the date when the cause of action accrues for limitation purposes should not necessarily be the date when the damage was first reasonably discoverable by the plaintiff (paragraph 2.38).

5. Minority apart there should be a statutory definition of disability for the purposes of limitation, and it should be based upon the definition of mental disorder in the Mental Health Act 1959 (paragraph 2.45).

6. There should be no change in the law relating to supervening disability (paragraph 2.48).

7. The normal limitation period should continue to be six years in length (paragraph 2.53).

8. The freedom of parties to abridge and to extend the limitation period by contract should be retained (paragraphs 2.57 and 2.58).

9. The 12-year limitation period of an instrument under seal should be retained (paragraph 2.59).

10. There is no need for a suspension of time during negotiations, otherwise than by contract (paragraph 2.61).

11. There is no need for a statutory definition of an acknowledgment (paragraph 2.64).

12. It should continue to be the law that an acknowledgment must be written and signed (paragraph 2.67).

13. No acknowledgment or part-payment made after expiration of the limitation period should be capable of reviving a remedy which has already been barred (paragraph 2.71).

14. The balance of advantage lies in retaining the issue of process as the step which stops time running against the plaintiff, even if the taking of that step may not immediately come to the defendant's notice (paragraph 2.81).

15. The question whether it should be necessary that the defendant be made

aware of the issue of process within a period shorter than 12 months deserves consideration (paragraph 2.82).

16. The rule that limitation has to be pleaded should be retained and, accordingly, limitation should continue to be a procedural rather than a substantive rule (paragraph 2.91).

17. Consideration should be given to the possible reform of the rules of private international law relating to limitation (paragraphs 2.93 and 2.96).

18. The rights of an owner of goods in respect of them should not be barred by lapse of time as against a thief or receiver; as against a *bona fide* purchaser of the stolen property, or a person claiming through him, the owner's title should be extinguished after six years from the purchase (paragraph 3.8).

19. There should be no limitation period in favour of a gratuitous transferee of stolen goods even if he is himself honest unless he can claim through a *bona fide* purchaser (paragraph 3.11).

20. There should be no change in the operation of section 3 of the Limitation Act 1939 in relation to finders of lost goods (paragraph 3.16).

21. Where money is lent, and no date is specified for repayment, time should not begin to run in favour of the borrower until a written demand for repayment is made (paragraph 3.26).

22. No recommendation is made on the conclusions of the Faulks Committee relating to limitation (paragraph 3.30).

23. Section 4 of the Limitation Act 1963 (which relates to contribution) is not in need of amendment (paragraph 3.34).

24. There should be no change in the various limitation periods relating to actions to recover land (paragraphs 3.38 to 3.42).

25. We are not agreed on the question whether the *St. Marylebone* decision should be reversed and we therefore make no recommendation (paragraph 3.46).

26. The law relating to adverse possession should be amended so as to ensure that no licence to possess the land is implied unless the evidence warrants it (paragraph 3.52).

27. In the case of land occupied under a tenancy at will, a gratuitous licence or a periodical oral tenancy, time should not begin to run in favour of the occupier until the tenancy or licence has been determined (paragraphs 3.55 and 3.56).

28. The sum of £1 in section 9(3) of the Limitation Act 1939 should be increased to £10 in respect of leases executed after the commencement of the change in the law (paragraphs 3.57 and 3.58).

29. There should be no change in the law relating to the running of time against persons entitled to future interests in land (paragraph 3.64).

30. The law of limitation as it applies to mortgages should not be altered (paragraph 3.70).

31. There should be no limitation period for claims for rectification of the land register (paragraph 3.72).

32. A claim for indemnity in cases of erroneous registration of title to land should not be defeated by a defence of limitation except where, had the land not been registered, the claim to the right itself would have been lost by lapse of time (paragraphs 3.77 to 3.79).

33. No change in the law of limitation relating to rentcharges is required (paragraph 3.80).

34. A trustee who is also a beneficiary and who has acted prudently and honestly in distributing trust property should be able to rely on a defence of limitation except in respect of the share which he would have had to pay to the late-comer had all the beneficiaries (including himself) been sued in time (paragraph 3.84).

35. Time should not be suspended in favour of a debtor who becomes administrator of his creditor's estate, and the rule in *Seagram* v. *Knight* should be reversed (paragraphs 3.92 and 3.93).

36. There should be no change in the law relating to acquiescence or laches (paragraph 3.100).

37. Section 210 of the Common Law Procedure Act 1852 (which provides a six month period within which relief may be claimed if a lessor has re-entered pursuant to a court order) should be extended to cases where there is no court order (paragraph 3.101).

38. The specific exceptions for Admiralty matters in the Limitation Act 1939 should be repealed (paragraph 4.5).

39. Any future review of Admiralty law should consider the law of limitation concerning sister-ships (paragraph 4.6).

40. The Maritime Conventions Act 1911 should be amended so as to include in personal injuries cases an extension of time as of right based upon 'a date of knowledge' (paragraph 4.7).

41. Section 28 of the Limitation Act 1939 (which relates to counter-claims) should be extended to Admiralty proceedings (paragraph 4.8).

42. Apart from a verbal amendment to section 27 of the Limitation Act 1939, no change in the law of limitation as it affects arbitration is required (paragraph 4.11).

43. The special 12-year period for an action on a judgment should be abolished (paragraph 4.16).

44. There should be no change in the law relating to the commencement of third party proceedings out of time (paragraph 5.10).

45. Section 28 of the Limitation Act 1939 (which relates to counter-claims) should be amended so as to apply to counter-claims made under the originating summons procedure (paragraph 5.11).

46. No change is required in the rules which enable a new cause of action to be added out of time (paragraph 5.12).

47. A plaintiff should be able to amend his pleadings out of time so as to sue in another capacity (including that of an administrator), and the rule-making

powers of the Supreme Court and County Court Rule Committee should be extended for this purpose (paragraph 5.15).

48. The rule making powers of the Supreme Court and County Court Rule Committees should be enlarged so as to confer power to enable parties to be added out of time, in specific cases, including those identified at paragraphs 5.20 and 5.21, if—

(*a*) the plaintiff's action is not properly constituted unless the new party is joined, and

(*b*) the plaintiff is not seeking substantive relief against the new party or, if he is seeking such relief, is seeking it against a person—

(i) who is jointly (but not severally) liable with an existing defendant, and

(ii) whose joinder is necessary if the plaintiff's claim against the defendant is to proceed (paragraph 5.28).

49. The exhaustive character of R.S.C. Order 20, rule 5(3), (4) and (5) should be clarified (paragraph 5.29).

ALAN S. ORR, *Chairman.*
HUGH GRIFFITHS.
RAYMOND WALTON.
W. GRANVILLE WINGATE.
T. H. BINGHAM.
A. G. GUEST.
C. A. HINKS.
DAVID HIRST.
LLOYD OF HAMPSTEAD
ANDREW MARTIN.
E. G. NUGEE.

M. C. BLAIR, *Secretary.*
J.A.C. WATHERSTON, *Assistant Secretary.*
July 1977.

ANNEX 1

Acknowledgments

A. The following bodies and individuals submitted memoranda in response to our questionnaire:

The Association of British Chambers of Commerce

Master R. E. Ball C.B., M.B.E., Chief Chancery Master

The Board of Inland Revenue

The British Insurance Association

The British National Committee of International Chambers of Commerce

The Chief Land Registrar

Circuit Judges assigned to Official Referee business

The Committee of London Clearing Bankers

The Council of Circuit Judges

The Department of Trade and Industry

The Honourable Mr. Justice Donaldson

Master J.B. Elton

The Engineering Employers' Federation

The General Council of the Bar

Professor M.J. Goodman

The Honourable Mr. Justice Goulding

The Honourable Mr. Justice Graham

Master E.R. Heward

The Hire Purchase Trade Association

The Institute

The Institute of Chartered Accountants

The Issuing Houses Association

Master I.H. Jacob, Q.C., the Senior Master, Queen's Bench Division

Professor J.A. Jolowicz

The Law Society

Lloyd's Underwriters

Professor F.A. Mann

D.A. Marshall, Esq.

M.J. Mustill, Esq., Q.C.

The National Coal Board

The National House-Builders Registration Council

Professor F.J. Odgers

The Official Solicitor

The Public Trustee

The Right Honourable Lord Reid, C.H.

The Right Honourable Lord Simon of Glaisdale

Messrs W.H. Thompson

The Trades Union Congress

The Honourable Mr. Justice Whitford

B. The following bodies and individuals gave other written evidence:

The Crown Estate Commissioners

The Duchy of Lancaster

The General Synod of the Church of England

Richard Hayden, Esq.

Professor R.F.V. Heuston

The Institute of Law Research and Reform of Alberta

The Law Commission

The National Federation of Building Trades Employers

The Prudential Assurance Company Limited

The Royal Institute of British Architects

His Honour Judge Ruttle

The Scottish Law Commission

The Treasury Solicitor

Keith Uff, Esq.,

Graeme Willis, Esq.

C. The following bodies and individuals submitted written evidence on Admiralty Law in response to our request (paragraph 4.1.):

The Admiralty Solicitors Group

The Honourable Mr. Justice Brandon, M.C.

The British Maritime Law Association

A.P. Clarke, Esq.

John Hobhouse, Esq., Q.C.

Barry Sheen, Esq., Q.C.

ANNEX 2

Special provisions

A. SPECIAL LIMITATION PERIODS IN THE INTERNATIONAL FIELD

I. Shipping

(i) *The Merchant Shipping (Oil Pollution) Act* 1971 implements the International Convention on Civil Liability for Oil Pollution Damage 1969 and applies to damage caused by the discharge or escape of persistent oil from a ship which is carrying it in bulk, and for the cost of, and any further damage resulting from, preventive measures. The United Kingdom ratified the Convention in 1975.

Section 9 of the Act provides that no action to enforce a claim shall be entertained by any court in the United Kingdom unless the action is commenced not later than **three years** after the claim arose, nor later than **six years** after the date of the first occurrence resulting in the discharge or escape by reason of which the liability was incurred.

(ii) *The Merchant Shipping Act* 1974, *Part I* makes provision for giving effect to the Convention on the Establishment of an International Fund for Compensation for Oil Pollution Damage, 1971. The Convention in effect extends and supplements the compensation available under the 1969 Convention referred to in (i) above. Section 7 of the Act, which is not yet in force, provides similar limitation periods as in (i) above for claims for compensation or indemnification against the Fund. The Convention may soon be ratified by the United Kingdom.

(iii) *The Maritime Conventions Act* 1911 gives effect to the International Convention for the unification of certain rules of law relating to collisions. Section 8 of the Act provides that no action is maintainable to enforce a claim or lien against a vessel or owner in respect of damage to a vessel or cargo, or in respect of salvage services, unless proceedings are commenced within **two years** from the date the damage or loss was caused or the salvage services were rendered. An action to enforce any contribution in respect of an overpaid proportion of damages must be brought within **one year** of overpayment. There is a discretion to extend these periods.

(iv) *The Carriage of Goods by Sea Act* 1924 (which gave effect to the Hague Rules of 1924 governing the relationship between the carrier and the shipper of goods by sea where a bill of lading or similar document of title is issued) provides, in Article III, that the carrier and the ship are not liable in respect of loss or damage to goods unless a suit is brought within **one year** of their delivery or of the date when they should have been delivered. *The Hague Protocol* of 1968 allows this period to be extended by agreement after the cause of action has arisen but the United Kingdom has not ratified this Protocol. A complete revision of the Hague Rules is now being prepared but it is not possible at this stage to say what the equivalent provision will be.

(v) The Athens Convention relating to the Carriage of Passengers and their Luggage by Sea of 1974 provides in Article 16 for a **two year** limitation period in respect of death or personal injury or loss of or damage to luggage, but this period may be extended by declaration of the carrier or agreement of the parties after the cause of action has arisen. This is similar to a provision in the predecessor Convention of 1961 which has not been ratified by the United

Kingdom. The United Kingdom intends to ratify the 1974 Convention but legislation will be required.

II. Aviation

The Carriage by Air Act 1961 gives effect to the Warsaw Convention as amended at the Hague 1955, which applies to the international carriage by air of persons, baggage and cargo for reward or gratuitously by an air transport undertaking. Similar principles are applied to international carriage by air as defined in the unamended Warsaw Convention by the Carriage by Air Act (Application of Provisions) Order 1967 (S.I. 1967 480) (not being carriage to which the amended Convention applies). Under Article 29, in each case, the right to damages is extinguished if any action is not brought within **two years** from the date of arrival at destination or from the date on which the aircraft ought to have arrived, or from the date on which the carriage stopped. Section 5(2) of the *Carriage by Air Act* 1961, as amended by Section 4(4) of the *Limitation Act* 1963, provides that Article 29 is not to be read as applying to any proceedings for contribution between joint tortfeasors.

III Road Transport

(i) *The Carriage of Passengers by Road Act* 1974 enables the United Kingdom to give effect to the Convention on the Contract for the International Carriage of Passengers and Luggage by Road to which the United Kingdom may be expected to accede in due course. Article 22(1) provides that the period of limitation for actions arising out of the death or wounding of, or out of any other bodily or mental injury to, a passenger should be **three years**. Article 22(2) of the Convention provides that the period of limitation for actions arising out of the carriage of luggage shall be **one year**, and shall run from the date on which the vehicle arrived at, or ought to have arrived at, its place of destination.

(ii) *Carriage of Goods by Road Act* 1965. The Act gives effect to the Convention on the Contract for the International Carriage of Goods by Road, which is scheduled to the Act. The period of limitation under Article 32 is **one year** save where there is wilful misconduct, or behaviour amounting to such, when it is extended to **three years**.

The period begins to run, in the case of partial loss, damage or delay in delivery from the date of delivery, in the case of total loss either **30 days** after an agreed time limit, or (if there is no agreement) **60 days** from the date on which the carrier took the goods over, and in all other cases **three months** after the contract for carriage was made. The limitation period is suspended where a written claim is made until it is rejected in writing by the carrier. Subject to these provisions, the extension of the period of limitation is governed by the law of the court seised of the case.

IV Rail Transport

(i) *Carriage by Railway Act* 1972 (*as amended by S.I.* 1974/1250) *Sched., Article* 17. The Act gives the force of law in the United Kingdom to the Additional Convention to the International Convention concerning the Carriage of Passengers and Luggage by Rail. The periods of limitation are, for an accident to a passenger, **three years** from the day after the accident and, where the claimant is not the passenger himself, **three years** from the day after the passenger's death or **five years** from the day after the accident, whichever is earlier. The limitation period is suspended where a written claim is made until it is rejected in writing by the railway. Subject to these provisions, the limitation of actions is governed by the law of the State on whose territory the accident to the passenger occurs, including the rules relating to conflict of laws.

(ii) *The International Convention concerning the Carriage of Goods by Rail (CIM)* 1970 *Article* 47 (incorporated by reference into each contract of carriage). The period of limitation for an action arising out of a contract of carriage is generally **1 year**. However, in some cases the period is extended to **two years**: for example, an action to recover net proceeds of a sale by the railway or where there is fraud or the damage is caused wilfully.

The *terminus a quo* varies, depending on the nature of the claim; for example, if the action is for late delivery, partial loss or damage, time runs from the date of actual delivery: whereas if the action is for the refund of carriage charges, the time runs from payment. In any cases for which no *terminus a quo* is specified it is the date on which the action accrues. Where a claim is made in writing to the railway the period of limitation is suspended until the claim is rejected. Subject to Article 47, the limitation law of the country in which the action is brought applies.

(iii) *The International Convention concerning the Carriage of Passengers and Luggage by Rail (CIV)* 1970 *Article* 43 (incorporated by reference into each Contract of Carriage). The period of limitation for an action arising out of a contract of carriage is **one year** unless the loss or damage claimed was caused wilfully or the action is for fraud, when the period is extended to **two years**. The *terminus a quo* varies depending on the nature of the claim; for example, if the action is for delay, partial loss or damage, it is the date of actual delivery; whereas in all cases where the action concerns the carriage of a passenger, it is the date of the expiry of the period of availability of the ticket. When a claim is made in writing to the railway the limitation period is suspended until the claim is rejected. Subject to Article 43, the national law of the country where the action is brought applies.

V. Other International Matters

(i) *The Uniform Law on International Sales Act* 1967 gives effect in the United Kingdom to the *Uniform Law on the International Sale of Goods*. The Uniform Law applies in the United Kingdom only to those contracts to which the parties have agreed it should apply. Under Article 39 of the Uniform Law a buyer loses the right to rely on a lack of conformity with the contract if he has not given notice of it within a period of **two years** from the date on which the goods were handed over, unless the lack of conformity constituted a breach of a guarantee covering a longer period. Under Article 49 a buyer loses his right to rely on lack of conformity with the contract at the expiration of **one year** after he has given notice under Article 39, unless he has been prevented from exercising his right because of fraud on the part of the seller.

(ii) *The Convention on the Limitation Period in the International Sale of Goods.* This Convention was adopted by the United Nations Conference on Prescription in the International Sale of Goods held in May of 1975. The United Kingdom has not signed the Convention and the period for signature has now expired.

(iii) *European Convention on Products Liability.* Article 6 of the Convention provides that proceedings for personal injuries arising from defective products are subject to a limitation period of **three years** from the date that the claimant becomes aware or ought reasonably to have been aware of the damage, the defect and the identity of the producer. Further, Article 7 provides that an action against a producer is extinguished if it is not brought within **10 years** from the date on which the defective product was put into circulation.

(iv) *EEC Draft Directive (Products Liability).* The Draft Directive proposes that in the case of action for personal injury and damage to property (excluding property used in a trade, business or profession) the limitation period should be **three years** from the date that the claimant knew or ought reasonably to have known of the damage, the defect and the identity of the producer (Article 8). An absolute limitation period of **10 years**, running from the date that the product was put into circulation, is proposed (Article 9).

(v) *The Convention on Civil Liability for Oil Pollution Damage resulting from Exploration for and Exploitation of Seabed Mineral Resources*, agreed at London in December 1976 contains, at Article 10, a twelve month limitation period based on a date of knowledge and an overall limitation period for **four years** from the date of the last occurrence.

B. SPECIAL PROVISIONS (ESPECIALLY IN THE CONSUMER FIELD) WHICH HAVE THE EFFECT OF PREVENTING CONTRACTING OUT OF A LIMITATION PERIOD

(i) *The Misrepresentation Act* 1967, section 3, provides that a provision excluding or restricting liability in respect of a misrepresentation made by a party before the contract, or any remedy available to another party to the contract by reason of such a misrepresentation, shall be of no effect except to the extent, if any, that the court may allow reliance on it as being fair and reasonable in the circumstances of the case.

(ii) *The Defective Premises Act* 1972, section 6(3), renders void any term of an agreement which purports to exclude or restrict the operation of, or any liability arising by virtue of, any of the provisions of the Act which impose on persons taking on work for, or in connection with, the provision of dwellings (by erection, conversion or enlargement) duties in relation to their standard of work. The building must be fit for habitation and the work must be done in a workmanlike or, as the case may be, professional manner.

Under section 1(5), a cause of action in respect of a breach of duty imposed by section 1 of the Act, which relates to standards of work, is deemed for the purpose of the Limitation Acts to have accrued at the time when the dwelling was completed or, in respect of further work done to remedy work already completed, at the time when the further work was finished.

(iii) *The Supply of Goods (Implied Terms) Act* 1973, section 4, amends section 55 of the Sale of Goods Act 1893 and makes void any term of a consumer contract which exempts from the implied terms as to the quality of the goods contained in sections 13–15 of the 1893 Act. Section 12 of the 1973 Act makes a similar provision for hire-purchase consumer agreements. The effect of the 1973 legislation on the law of limitation is that any purported attempt, in any consumer contract protected by the Act, to cut down a limitation period in respect of any cause of action arising under sections 13–15 of the 1893 Act will be void. In the case of non-consumer sales and hire-purchase agreements the limitation period can be cut down by agreement only if it is fair and reasonable to do so.

(iv) *Contracts for services, etc.* The Unfair Contract Terms Bill which implements the Law Commissions' *Second Report on Exemption Clauses* (Law Com. No. 69, Scot. Law Com. No. 39; H.C. 605 (1974–75)), would render ineffective certain terms in contracts which are entered into with a consumer or on standard terms unless it would be fair or reasonable to allow reliance on the term. The terms controlled would be those enabling liability for breach to be excluded or performance substantially different from that expected, or indeed no performance, to be rendered. Clause 2 would render void certain terms and notices which purport to exclude or restrict liability for negligence causing personal injury. Both these proposed provisions, and others in the Bill, would thus affect special periods of limitation in contracts, or in some cases in notices.

Law Reform Committee
Twenty-Fourth Report

LATENT DAMAGE

To the Right Honourable the Lord Hailsham of St. Marylebone, C.H., F.R.S., D.C.L.,
Lord High Chancellor of Great Britain

Part I

INTRODUCTION

Terms of reference

1.1 In August 1980 you invited us 'to consider the law relating to—

(i) the accrual of the cause of action, and

(ii) limitation

in negligence cases involving latent defects (other than latent disease or injury to the person) and to make recommendations.'

1.2 Our study is, therefore, confined to a very limited class of negligence case. First, those involving personal injury are excluded. Secondly, we are concerned only with 'negligence cases involving latent defects'. Such defects might arise in a number of different circumstances. For instance, a builder may act negligently in putting into a building inadequate or otherwise unsound foundations, but the owner of the building may be unaware of the damage for many years; indeed he may sell to another before he becomes aware of any such damage. Equally a solicitor, a surveyor, or an accountant may give unsound advice upon which the client acts in the belief that it is sound only to discover years later that the advice was bad. Very serious damage, physical or financial, may be suffered in such cases, without any deliberate concealment on the part of the wrong-doer and without the victim becoming aware of the defective work or advice or even of the damage done until under the existing law relating to limitation of actions he is barred by lapse of time from obtaining a remedy in the courts. Another possibility is that an inherent defect, for instance in the foundations of a building, does not result in damage until many years after the breach of duty which caused it. In this case, at present, the plaintiff will not necessarily be barred from action, because under existing law he will not be in a position to sue in negligence until he suffers damage (until, in the technical language of the law his 'cause of action accrues'), and, so long as he commences his proceedings within six years of that date[1], he will still be in time. However in this type of case the defendant may be at a considerable disadvantage through having to fight a stale claim which he no longer has the evidence to contest. We believe that our terms of reference require us to examine both types of situation that is to say, those cases where damage occurs but is not discoverable until much later and those where the damage itself does not occur until long after the breach of duty to which it is attributable. Our task is to make proposals that will so far as possible secure justice for both plaintiffs and defendants.

1.3 We originally considered the problems of latent damage in our 21st Report which dealt with the law of limitation generally[2]. However, two of the most important cases on the problem[3] were reported only shortly before we submitted that Report, and there have been a number of significant developments since then[4]. The present reference has afforded us an opportunity to reconsider the law and the tentative conclusions that we reached in the 21st Report[5].

The Consultative Document

1.4 For the purpose of this review we set up a Sub-Committee which in July 1981 issued a Consultative Document[6]. The document set out the law as it was then understood and the problems to which it was believed to give rise. It went on to canvass a number of different approaches to a solution of these problems, and to invite views. It was widely circulated amongst professional bodies and others known to have a special interest in the particular area of law in question. In total over 140 individuals and bodies responded to our request for comments and their names are listed in the Appendix to this Report. We found the memoranda that we received extremely helpful and we would like to take this opportunity of thanking all those who assisted us for the trouble that they took in responding to our request.

Recent developments in the law

1.5 Since the Consultative Document was published, and indeed since most of the comments that we received were written, there have been a number of court decisions in the field of latent damage. Of these the most important is *Pirelli General Cable Works Ltd.* v. *Oscar Faber and Partners*[7] in which the House of Lords has ruled that in the case of latent damage to buildings a plaintiff's cause of action accrues, and time starts to run against him, when physical damage occurs to the building, although it may not be discovered, or reasonably discoverable, until later. It is, for this reason, that under the existing law a plaintiff may find himself barred from suing before he even knows that he has suffered damage or loss. The effect of the ruling, which we discuss in more detail in Part II of this Report, has been to alter radically the direction in which the law prior to *Pirelli* was generally understood to be developing. Two of their

---

[1] Limitation Act 1980, s. 2.
[2] *Final Report on Limitation of Actions*, (1977) Cmnd. 6923.
[3] *Sparham-Souter* v. *Town and Country Developments (Essex) Ltd* [1976] 1 Q.B. 858; *Anns* v. *Merton London Borough Council* [1978] A.C. 728.
[4] See further para. 1.5. below.
[5] At paras. 2.34–2.38 of that Report: see para. 3.6. below.
[6] Latent Damage (July 1981).
[7] [1983] 2 A.C. 1.

Lordships, however, expressed considerable misgivings, and in particular Lord
Fraser of Tullybelton said (at p. 19):—

> 'I am respectfully in agreement with Lord Reid's view expressed in *Cartledge*
> v. *E. Jopling and Sons Ltd.* [1963] A.C. 758, that such a result appears to
> be unreasonable and contrary to principle, but I think the law is now so
> firmly established that only Parliament can alter it. Postponement of the
> accrual of the cause of action until the date of discoverability may involve
> the investigation of facts many years after their occurrence—see, for example.
> *Dennis* v. *Charnwood Borough Council* [1983] Q.B. 409—with possible
> unfairness to the defendants, unless a final longstop date is prescribed, as
> in sections 6 and 7 of the Prescription and Limitation (Scotland) Act 1973.
> If there is any question of altering this branch of the law, this is, in my
> opinion, a clear case where any alteration should be made by legislation,
> and not by judicial decision, because this is, in the words of Lord Simon
> of Glaisdale in *Miliangos* v. *George Frank (Textiles) Ltd.* [1976] A.C. 443,
> 480: "a decision which demands a far wider range of review than is available
> to courts following our traditional and valuable adversary system—the sort
> of review compassed by an interdepartmental committee". I express the hope
> that Parliament will soon take action to remedy the unsatisfactory state of
> the law on this subject.'

Matters outside our terms of reference

1.6 In the introduction to the Consultative Document the Sub-Committee
drew special attention to the limited character of our terms of reference[8]. In
particular it noted that the Committee is not empowered to examine the question
of who should be liable in respect of a particular type of loss. In the event
a number or those who submitted comments to us did seek to open up this
area. Another proposal made by a number of commentators was that there
should be a system of compulsory insurance against latent damage during the
period of a contractor's liability and that this should be taken into account
in the price paid by the purchaser[9]. These ideas, particularly the insurance
suggestion, are interesting, and we think it desirable that they should be considered
by an appropriately qualified body at some future date. However, they have
very wide implications and we would be travelling far outside our terms of
reference if we were to attempt in the present study to explore the fields of
business and law opened up by such proposals. They are therefore not covered
in the recommendations which we make for the reform of the law. We have
also refrained from making recommendations for a more general overhaul of
the law in respect of accrual of causes of action—but for a different reason.
We are satisfied that the proposals which we put forward for reform by amendment
to the Limitation Act 1980 should achieve a substantial improvement in the
law and can be enacted without a major overhaul of the law of tort. If a more
general survey of the substantive law relating to the cause of action in negligence

---

[8] At para. 3.
[9] See also the suggestion that there might be a form of national insurance to cover cases
where a victim of latent damage is unable to claim (1983) 127 S.J. 1: and see further
the observations made by Lawton L.J. in *Dennis* v. *Charnwood Borough Council* [1983]
1 Q.B. 409, 424.

cases is believed to be necessary, it should be undertaken upon terms of reference not limited to cases involving latent defects.

Scheme of the Report

1.7 The scheme that we have adopted is as follows. In Part II we discuss the existing law and its difficulties, giving particular attention to the developments that have taken place since the Consultative Document was published. In Part III we outline the possible alternatives to the present law. Part IV contains our recommendations for a change in the law. In Part V we summarise our conclusions and recommendations.

Part II

THE PRESENT LAW AND ITS DIFFICULTIES

The present law

2.1 The general principle of the English law of limitation is that a plaintiff must commence his action within a particular period beginning with the date of accrual of his cause of action. The period is known as the limitation period. In cases founded on tort, which include actions for negligence, the limitation period is generally[10] six years[11]. The cause of action in negligence cases accrues on the date when damage is caused[12]. This will often be the same date as the date on the defendant's breach of duty. Sometimes, however, the defendant's negligence, or its effects, may lie hidden for years. For instance the existence of defects in foundations may not become apparent until many years after the building in question was designed and built. The problem in such cases is to determine when the plaintiff suffers damage so as to start the limitation period running against him. In a building case, for instance, is it the date on which damage to the structure first occurs, or the date on which the plaintiff acquires a negligently designed building, or the date on which he first discovers, or could reasonably have discovered, that the foundations are unsound? After the decisions of the Court of Appeal in *Sparham-Souter* v. *Town and Country Developments (Essex) Ltd.*[13] and the House of Lords in *Anns* v. *Merton London Borough Council*[14] it was widely believed that courts would favour the date of discovery or discoverability;[15] but the point was never entirely free from doubt[16]. For instance in a number of cases involving purely economic loss (as opposed to physical damage to a building) the courts have held that the plaintiff suffered damage, and time began to run against him, from the moment that he acted to his detriment in reliance on the negligent advice[17]. However, any further developments in the direction of treating the cause of action as accruing on the date of discovery or discoverability were finally halted by the decision of the House of Lords in *Pirelli General Cable Works Ltd.* v. *Oscar Faber and Partners*[18] in which their Lordships held that in cases of latent damage to buildings the plaintiff's cause

---

[10] There are special rules in relation to actions for damages for personal injuries or death; see Limitation Act 1980, ss. 11 and 14. We are not concerned with these.

[11] Limitation Act 1980, s. 2.

[12] Contrast an action founded on contract in which the cause of action accrues and the limitation period starts to run at the date of the breach of contract.

[13] [1976] Q.B. 858.

[14] [1978] A.C. 728

[15] The approach adopted in *Sparham-Souter* was broadly followed in a number of cases including *Eames London Estates Ltd.* v. *North Herts. District Council* (1981) 18 Build. L.R. 50; (1981) 259 E.G. 491, *Crump and Another* v. *Torfaen UDC* (1982) 261 E.G. 678, and *Dennis* v. *Charnwood Borough Council* [1983] 1 Q.B. 409.

[16] See for instance the discussion of these cases in paragraphs 2.12–2.20 of the *21st Report (Final Report on Limitation of Actions)*, (1977) Cmnd. 6923.

[17] E.g. *Forster* v. *Outred* [1982] 1 W.L.R. 86; *Melton* v. *Walker and Stanger* (1981) 125 S.J. 861; *Baker* v. *Ollard and Bentley* (1982) 126 S.J. 593. All of these cases concerned legal advice.

[18] [1983] 2 A.C. 1. Their Lordships' decision was applied by Hodgson, J. in *Dove* v. *Banhams Patent Locks Ltd.* [1983] 1 W.L.R. 1436.

of action will accrue[19] when damage occurs, no sooner and no later and irrespective of discoverability. Their Lordships disapproved of the approach adopted in *Sparham-Souter* and doubted whether a majority in the House of Lords in the *Anns* case had favoured the discovery/discoverability principle. Their conclusion was in line with the approach taken in their earlier decision in *Cartledge* v. *Jopling*,[20] which concerned latent injury to the person.

2.2 Before we turn to consider the problems to which the present law on latent damage gives rise, three particular points need to be made by way of background. The first is that our discussion of limitation periods in relation to latent damage assumes that there has been no fraud or deliberate concealment. Section 32 of the Limitation Act 1980[21] makes particular provision for actions based on fraud or where there has been concealment, which is extended to include certain deliberate breaches of duty, in the following terms:—

'(1) Subject to subsection (3) below, where in the case of any action for which a period of limitation is prescribed by this Act, either:—

   (a) the action is based upon the fraud of the defendant; or

   (b) any fact relevant to the plaintiff's right of action has been deliberately concealed from him by the defendant; or

   (c) the action is for relief from the consequences of a mistake;

   the period of limitation shall not begin to run until the plaintiff has discovered the fraud, concealment or mistake (as the case may be) or could with reasonable diligence have discovered it . . .

(2) For the purpose of subsection (1) above, deliberate commission of a breach of duty in circumstances in which it is unlikely to be discovered for some time amounts to deliberate concealment of the facts involved in that breach of duty'.

For example, a builder who deliberately commits a breach of duty in the construction of the foundations of a house without taking active steps to conceal it but in circumstances in which it is unlikely to be discovered for a long time will not be able to rely on the general law; time will not begin to run against the plaintiff until the concealment is discovered or ought to have been discovered. The law dealing with such concealment (and/or mistake) is well established; section 32 of the 1980 Act was not generally criticised[22] on consultation and we make no recommendations for its amendment.

2.3 The second point is that a breach of duty may give rise to liability in both contract and tort and the fact that someone who has suffered loss may

---

[19] Lord Fraser went on to observe (at p. 16) that 'There may perhaps be cases where the defect is so gross that the building is doomed from the start, and where the owner's cause of action will accrue as soon as it is built, but it seems unlikely that such a defect would not be discovered within the limitation period. Such cases, if they exist, would be exceptional'. For a criticism of this approach see Baxter, 'Latent Damage in Defective Construction Work' (1983) 133 N.L.J. 414, 437.

[20] [1963] A.C. 758.

[21] Originally section 26 of the Limitation Act 1939 but re-formulated as a result of our 21st Report. (1977) Cmnd. 6923, paras. 2.22–2.24 and 2.35.

[22] See further para. 4.20, below.

have, or may have had, a right of action in contract against the person who
has injured him will not of itself prevent him, from bringing an action in tort[23].
Thus in the case, for instance, of a builder who is negligent in constructing
a house for a client, the client may sue him in contract within six years of
the date of breach of contract, or twelve if the contract is a speciality contract
(i.e. one entered into by deed), or he may sue in tort within six years of the
date when damage occurs, which might of course be very much later than the
date of the negligent act.

2.4 The third and final point is the considerable extension in recent years
of the range of the action for damages for negligence. It is in no way confined
to personal injury or damage to property. It extends to financial loss arising
from, amongst other matters, bad professional advice. In *Ross* v. *Caunters*[24]
for instance a solicitor was held to owe a duty not only to his client (to whom
he would also have been liable in contract) but also to the intended beneficiary
under the client's will. More recently in *Yianni* v. *Edwin Evans and Son*[25] a surveyor
preparing a valuation report for a building society for the purpose of ascertaining
whether a property would provide sufficient security for a loan to mortgage
applicants was held to owe a duty of care to the applicants. There are also
other examples of the extension to new situations and relationships of tortious
liability in negligence[26]. A matter, therefore, which we have had to consider
is whether our recommendations for reform should be generally applicable or
limited, say, to building and civil engineering cases[27].

Problems arising out of the present law

2.5 In the Consultative Document our Sub-Committee suggested that there
were two main criticisms of the law as it then appeared[28]. First it seemed to
place an unduly heavy burden on professional advisers who in theory might
be open to claims for negligence for an indefinite period of time. In such
circumstances the cost of obtaining insurance could be formidable and there
could also be difficulties in obtaining sufficiently comprehensive insurance.
Secondly the Sub-Committee criticised the law on the ground of uncertainty,
in particular the uncertainty as to whether the effect of the *Sparham-Souter*
and *Anns* cases was to make the accrual of the plaintiff's cause of action dependent
upon the discoverability of the damage.

2.6 Broadly the comments that we received in response to the Consultative
Document reinforced these criticisms. Extremely few of those who wrote to us
thought that the law (as it was then understood)[29] was satisfactory. The main
complaint was uncertainty—both uncertainty as to the substance of the law

---

[23] See e.g. *Midland Bank Trust Co. Ltd.* v. *Hett, Stubbs and Kemp* [1979] 1 Ch. 384, 417,
433 and *Forster* v. *Outred* [1982] 1 W.L.R. 86, 99. But see, more recently, *William Hill
Organisation Ltd.* v. *Bernard Sunley and Sons Ltd.* (1983) 22 Build. L.R. 1 (C.A.).
[24] [1980] 1 Ch. 297.
[25] [1982] 1 Q.B. 438.
[26] See, for example, *J.E.B. Fasteners Ltd.* v. *Marks, Bloom and Co* [1981] 3 All ER 289;
Harrison v. *British Railways Board* [1981] 3 All ER 679: *The Irene's Success* [1983] 1 All
ER 218.
[27] See further para. 4.22 below.
[28] I.e. after the decisions in *Sparham-Souter* and *Anns*, but before the decision in *Pirelli*
[29] I.e. after the decisions in *Sparham-Souter* and *Anns*, but before the decision in *Pirelli*

and uncertainty about the length of time during which a person might remain liable for past acts or omissions. The difficulty of obtaining satisfactory insurance cover in respect of latent damage was also mentioned by many commentators and particular concern was voiced about the problems faced by retired professional people who felt impelled to keep up expensive insurance policies long after their retirement. A number of the submissions also mentioned the practical problems, especially in terms of evidence, of defending an action many years after the events giving rise to it and some suggested that these had led to a growing number of insubstantial claims. Many commentators were pessimistic about where these problems would lead and a significant number expressed anxiety about the effect that an apparently 'open-ended' liability would have on the development of new methods of technology and on the ultimate cost charged to consumers.

2.7 As we have already noted, both our analysis of the present law and the majority of the submissions that we received were written prior to the decision of the House of Lords in the *Pirelli* case[30]. In the next few paragraphs we discuss the extent to which this case and the other recent developments which we have mentioned had resolved the criticisms that were levelled at the earlier law, and the extent to which they have created new problems.

The burden on defendants

2.8 As far as criticism of unfairness to professional advisers is concerned, the recent developments outlined above have done much to redress the balance in their favour. In *Forster* v. *Outred*,[31] for instance, where the plaintiff had suffered loss through the negligent advice of her solicitor about a mortgage, the Court of Appeal held that actual damage was suffered (and the limitation period therefore started to run) on the date on which she entered into the mortgage and thereby encumbered her property with a liability. It was immaterial that she did not feel the loss in cash terms until much later and that she was not until then aware of the facts necessary for making a case against her solicitor. The decision has since been followed in a number of other cases involving 'economic loss'[32]. Additionally, as a result of the *Pirelli* decision, the overall period during which defendants might in theory be exposed to an action for negligence in relation to a latent defect in a building has been shortened, to the extent that the six year limitation period now runs from the date of damage, and not from the date of its discoverability. As a result of these developments however, many would argue that the balance in certain cases has been shifted too far in favour of defendants.

Uncertainty

2.9 The substance of the law is more certain following the *Pirelli* decision. Unless a building is so defective as to be 'doomed from the start'[33] a plaintiff's cause of action will accrue at the moment that physical damage occurs to it. The element of discovery or discoverability has been ruled out as irrelevant

---

[30] [1983] 2 A.C. 1.
[31] [1982] 1 W.L.R. 86.
[32] See n. 8, above.
[33] [1983] 2 A.C. 1. 16. *per* Lord Fraser. Some difficulty about the meaning of this qualification was expressed by Hodgson. J. in *Dove* v. *Banhams Patent Locks Ltd.* [1983] 1 W.L.R. 1436.

in determining when the cause of action accrues. Hence as soon as damage as a matter of fact occurs time will start to run in favour of the defendant and six years later the plaintiff's action will be statute barred. The law has been clarified: but the difficulties of establishing the date of the occurence of latent damage—which are difficulties arising out of the facts in each and every case—remain as severe as ever. Where there is disagreement neither a plaintiff nor a defendant can be certain as to this date until a court has ruled on it. The sad truth is that no reform of the law can eliminate the factual uncertainties which are likely to arise in cases of latent damage.

2.10 The facts in *Pirelli* concerned latent defects in a building but the decision in relation to the law of limitation of actions may extend far wider. A significant feature of the modern law has been the extension[34] of the tort of negligence to cover cases other than those of personal injury and physical damage. This extension presents problems in the law relating to limitation. If a solicitor gives his client bad advice and the client acts on it but in the result does not suffer financial loss until very much later, does the cause of action accrue and the period of limitation run from the time when the client acts on the advice or from the time when he first suffers financial loss? It is not much help to the client to be told that the limitation period runs from the date of damage unless it is possible to identify damage and its date. Despite its general application, therefore, *Pirelli* offers no guidance in solving such problems and uncertainties in the limitation law.

2.11 *Pirelli* has also had a quite distinct salutary effect. It has removed the possibility initially discussed in the *Sparham-Souter*[35] case and subsequently expanded upon in *Eames London Estates Ltd.* v. *North Herts. District Council*,[36] that in the case of successive owners of property time might not begin to run against the plaintiff until the later of *either* the date on which damage becomes detectable *or* the date on which he acquired his interest in the property. This interpretation of the law was much criticised[37] as opening the way to indefinite liability on the part of defendants, and almost all of those who submitted comments on the case expressed concern about its implications. In rejecting such a rule in *Pirelli* Lord Fraser observed[38]

> 'I think that the true view is that the duty of the builder and of the local authority is owed to owners of the property as a class, and that if time runs against one owner, it also runs against all his successors in title. No owner in the chain can have a better claim than his predecessor in title.'

Remaining problems: our view

2.12 Considerable problems therefore remain. As far as plaintiffs are concerned, they are now in a position in which they may well become barred from action before they know, or could even be in a position to know, that they have suffered damage. As far as defendants are concerned, they are faced with very great uncertainty. They have no way of telling in advance how long

---

[34] See para. 2.4, above.
[35] [1976] 1 Q.B. 858.
[36] (1982) 18 Build. L.R. 50; (1981) 259 E.G. 491.
[37] See e.g. (1982) 126 S.J. 775, 776.
[38] [1983] 2 A.C. 1. 18.

they will remain liable and, where damage does not occur until long after the events giving rise to it, they are likely to be faced with the practical difficulties of contesting a stale claim. In addition to the problems that are being faced by the parties to a claim for latent damage, courts are now being required to perform the time consuming, expensive and sometimes impossible task of ascertaining exactly when damage occurred. We do not think that this situation can be justified. We believe, however, that the law can be reformed without too much difficulty so as to secure a fair measure of justice between litigants. We therefore turn now to examine the alternatives to the present law in the light of the comments made to us on consultation.

Part III

FIELD OF CHOICE FOR REFORM

Introduction

3.1 In the Consultative Document our sub-Committee suggested a number of different approaches to the problem of latent damage. The possibilities canvassed were directed to possible modification of the long established rule that the limitation period starts to run on the date when a plaintiff's cause of action accrues. Thus it was suggested that in a case involving latent damage, a cause of action could be treated as accruing on any one of the following dates:—

    (a) the date on which the relevant breach of duty occurred; or

    (b) the date on which the relevant damage as a matter of fact occurred; or

    (c) the date on which the plaintiff could with reasonable diligence have discovered his loss (which might or might not be the same as the date on which he actually discovered it).

Additionally it was suggested that a new rule for determining when the limitation period begins to run could be combined with either an absolute bar on the bringing of proceedings after a fixed period of time (a 'long stop'), or a discretion for the court, in appropriate cases, to override what would otherwise be an effective defence of limitation, or with both a long stop and a discretion. A further possibility would be a scheme similar to that which presently obtains for personal injury claims[39]. In this Part of the Report we re-examine the main possibilities in the light of the comments that have been submitted to us.

(a) *Date of Breach of Duty*

3.2 This proposal is that a plaintiff's cause of action should be treated as accruing on the date of the defendant's breach of duty and that the limitation period should run from that date. We have already pointed out[40] that in the majority of cases where damage results from a negligent act or omission, the date of the breach of duty and the date of damage will be the same and the cause of action will accrue on that date. It might therefore be argued that the accrual of the cause of action should always coincide with the date of the relevant breach of duty; this would be comparable with the position in contract, where it is the date of the breach of contract that sets time running against the plaintiff. Additionally it might be said for this approach that in most cases there will be no difficulty in ascertaining the date on which the defendant's breach of duty took place. This in turn would make the maximum duration of a person's

---

[39] S. 11 of the Limitation Act 1980 provides for a three-year limitation period in relation to claims for personal injury, running from the date on which the cause of action accrued or the date of knowledge, as defined in section 14, of the injured person, whichever is the later. Section 33 however gives the court a discretion to allow an action to proceed notwithstanding the expiry of the three-year period and provides guidelines for the court's use in exercising the discretion.

[40] See para. 2.1, above.

liability in respect of a particular set of dealings relatively easy to predict or determine.

3.3 The main disadvantage of this approach is that, when applied in the context of latent defects or damage, it could mean that the limitation period would start to run at a time when the relevant defect has not emerged as the plaintiff has not yet suffered any damage. It was for this reason that most of those who wrote to us rejected a simple breach of duty approach. There is also the difficulty of legal principle in that negligence is not actionable unless actual damage has been suffered.

3.4 One possible way of overcoming the difficulties of principle inherent in this approach would be to allow the court a discretion to override a defence of limitation in appropriate cases. On the other hand any discretion, however tightly formulated, would introduce an element of uncertainty. It would never be entirely predictable either when it might be exercised or on what terms; and thus matters could never certainly be treated as closed. Another possibility would be to have a longer period of limitation that the present six years. This would have the advantage of catering for many hard cases where a plaintiff does not discover that he has suffered damage until some time after the defendant's breach of duty. But this would not answer the argument of legal principle, and it would be overgenerous to the plaintiff who discovered the damage soon after the defendant's breach of duty.

3.5 Although this approach did find favour with a number of those who wrote to us, especially those who were concerned that the duration of liability should be finite, most felt that it would work unreasonably as far as the plaintiffs were concerned and that a discretion would be too uncertain to make it acceptable. We accept these criticisms. We therefore reject 'breach of duty' as the date from which the limitation period should run. But we return to consider breach of duty as the date from which a possible 'long stop' period might run.

(b) *Date of Damage*

3.6 If the 'date of damage' approach were to be adopted a plaintiff's cause of action would accrue on the date on which damage as a matter of fact occurs, irrespective of whether it is discovered, or even discoverable. This is the existing law (the *Pirelli* case[41]) and it was the solution that we favoured in our 21st Report, if our interpretation in that report of the House of Lords decision in *Anns* v. *Merton London Borough Council*[42] should prove to be wrong. We there[43] expressed the view that the occurrence of damage should be treated as 'a question of fact to be determined by the evidence, without the interposition of a rule of law to the effect that damage does not occur until it is reasonably discoverable.' The approach could be used alone (as it is in the existing law) or it could be combined with either a discretion, or a long stop, or with both a discretion and a long stop.

3.7 There are two advantages in treating the plaintiff's cause of action as accruing on the date of damage. First it is consistent with established legal principle. Secondly, on the assumption that in many cases damage will be

[41] [1983] 2 A.C. 1.
[42] [1978] A.C. 728
[43] *Final Report on Limitation of Actions*, (1977) Cmnd 6923, para. 2.38.

discoverable within a short time of its actual occurrence, the approach is probably more often than not fair to plaintiffs.

3.8 However, in the context of latent damage, as we have seen[44], the date of damage approach is open to a number of substantial objections. It is significant that it was favoured by very few of those who wrote to us. Determining exactly when damage takes place may, in itself, prove difficult, and sometimes even impossible. In *Pirelli*, a building case, the court chose the moment at which physical damage occurred to the structure. Another possibility would be to say that damage occurs on the date on which, for instance, a badly-constructed building is completed or first acquired, on the basis that the building owner or the purchaser is not getting the sound building that he bargained for[45]. But if either or both of the proposals were to be adopted the plaintiff might not suffer any financial loss (e.g. expenditure in making good a defect or a reduction in the market value of the property) until after the date on which the damage was discovered or became discoverable. More important however than the problems inherent in identifying the precise date of damage, is the fact that the approach secures justice for neither plaintiffs nor defendants. As we have pointed out[46] in our discussion of the present law, a limitation period based on the date of damage raises the possibility that plaintiffs may become barred from action before they even know that they have suffered any damage and, as far as defendants are concerned, there is always the possibility that where the damage occurs long after the relevant breach of duty they will have to fight stale claims for which they are practically and financially unprepared.

3.9 One way, of course, of dealing with cases where a plaintiff has become barred before he even knows that he has suffered damage might be to allow the court a discretion to let him proceed in particular circumstances. On the other hand a discretion would erode certainty. It would also make the difficulties which defendants already face under the present law worse because there would be an even greater degree of uncertainty about the duration of their liability. A possible solution might be to couple a discretion with an overall long stop. We can see some attractions in the approach. However by introducing a discretion one would in effect be introducing a discoverability approach for certain cases since the exercise of the discretion would in practice very probably be much influenced by discoverability. Arguably an approach to the problem based on discoverability would be a more straightforward solution and to this we now turn.

(c) *Date of Discovery or Discoverability*

3.10 This approach can be formulated in either of two ways. The first, and in our view less acceptable, way is to reform the law of negligence by making an exception to the general rule and enacting that in latent damage cases the discovery (or discoverability) of the damage is to be the date of the accrual of the cause of action. The second is simply to amend the limitation law by prescribing that a plaintiff shall have an extension of time in which to sue after

---

[44] See para. 2.12, above.
[45] Cf the 'economic loss' cases where the date on which the plaintiff acted to his detriment seems to be the approach which has found judicial acceptance: *Forster* v. *Outred* [1982] 1 W.L.R. 86. See also para. 2.1. above.
[46] See paras. 2.9–2.12. above.

he has discovered, or ought reasonably to have discovered, the existence of damage.

3.11 The discoverability approach was favoured by the Court of Appeal in *Sparham-Souter* v. *Town and Country Developments (Essex) Limited*[47] and it is the basis of the Scots approach to latent damage[48]. It can be applied by itself and without qualification, as in *Sparham-Souter* and the cases that followed it. It can be made subject to a discretion or to a long stop, or to both. In Scotland the discoverability principle is subject to an absolute bar 20 years after the date on which damage occurred[49] (long negative prescription). A significant number of those who wrote to us favoured this type of solution.

3.12 Its chief attraction is that it would usually prevent a diligent plaintiff from suffering injustice. On the other hand it can cause injustice to a defendant who, having no reason to suppose that he may have incurred a liability, has destroyed his records. Further, by itself it is bound to lead to a degree of uncertainty because the date on which damage will become discoverable will not be known in advance, and may prove difficult to determine later when the issue arises in litigation. Thirdly unless specifically dealt with, it opens the way for difficulties such as arose in the *Eames* case[50].

3.13 In the view of those who wrote to us the main difficulty with the discoverability approach by itself is the possibility of injustice to defendants and the element of uncertainty. Most of them however agreed that these problems could to a great extent be overcome by making a limitation period based on discoverability subject to a long stop whereby a defendant's liability would in effect be at an end a certain number of years after either the date of breach of duty or the completion of the defendant's work. On the assumption that the long stop period would be sufficiently long, our correspondents argued that only a very small number of plaintiffs would be denied a right of action before they realised that they had suffered damage. A long stop would also reduce the extent to which a discoverability approach would cause the sort of problems that arose in the *Eames* case[51] although it would equally well be possible to formulate the law so that once time had started to run a prospective plaintiff's successor in title could claim no better right to sue than his predecessor (as, it would seem, is the case under the existing law.[52])

Our view on the field of choice

3.14 In the Consultative Document the Sub-Committee indicated no preference as between the three approaches. In our 21st Report however we unanimously rejected the discoverability approach on the basis that it was too uncertain and

---

[47] [1976] 1 Q.B. 858.
[48] Section 11(3) of the Prescription and Limitation (Scotland) Act 1973 provides in relation to obligations to make reparation that where 'the creditor was not aware, and could not with reasonable diligence have been aware, that loss, injury or damage caused as aforesaid had occurred', the relevant period of prescription runs from 'the date when the creditor first became, or could, with reasonable diligence have become so aware'.
[49] Prescription and Limitation (Scotland) Act 1973, s. 7.
[50] (1982) 18 Build. L.R. 50: (1981) 259 E.G. 491. See para. 2.9 above.
[51] *Ibid.*
[52] See Lord Fraser's observations in *Pirelli General Cable Works Ltd.* v. *Oscar Faber and Partners* set out in para. 2.11 above.

could cause injustice to defendants. A majority of us favoured making no special provision for cases of latent damage; a minority favoured granting the court a residual discretion to override a defence of limitation in a limited class of case. We did not then consider the possibility of using a long stop to mitigate the disadvantages of the discoverability principle. For the reasons outlined above[53] we do not now think that it is possible to make no provision at all for cases of latent damage. On the other hand we are impressed by the weight of argument that has been put to us against any form of discretion and we are persuaded that it would not provide the right balance between certainty and justice.

3.15 For the reasons developed in the preceding paragraphs we reject the proposal that the period of limitation should begin to run against a plaintiff as from the date of breach of duty, save only that the date can be used to determine the moment from which time is measured before the imposition of an ultimate long stop (a matter which we examine later.[54]) We believe that the existing law (as laid down in *Pirelli*) under which the period of limitation begins with the date of damage should remain, and should be of general application. But we think an extension of the period of limitation must be made available in cases of latent damage. Finally we reject the proposal for a judicial discretion:[55] but we believe that an ultimate 'long stop' has merit.

3.16 Our proposal will be found to be two-fold. First, we recommend that there be in cases of latent damage a special extension of the limitation period which is to run from the date of discovery or discoverability. Secondly, we recommend the introduction into the law of a long stop after which a plaintiff in a case involving latent defect or damage would be barred from bringing an action. The proposed special extension—and the proposed long stop—would be limited to cases of latent damage and the long stop would be no more than a bar to action. We do not recommend that it should extinguish the plaintiff's right: this is in accordance with the basic principle of our law that limitation of actions is procedural law only. Finally we believe that the long stop should operate whether it is the defect, the damage or its discoverability that is delayed: if damage arises or is discovered after the point at which the long stop expires, the defendant should be protected save only in cases of fraud or concealment. We develop our proposals in detail in the next Part of this Report. Before we do so, we think it necessary, however, to mention two approaches to reform that were suggested to us by those who commented on the Consultative Document, but which we had not ourselves initially considered.

Other proposals for reform

3.17 Most of those who wrote to us favoured one or other of the approaches suggested in the Consultative Document. Of the other proposals that were made the two most significant were:

(a) *A limitation period running from the date of 'completion'*

By this proposal a plaintiff would be barred from action a fixed number of

---

[53] In Part II of this Report.
[54] See para. 4.12, below.
[55] See para. 3.4 above, and paras. 3.17 and 4.19 below.

years after the date on which the work in question had been completed. It is broadly similar to the date of breach of duty approach described above[56] but is intended to overcome any problems in defining the date on which a breach of duty occurs. The disadvantages of such an approach are generally the same as with the breach of duty approach; additionally we are not persuaded that 'completion' is a concept that can be readily adapted to all the types of circumstance in which latent damage may arise[57]. For these reasons therefore we have rejected this proposal.

(b) *The Law Society's proposal*

In their submission to us The Law Society proposed a rule whereby in all actions (whether in contract or tort), other than personal injury actions and actions where there had been fraud or mistake, a plaintiff would be required to commence proceedings within either:

(i) a basic limitation period of six years from the date of the defendant's breach of duty or

(ii) an extended limitation period of one or two years from the date of the plaintiff's 'date of knowledge'[58] where the plaintiff has not started proceedings within the basic period. This extended period however would be subject to a long stop of fifteen years from the date of the defendant's breach of duty.

In addition the court would be allowed a limited discretion, subject to the long stop period, to extend either the basic period or the extended period where proceedings have not been started due to the plaintiff's or his adviser's inadvertence *and* hardship would be caused to the plaintiff but not to the defendant if the action could not proceed. The proposal, notwithstanding the departure it involves from established legal principles, has much to commend it. The combination of the two periods of limitation with a long stop balances the interests of plaintiffs and defendants and the importation of a limited discretion provides a possible safety net for particularly hard cases. The proposal, however, presents formidable difficulties.

First, the ordinary, or basic, limitation period would run from breach of duty: we have already given our reasons for rejecting this proposal[59]. Secondly, as we have already said, we have been impressed by the weight of argument that has been put to us against any form of discretion and, on the assumption that the initial period of limitation is a fair one, we believe the addition of a discretion would only create uncertainty[60]. We have, however, drawn substantially upon the views of The Law Society. We accept the principle of an extended period

---

[56] At paras. 3.2–3.5.
[57] Many of those who made this suggestion directed their attention to building and engineering cases. But there are many other very different situations in which latent damage can follow a breach of duty, notably those of professional advice: see paras. 1.2 and 2.1 above.
[58] The Law Society suggest that the definition of date of knowledge contained in the Limitation Act 1980, s. 14 might be adapted for this purpose. A summary of the Society's evidence to us was published in (1982) 79 Law Soc. Gaz. 390.
[59] See paras. 3.3 and 3.5 above.
[60] See further para. 4.19, below.

Part IV

RECOMMENDATIONS FOR REFORM

Recommendations

4.1 In our view, the problem of limitation in 'negligence cases involving latent defects' can be solved by amendment of the existing limitation statute, i.e. the Limitation Act 1980. We recommend in such cases:—

(i) that the ordinary period of limitation should be subject to an extension which would allow the plaintiff three years from the date on which he discovered or could reasonably have discovered that he had suffered significant damage; but

(ii) that there should be a long stop which, we suggest, should operate to bar all negligence claims involving latent defects or damage that are brought more than fifteen years from the date of the defendant's breach of duty.

Our general approach

4.2 Three principles are of critical importance in this branch of the law. They are:—

(i) that plaintiffs must have a fair and sufficient opportunity of pursuing their remedy;

(ii) that defendants are entitled to be protected against stale claims;

(iii) that uncertainty in the law is to be avoided wherever possible.

We would not find any proposal for reform of the law acceptable which failed in any significant respect to satisfy these criteria.

4.3 In the second Part of our Report we have suggested that the existing law achieves neither justice nor certainty,[61] and in our examination of the various alternatives to the present law we have found that most approaches fall short in one or other respect. We accept that limitation of actions represents a compromise between conflicting interests and that complete certainty is not possible in a branch of the law where the gist of the cause of action is the suffering of damage or loss. Nevertheless we believe that the limitation law can be reformed so that it achieves an acceptable balance between the principles stated in paragraph 4.2 above.

4.4 We consider that a plaintiff who has no means of knowing that he has suffered damages should not as a general rule be barred from taking proceedings by a limitation period which can expire before he discovers (or could discover) his loss. But we are equally convinced that defendants require protection from stale claims and that a time limit must be set to legal action by a plaintiff. In our view therefore two reforms are necessary. The first is the introduction of an extension to the ordinary period of limitation so as to give a plaintiff in a negligence case involving latent damage an additional period of years from the date on which he knows (or ought reasonably to have known) that he has

---

[61] See paras. 2.8–2.12, above.

suffered significant damage. In paragraphs 4.5 to 4.9 below we discuss in detail the precise type of knowledge we consider a plaintiff should have before time will run against him and the exact length of the special extension. The second reform is the introduction of a long stop which would operate to bar legal action in cases of latent defect or damage after a defined period of years. This proposal, and in particular its application to certain cases where the plaintiff's cause of action has not even accrued (because the occurrence of actual damage is long delayed) is fully discussed in paragraphs 4.10 to 4.14 below. We should however point out at this stage that we are not in this Report recommending any change to the general rules governing the accrual of the cause of action. In cases involving negligence, a plaintiff's cause of action might accrue at different dates depending upon whether the negligence was in the performance of a contractual duty, or a statutory duty[62] or a duty of care at common law[63] and this can lead to complications. Indeed a single set of facts could in theory give rise to claims for breach of duty under all three heads, with three limitation periods. This situation was criticised by a number of those who wrote to us. Our terms of reference on the other hand are limited to the relatively narrow band of 'negligence cases involving latent defects' and we consider that it would be quite inappropriate for us to make general recommendations, applicable for instance in the contract field, in the context of the present review.

The extension of time in latent damage cases

(i) *Definition of the date of knowledge*

4.5 We have considered three possible approaches to defining the knowledge that a plaintiff under our proposals must have before the special period of limitation starts to run against him. The first would be to define knowledge fairly generally.

This is what is done for instance in the Scottish law on latent damage where section 11(3) of the Prescription and Limitation (Scotland) Act 1973 provides (in relation to obligations to make reparation) that where a 'creditor was not aware, and could not with reasonable diligence have been aware, that loss, injury or damage caused as aforesaid has occurred', the relevant period of prescription runs from the 'date when the creditor first became, or could with reasonable diligence have become, so aware'. The special provision contained in the Limitation Act 1980 for cases of fraud, concealment and mistake also adopts this approach.[64] The second possibility would be to adapt the very much more precise formulation that is used in the 1980 Act in cases of latent personal injury where the limitation period runs from the date of the accrual of the cause of action or the 'date of knowledge'. Section 14 provides that:

'(1) ... references to a person's date of knowledge are references to the date on which he first had knowledge of the following facts:—

(a) that the injury in question was significant; and

(b) that the injury was attributable in whole or in part to the act

---

[62] *Dennis* v. *Charnwood Borough Council* [1983] 1 Q.B. 409, 420, *per* Templeman, L.J.
[63] See para. 2.1, above.
[64] Limitation Act 1980, s. 32

or omission which is alleged to constitute negligence, nuisance or breach of duty; and

(c) the identity of the defendant; and

(d) if it is alleged that the act or omission was that of a person other than the defendant, the identity of that person and the additional facts supporting the bringing of an action against the defendant;

(2) For the purposes of this section an injury is significant if the person whose date of knowledge is in question would reasonably have considered it sufficiently serious to justify his instituting proceedings for damages against a defendant who did not dispute liability and was able to satisfy a judgment.

(3) For the purposes of this section a person's knowledge includes knowledge which he might reasonably have been expected to acquire—

(a) from the facts observable or ascertainable by him; or

(b) from the facts ascertainable by him with the help of medical or other appropriate expert advice which it is reasonable for him to seek;

but a person shall not be fixed under this subsection with knowledge of a fact ascertainable only with the help of expert advice so long as he has taken all reasonable steps to obtain (and, where appropriate, to act on) that advice.'

The third possibility would be to disregard constructive knowledge altogether and to define knowledge solely in terms of what the plaintiff actually knows.

4.6 We have little hesitation in rejecting the third of these approaches. It would in our view be grossly unfair to defendants, it would favour dilatory plaintiffs and it would effectively hand to claimants the option of choosing when the special limitation period should start to run against them.

4.7 As between the first and second approaches however each has certain advantages. The first has the advantage of simplicity. On the other hand we think that it could in practice operate harshly against plaintiffs in the special circumstances of a case involving latent damage. In the first place, although the point has not, as far as we are aware, been tested in the Scottish courts, it is at least arguable that section 11(3) of the 1973 Act is confined to lack of knowledge of the damage, and does not cover lack of knowledge of its causation, or the identity of the person (or persons) liable.[65] By comparison awareness of such matters, which could sometimes be difficult to ascertain in a latent damage context, is specifically included in the definition of knowledge contained in section 14 of the 1980 Act. Secondly, the first approach gives no indication of the severity of damage required to be within the plaintiff's knowledge before time will run out against him. Section 14 on the other hand requires the damage to be 'significant' which in turn is defined as 'sufficiently serious to justify . . . instituting proceedings for damages against a defendant who did not dispute liability and

---

[65] See the Scottish Law Commission's *Report on the Reform of the Law Relating to Prescription and Limitation of Actions* (1970) Scot. Law Com. No. 15, para. 97, on which the 1973 Act is based.

was able to satisfy a judgment.' We think that the substance of this requirement is a particularly important one, and that there is a strong argument for refining it further to refer not only to 'proceedings' but to the very proceedings in question. Latent damage is by definition hard to detect and may in many cases be heralded by defects that at first appear to be minor and isolated. It may not be until much later that the full significance of these early defects becomes apparent and it might be harsh if an extended period of limitation based on discovery or discoverability started to run against the plaintiff from the moment that the first apparently trivial damage appeared.

However the second approach does have its disadvantages too.[66] It is a complicated formulation and the present definition of 'significance' requires the court to make an assessment of the plaintiff's injury by reference to both subjective and objective criteria.[67] One could also argue that the subjective element of the definition goes too far in the direction of a requirement of actual knowledge, an option that we have already rejected on the grounds of unfairness to defendants.[68]

4.8 Having considered in detail the advantages and disadvantages of the first two approaches mentioned in paragraph 4.5 above, our conclusion is to favour the second, namely the adaptation of section 14 of the 1980 Act to cases of latent defect other than those of personal injury. We recognise, however, that difficulties of drafting and presentation will arise in the preparation of legislation adapting section 14 of the 1980 Act to property damage or loss. It will for instance be necessary, while excluding references to injury and medical advice, to ensure that the drafting takes account of the different sorts of loss or damage which can occur in latent damage cases. Secondly, the draftsman must be astute to prevent a revival of the *Eames* difficulty, which the *Pirelli* case has exorcised from the existing law.[69] Thirdly, though it will in evitably fall to the judges to determine what is 'significant' damage, the legislation must contain a definition, or guidelines, sufficiently detailed to assist not only the judges but the parties and their advisers in reaching a view on this critical question. In this respect we believe that the objective should be for the special period of limitation to start to run when the plaintiff knows, or might reasonably be expected to know, that he has suffered such damage as would justify a reasonable plaintiff in initiating the proceedings in hand against a defendant who did not dispute liability and was able to satisfy a judgment.

(ii) *Length of the period of limitation*

4.9 We have considered various possible lengths for the special limitation period and we have concluded that a period of three years from the date of

---

[66] For a recent criticism of section 14, see Davies. 'Limitations of the Law of Limitation' (1982) 98 L.Q.R. 249.

[67] In this context the meaning of the word 'would' was questioned by Geoffrey Lane, L.J. in *McCafferty* v. *Metropolitan Police District Receiver* [1977] 1 W.L.R. 1073. 1081. See also Davies, 'Limitations of the Law of Limitation' (1982) 98 L.Q.R. 249.

[68] In practice the courts seem to have adopted a fairly restrictive approach to the subjective element now contained in section 14(2): see e.g. *Buck* v. *English Electric Co. Ltd.* [1977] 1 W.L.R. 806, 809: *McCafferty* v. *Metropolitan Police District Receiver* [1977] W.L.R. 1073, 1082.

[69] [1983] A.C.1, 18. See further para. 4.21 below.

knowledge (as defined above) would be the most appropriate. The ordinary period for tort cases is six years, and the fact that this is the period with which people are most familiar is a substantial, although by no means conclusive, argument for adopting a similar period for the extension of time in latent damage cases.[70] However where the plaintiff knows, or is assumed to know, that he can take proceedings the law sometimes imposes a more stringent time limit on him. In the field of personal injuries, for instance, it is (subject to the court's discretion) three years,[71] and in contribution proceedings the limitation period is two years from the date on which judgment is given.[72] The plaintiff's knowledge of significant damage is the cornerstone of our recommendations for an extended period of limitation and, although we accept that under the general law a plaintiff is entitled to a full six years in which to commence proceedings, regardless of his state of knowledge, we think that it would be fairer to defendants and that it would not be unreasonable to plaintiffs, to require claimants in latent damage cases to bring their proceedings within a shorter period than six years from the date of knowledge.

The long stop

4.10 Our second recommendation is that the law should fix a point beyond which a plaintiff in a negligence case involving latent defect or damage should no longer be able to commence proceedings. As we have said above we consider that this is essential if effect is to be given to the second principle set out in paragraph 4.2(ii) above that defendants are entitled to be protected against stale claims. A long stop is of course a relatively novel concept in English Law[73] and the paragraphs that follow therefore set out in some detail the way in which we see our proposed long stop working in the context of negligence cases involving latent defects. Four particular aspects require discussion:

(i) the application of the long stop;

(ii) the date from which it is to be reckoned;

(iii) its length; and

(iv) its effect.

---

[70] Cf. Prescription and Limitation (Scotland) Act 1973 where the period of short negative prescription is five years whether the obligation becomes enforceable at the date of damage (under section 11(1)) or the date of the creditor's first awareness of his loss (under section 11(3)).
[71] Limitation Act 1980, section 11(4).
[72] *Ibid.* section 10.
[73] A 'long stop' was recommended by the Tucker Committee on the Limitation of Actions in 1949 in the context of personal injuries (Cmnd. 7740, para. 22) but the proposal was not implemented. We considered such an approach again in 1974 in our *Report on Limitation of Actions in Personal Injury Claims* (Cmnd. 5630, para. 36) but rejected it on the basis that it would 'either be too long to serve any very useful purpose in the majority of cases or too short to cover those with which we are particularly concerned, namely insidious diseases.' A long stop is however to be found in section 15(1) Nuclear Installations Act 1965 and it is also not unlike the Scottish twenty year period of long negative prescription: Prescription and Limitation (Scotland) Act 1973, s. 7.

(i) *The application of the long stop*

4.11 The possibility that a defendant might be faced with a very stale negligence claim in respect of a latent defect might arise, as we have seen,[74] in one of two situations. In the first place damage might occur but remain undiscoverable for such a long period that the defendant is no longer in a position to contest the plaintiff's allegation of negligence. Secondly the damage itself might not occur until long after the events giving rise to it. As we said in the Introduction to this Report, we consider that our terms of reference require us to examine both types of situation. In practice we can see little to differentiate between them. In both, defendants may be confronted with allegations of negligence at an impossibly remote date and be quite unable to meet them either evidentially or financially. There is also the problem of whether they will have been able to insure themselves adequately. There are therefore strong arguments for applying a long stop in both types of situation. However there is also an important objection of legal principle to a long stop in cases of delayed damage because it might expire before damage even occurs and before the plaintiff has ever been in a position to claim. We believe that this is a substantial difficulty and we can see that there is much to be said for either applying the long stop only in relation to the three year extended period of limitation (thus leaving the ordinary period of limitation running from the date of damage unaffected) or providing that the long stop should only have effect once damage has occurred. However either of these approaches would be open to the objection that stale claims would still be possible. Additionally they would differentiate between defendants in an undesirable way: defendants in cases where damage occurred but remained undiscoverable for an excessive period would be able to claim the benefit of the long stop, but not defendants in cases where the occurrence of the damage itself was delayed. We have found this a particularly difficult choice and have discussed it at some length. Our conclusion is to favour a long stop applicable to all negligence cases involving latent defects—whether or not the defect has manifested itself in damage by the time that the long stop expires. We consider it important that the law should provide some degree of finality and we think that any concern lest the long stop should operate to deprive plaintiffs of worthwhile causes of action can be met by selecting a sufficiently lengthy period. We discuss this question at paragraph 4.13, below.

(ii) *Date from which the long stop period is to be reckoned*

4.12 We initially considered three possible points from which the long stop might run. These were:—

(1) the date of damage;[75]

(2) the date of the defendant's breach of duty;

(3) the date of the completion of the work in question.

For the reasons given in the previous paragraph however we decided that the

---

[74] See para. 1.2, above.

[75] Cf. the Scots period of long negative prescription which starts to run on the date on which 'the obligation becomes enforceable' which in relation to obligations to make reparation is the date on which damage occurs: Prescription and Limitation (Scotland) Act 1973, ss. 7 and 11.

date of damage would not be a satisfactory starting point. Although it would accord with legal principle it would provide no certainty and might well permit many stale claims. Accordingly we view the choice as lying between the date of breach of duty and the date of completion. As far as the first of these dates is concerned it is, of course, already well established in English Law. In contract the limitation period runs from the date of the defendant's breach of contract and courts and litigants are therefore already familiar with the concept. In theory difficulties can arise where there has been a course of dealing between plaintiff and defendant or a series of breaches of duty; and where the breach consists of an omission to do something it would appear to be settled law that time does not begin to run until the duty is no longer capable of performance.[76] We do not however consider that these are substantial objections, and in the majority of cases we think that the date of breach of duty will be readily ascertainable by the parties. A number of those who wrote to us—especially those involved in the construction industry—suggested that the date of completion would be even easier to ascertain than the date of breach of duty. Section 1(5) of the Defective Premises Act 1972, for instance, provides that for the purposes of proceedings under the Act a cause of action shall be deemed to have accrued 'at the time when the dwelling was completed'. We are doubtful though whether this is really a satisfactory alternative and in particular we can see formidable difficulties in adapting the concept of completion to all the types of circumstances (other than personal injury) where latent damage might arise. There is also the possibility of injustice to defendants where 'completion', on a very large project for instance, takes place many years after the relevant breach of duty. Accordingly we recommend that the long stop should start to run at the date of the defendant's breach of duty.

(iii) *Length of the long stop*

4.13 The question of the length of the long stop is difficult: it must not be so long that it has no useful effect and it must not be so short that it will cause injustice. The latter factor, as we have said above,[77] is of particular importance in the light of our recommendation that the long stop should apply to cases of delayed damage, as well as to cases of undiscoverable damage. In the final analysis the question of length is one of judgment. In the draft European Community Product Liability Directive[78] it is provided that a producer's liability is extinguished ten years from the end of the calendar year in which the defective article was put into circulation. In Scottish Law the period of long negative prescription, which operates as a long stop, is twenty years, but it runs from the date of damage rather than the date of breach as we are suggesting. We have considered periods of twelve years, fifteen years and twenty years. We have come to the conclusion that a period of twelve years, although it would probably work satisfactorily in most cases, might also bar some worthy claims. At the other extreme we think that a twenty year period might permit some very stale claims and expose many defendants to the risk of litigation for an

---

[76] *Midland Bank Trust Company Ltd.* v. *Hett. Stubbs and Kemp* [1979] Ch. 384.

[77] At para. 4.11

[78] The text of the proposal for a directive which was presented to the Council of the European Communities in 1976 is reproduced as Appendix B to the *Report on Liability for Defective Products* made by the Law Commission and the Scottish Law Commission in 1977 (Law Com. No. 82 and Scot. Law Com. No. 45, Cmnd. 6831).

unreasonable length of time. We have concluded that a fifteen year period strikes the right balance between justice for plaintiffs and certainty for defendants and we so recommend.

(iv) *Effect of the long stop*

4.14 Should the long stop extinguish the plaintiff's right, or should it merely bar his remedy? We believe that it should do the latter. With a few exceptions[79] the periods of limitation contained in the Limitation Act 1980 bar the remedy without extinguishing the right itself. In practice the distinction is usually of little importance although barring the remedy means that payment of most, though not all, statute barred debts cannot thereafter be attacked as improper, and that a lien, charge or other security may be enforced even though the debt itself is statute barred. The distinction is however of importance in the context of contribution proceedings. The general rule in such proceedings is that a defendant who is sued within the statutory period may seek a contribution or an indemnity from a third party even though an action by the plaintiff against such a third party would by then have been statute barred. If however the plaintiff's rights against the third party should have been extinguished by effluxion of time a defendant would have no right of action at all against the third party for a contribution.[80] A long stop which extinguished the plaintiff's right might therefore bar an action for a contribution between joint wrongdoers. This would, we think, be unfortunate. Additionally we believe that there can be circumstances in which defendants may prefer to treat an action on the merits rather than rely on the long stop defence. This they could not do if the expiry of the long stop served to extinguish the plaintiff's right. The effect of our recommendation that the long stop should operate to bar the plaintiff's remedy will, of course, mean that it will operate as a 'procedural' rule and will have to be specifically pleaded by way of defence.

Extension of time where the plaintiff is under a disability

4.15 One matter that we have not so far discussed is the question whether either the additional limitation period or the long stop should be capable of extension by reason of the plaintiff's disability. Under the present law (section 28 of the 1980 Act), where a person is under a disability (i.e. a minor or of unsound mind)[81] at the time at which his right of action accrues, he is allowed (subject to certain exceptions) a period equivalent to the appropriate limitation period, calculated from the date on which he ceases to be under the disability, in which to commence his proceedings.[82] For example, in the case of a person who suffers a latent personal injury which he discovers (as provided for by sections 11(4) and 14 of the 1980 Act) whilst still a minor, time will not begin to run against him until he reaches 18. In Scotland it would appear that in cases of latent damage the period of short negative prescription is capable of

---

[79] The most frequently encountered exceptions are the provisions governing extinction of title in relation to land (Limitation Act 1980, s. 17) and to chattels (*ibid.* s. 3(2)). See also section 15(1) of the Nuclear Installations Act 1965.
[80] Civil Liability (Contribution) Act 1978, s. 1(3).
[81] Limitation Act 1980, section 38(2).
[82] *Ibid.*, section 28(1).

suspension by reason of a creditor's disability, but not so the twenty year period of long negative prescription.[83]

4.16 Taking first the case where the plaintiff is under a disability at the time that the special limitation period would otherwise have started to run, we would make the preliminary observation that in the ordinary way a plaintiff who was under disability when the damage that he had suffered became discoverable would be fully protected by the general law. One might however have an exceptional case where the disability came into existence between the date of damage when the cause of action accrued and the date of discovery or discoverability. In such a case we think that it is right that the disabled plaintiff should be given extra time in which to commence his proceedings.

4.17 But should disability postpone the commencement of the long stop period? We think not for a number of reasons. The first is that, if it did, it would diminish the certainty and the effectivness of the long stop. The second is that it is doubtful whether the possibility of a postponement of the long stop would greatly assist many disabled plaintiffs. A plaintiff who is under a disability at the date of damage will also be protected by section 28 of the Limitation Act and will have six years from the date on which his disability ceases in which to commence proceedings. We think that the right conferred by section 28 on a disabled plaintiff should remain, notwithstanding the introduction into the law of a long stop; the section should, we think, override the long stop. The proposed long stop will not affect his rights under the general law. We would also observe that such precedents for 'cut off' periods as we are aware of do not provide for any extension on the ground of disability at the date of their commencement.[84] We recommend, therefore, that subject to the operation of section 28, the fact of disability should have no effect on the commencement or duration of the long stop period. Accordingly, our recommendations as to the effect of disability are:—

(a) the operation of section 28 should not be affected by our proposals. Accordingly, where a plaintiff is under a disability when damage occurs and the cause of action accrues, time should not start to run until the disability ceases.

(b) Where a plaintiff becomes subject to a disability after the damage occurs but before it becomes discoverable he should be entitled to the benefit of the three year extension which we propose as from the cesser of the disability if this provides a longer period than is available under the general law.

(c) The extension of the limitation period by section 28 in cases of disability should remain unaffected by the long stop but subject to this the existence of disability during the long stop period should have no effect upon its duration or effect. Thus disability which ended before the cause of action accrued and disability which arose after it had accrued would not extend the long stop period.

4.18 We appreciate that recommendation (c) in the foregoing paragraph may

---

[83] Prescription and Limitation (Scotland) Act 1973, s. 14(1)(b).
[84] See e.g. Prescription and Limitation (Scotland) Act 1973, s. 14(1)(b): Nuclear Installations Act 1965, s. 15(1): and the draft European Product Liability Directive, Article 9.

appear to some to draw an unjustifiable distinction between the plaintiff who, being disabled when the latent damage occurred, has the benefit of section 28 and the plaintiff who, though disabled when the damage was discovered, was under no disability when the damage (unknown to him) occurred and does not have the benefit of section 28. The question is one of policy, and the reasons for our view are to be found in paragraph 4.17. If the other view should prevail, it would be a simple matter to amend section 28 so as to cover a plaintiff under no disability when damage occurred but disabled by the time it became discoverable.

Extension of time at the discretion of the court

4.19 We have considered whether there should be a discretion to extend the new limitation periods that we are proposing. The value of the long stop would be lost if there was a judicial discretion to postpone it. But the three-year extension of time which we propose a plaintiff shall have from when he discovers (or ought to discover) the existence of damage clearly could be made subject to a judicial discretion. The court could have either a general discretion, subject to the long stop, to extend the period in which proceedings might be commenced, or a discretion subject to particular guidelines[85] Most of those who wrote to us rejected the idea of a general discretion on the basis that it introduces an element of doubt, and as we have explained above this is a view that we share.[86] In cases of latent personal injury, the court does have a discretion to extend the limitation period, but such cases are we think different from the type of latent damage that we are presently discussing and require a different balance to be drawn between plaintiffs and defendants. In the present context we believe that a period of three years from the date of (presumed) knowledge is long enough to dispense with the need for a discretionary power of extension and it is much less uncertain in operation. We therefore make no recommendations in this regard.

Extension of time under section 32 of the 1980 Act (Fraud, Concealment, Mistake)

4.20 Special provision is already made in the general law for actions involving fraud, deliberate concealment or mistake[87] with the result that in such cases the period of limitation does not begin to run until the plaintiff discovers the fraud, concealment or mistake (or could with reasonable diligence have discovered it). In such cases the plaintiff's cause of action could in theory be indefinitely postponed. It can, however, be argued that our proposed long stop should also apply to actions involving fraud, deliberate concealment and mistake. We do not think that this would be appropriate, and it is interesting that very few of those who submitted comments to us suggested that there should be any change in section 32 of the 1980 Act. The essential feature of the section is that it is based on some degree of responsibility on the part of the defendant

---

[85] See for instance the form of discretion that was recommended to us by The Law Society set out in paragraph 3.17(b), above.
[86] See paras 3.4 and 3.9 above.
[87] Limitation Act 1980, s. 32 set out in paragraph 2.2 above. For a recent case on common mistake see *Peco Arts Inc.* v. *Hazlitt Gallery Ltd.* [1983] 1 W.L.R. 1315 involved the sale of a drawing which both sides believed, mistakenly, to be an original but which turned out to be a copy.

beyond his mere failure to comply with his legal obligations, and the traditional view taken by the courts of such conduct is that it would be 'against conscience'[88] to allow a defendant to take advantage of such behaviour by lapse of time. We believe that it would be no less repugnant to most people's sense of justice to allow such defendants to take advantage of a long stop provision, and we therefore make no recommendation in this area. Accordingly, the long stop will come into play in those latent damage cases where there has been negligence by inadvertent or careless acts or omissions but not where there has been, in the words of section 32(2) a 'deliberate commission of a breach of duty in circumstances in which it is unlikely to be discovered for some time'.

Successors in title

4.21 In our discussion above[89] of the present law and its background we mentioned the case of *Eames London Estates Ltd.* v. *North Herts. District Council*[90] in which it was held at first instance that time did not begin to run until the date on which the damage became detectable or the date on which the plaintiff acquired his interest, whichever was the later. The decision was criticised by most of those who wrote to us and it has now been disapproved by the House of Lords in *Pirelli General Cable Works Ltd.* v. *Oscar Faber and Partners.*[91] However it does illustrate a particular difficulty inherent in the date of knowledge approach, namely that a successor in title will not be in a position to discover that he has suffered damage until, at the earliest, the date on which he acquires the property in question. Nevertheless we share the view expressed by Lord Fraser (and his reasoning) in the *Pirelli* case that once time begins to run it should run not only against the plaintiff but also his successors in title and we recommend that, for the avoidance of doubt, the legislation which implements our recommendations should specifically so provide.

Application of our recommendations

4.22 Much of the case law that has developed on the subject of latent damage has been confined to the field of building and construction work and a significant number of those who commented on the Consultative Document restricted their submission to this sphere. A number also suggested that any recommendations for change should be confined to these areas. In our 21st Report the minority amongst us who favoured a residual discretion to override a defence of limitation suggested that it might be limited to the 'class of case in which problems of latent damage in practice arise (namely, professional advice and building and engineering contracts)'.[92] We have given this suggestion particularly careful consideration and we can see its attractions. It is probably true to say that the majority of claims for latent damage arise out of building and construction work and consequently a solution limited to these areas of activity would resolve much of the present difficulty in the law and could be tailored precisely to meet the needs of that industry. It would also avoid imposing upon professional advisers outside the construction industry any more lengthy liability than they

---

[88] *William Hill Organisation* v. *Bernard Sunley and Sons* (1983) 22 Build. L.R. 1 (C.A.).
[89] See para. 2.11 above.
[90] (1982) 19 Build. L.R. 50: (1981) 259 E.G. 491.
[91] [1983] 2 A.C. 1, 18; see also para. 2.11 above.
[92] (1977) Cmnd. 6923. para. 2.36.

already bear. However we do not find these arguments convincing. Although the majority of claims for latent damage occur in relation to building and construction work there is no doubt that such damage can also occur in other fields, and we can see no reason in principle why a plaintiff who has, for instance, suffered damage as a result of a negligently drawn lease should be in any worse a position than a plaintiff whose house has defective foundations. Similarly we are not troubled by the fact that our proposals will sometimes impose upon professional advisers a longer period of liability than they might bear at present. It is the object of the reforms that we are suggesting to do justice to both plaintiffs and defendants and it should not be forgotten that we are also proposing a long stop which will provide defendants with a substantial benefit in cases of long delay. Accordingly we recommend that there should be no restriction in the areas of activity to which our proposed reforms should apply.

Transitional problems

4.23 Transitional problems are raised when legislation amends the law of limitation because, although limitation is formally classified as 'procedural' (so that any change is *prima facie* properly applied to accrued causes of action and to pending proceedings), in reality it is a matter of substance and the normal rule is that changes in substantive law do not apply to accrued causes of action, whether or not there are pending proceedings.

4.24 The changes that we are recommending will have a substantial effect in cases where damage is delayed or undiscoverable. In probably what will prove to be the majority of cases plaintiffs will be in a better position that they are at present because they will have longer in which to bring their proceedings. In cases where damage itself is delayed however they may be less well off to the extent that they will not be able to proceed after the fifteen year long stop period we propose has expired. Some transitional cases may be caught. Four situations need to be considered:

(a) the position where the normal limitation period is already running at the commencement of the new legislation.

  (i) should the plaintiff be able to avail himself of the new three year extension of time? and

  (ii) should the defendant be able to take advantage of the long stop in a case of delayed damage?

(b) the position where the plaintiff is already statute barred at the date of commencement. Should he be able to avail himself of the new legislation?

(c) the position where proceedings are already pending at the date of commencement. Should the plaintiff be able to take advantage of the new legislation?

(d) the position where judgment has been given prior to commencement but where the time for appeal has not yet expired.

4.25 The general approach to these possible situations is illustrated by section 12 of the Limitation Amendment Act 1980 which provided as follows:—

'(1) Nothing in any provision of this Act shall—

(*a*) enable any action to be brought which was barred by the principal Act before that provision comes into force; or

(*b*) affect any action or arbitration commenced before that provision comes into force or the title to any property which is the subject of any such action or arbitration.

(2) Subject to subsection (1) above and sections 3(3) and 6(5) of this Act, the provisions of this Act shall have effect in relation to causes of action accruing and things taking place before, as well as in relation to causes of action accruing and things taking place after, those provisions respectively comes into force.'

Exceptionally however a rather different approach has been adopted in relation to personal injuries legislation[93] where it has in recent years been accepted that a change in the law of limitation that is beneficial to plaintiffs should apply notwithstanding both that the relevant cause of action arose before the change of the law and that by then the plaintiff's claim was, under the old law, already statute barred.[94] The argument in favour of the general approach is that revival of old claims would frequently produce unjust and inconvenient results. The argument in favour of the exception, which has so far been confined to the field of personal injuries, is that if the law is changed with the object of remedying a specific hardship suffered by plaintiffs, the change would in part be frustrated if it applied only where the plaintiff was not already barred by the pre-existing law.

4.26 In the present context of cases of latent damage not involving personal injury, we are of the opinion that the general approach is to be preferred. We accept that the present law is unsatisfactory and there may be some hard cases where plaintiffs have become statute barred before commencement and before they could have discovered that they had suffered damage. On the other hand a retrospective provision would undoubtedly cause hardship and injustice to defendants who have arranged their affairs on the basis that the plaintiff in their particular action had become statute barred, and we are not convinced that the arguments that have prevailed in recent years in relation to personal injuries legislation should be given the same weight in the present context. Our conclusion therefore is that whilst our recommendations should apply to causes of action accruing before as well as to those accruing after they come into force, it should not be possible for a plaintiff to avail himself of them where his claim was either already barred at the date of commencement or where his claim was pending at that date. The effect of this proposal can conveniently be illustrated by reference to the four hypothetical situations postulated in paragraph 4.24

---

[93] See e.g. Limitation Act 1975, section 3 of which provided as follows:

'(1) The provisions of this Act shall have effect in relation to causes of action which accrued before, as well as causes of action which accrue after, the commencement of this Act, and shall have effect in relation to any cause of action which accrued before the commencement of this Act notwithstanding that an action in respect thereof has been commenced and is pending at the commencement of this Act.

(2) For the purposes of this section an action shall not be taken to be pending at any time if a final order or judgment has been made or given therein, notwithstanding that an appeal is pending or that the time for appealing has not expired.'

[94] The arguments for and against this approach are discussed in our *Twentieth Report on Limitation of Actions in Personal Injury Claims*, (1974) Cmnd. 5630, paras. 137–146.

above. In the first, where the normal limitation period is already running at the date of commencement, a plaintiff will be able to proceed either under the general law, or if it is more generous, under the special three year period— subject always of course to the long stop. In the second situation, where the plaintiff is statute barred at the date of commencement he will be unable to benefit from our recommendations. In the third situation, where proceedings are already pending at the date of commencement, the action will be continued under the pre-existing law. In the fourth situation, where judgment has already been given but the time for appealing has not yet expired, neither party will be able to invoke the provisions of the new legislation.

Part V

CONCLUSIONS AND RECOMMENDATIONS

5.1 The present law is unjust to plaintiffs and defendants. In our view, it requires reform which will take care of the interests of both. Reform is, therefore, bound to be, in effect, a compromise between conflicting interests.

5.2 Suggestions were made to us by some of those whom we consulted for reforms more wide ranging than we have felt able to recommend.[95] We recognise the value of these suggestions and we believe that some of them deserve further consideration. Our terms of reference are limited to 'negligence cases involving latent defects' and our recommendations are designed to improve the law of limitation in respect of that class of case.

5.3 Our recommendations can be summarised as follows:—

(a) there should be no change in the general rule of substantive law whereby a cause of action in negligence accrues at the date on which the resulting damage occurs (paragraph 4.4);

(b) in negligence cases involving latent defects the existing six year period of limitation should be subject to an extension which would allow a plaintiff three years from the date of the discovery, or reasonable discoverability, of significant damage (paragraphs 4.5–4.9);

(c) there should be a long stop applicable to all negligence cases involving latent defects which should bar a plaintiff from initiating court action more than 15 years from the defendant's breach of duty (irrespective of whether damage has occurred) (paragraphs 4.10–4.13);

(d) the effect of the long stop should be to bar the plaintiff's remedy, not to extinguish his right (paragraph 4.14);

(e) where the plaintiff is under a disability at the 'date of knowledge' it should be possible for his action to be commenced within three years of the date that his disability ceases, or he dies, whichever is the sooner; the existence of the plaintiff's disability during the long stop period should have no effect on its duration; but the extension of the limitation period by section 28 of the Limitation Act 1980 in case of disability should remain unaffected by the long stop (paragraphs 4.15–4.17);

(f) the long stop should not apply to cases of latent damage involving fraud, deliberate concealment or mistake (paragraph 4.20);

(g) the extended limitation period should run not only against the plaintiff but also against his successors in title (paragraph 4.21);

(h) the preceding recommendations should be of general application to cases of latent damage and not confined to, say, building, construction or engineering cases (paragraph 4.22);

(i) our recommendations can be effected by amendments to the Limitation Act 1980 and should be subject to the transitional provisions proposed in paragraphs 4.23–4.26.

---

[95] See paras. 1.6 and 3.17 above.

Index

243